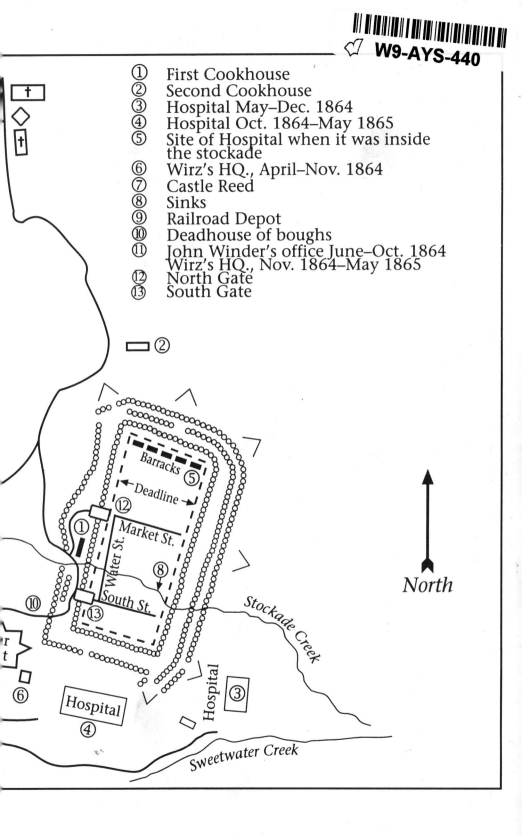

① First Cookhouse
② Second Cookhouse
③ Hospital May–Dec. 1864
④ Hospital Oct. 1864–May 1865
⑤ Site of Hospital when it was inside the stockade
⑥ Wirz's HQ., April–Nov. 1864
⑦ Castle Reed
⑧ Sinks
⑨ Railroad Depot
⑩ Deadhouse of boughs
⑪ John Winder's office June–Oct. 1864
  Wirz's HQ., Nov. 1864–May 1865
⑫ North Gate
⑬ South Gate

Barracks ⑤
←Deadline→
⑫ Market St.
① Water St.
⑧
South St.
⑩
⑬
r t
⑥
Hospital ④
Hospital ③
Stockade Creek
Sweetwater Creek

North

ANDERSONVILLE JOURNEY

By

Edward F. Roberts

 Burd Street Press

This Burd Street Press publication
was printed by
Beidel Printing House, Inc.
63 West Burd Street
Shippensburg, PA 17257-0152 USA

In respect for the scholarship contained herein, the acid-free paper used in this book meets the guidelines for permanence and durability of the Committee on Production Guidelines for Book Longevity of the Council on Library Resources.

For a complete list of available publications
please write
Burd Street Press
Division of White Mane Publishing Company, Inc.
P.O. Box 152
Shippensburg, PA 17257-0152 USA

Library of Congress Cataloging-in-Publication Data

Roberts, Edward F. , 1945–
     Andersonville journey / by Edward F. Roberts.
          p.   cm.
     Includes bibliographical references and index.
     ISBN 1-57249-059-4
     1. Andersonville Prison. 2. United States--History--Civil War, 1861-1865--Prisoners and prisons, Confederate. 3. Prisoners of war--Confederate States of America. 4. Prisoners of war--United States--History--19th century.   I. Title.
E612.A5R63   1998
973.7'71--dc21   97-32642
                                                                                    CIP

For

YUKI

My wife and the wind beneath my wings.

This work is respectfully dedicated to the memory of:
Private Edward Roberts,
Company K, 4th Massachusetts Cavalry,
who died at Andersonville, Georgia,
September 21, 1864,
Grave Number 9,448

TABLE OF CONTENTS

ILLUSTRATIONS

Andersonville National Cemetery

FOREWORD

A Small Town in Georgia

Andersonville is a small village in the southwestern part of the state of Georgia, located about one hour's drive west of busy Interstate 75 on Georgia State Road 49. It is easy to bypass the small village of Andersonville as you speed along Georgia's peaceful highways, admiring the well-tended cotton fields and lush green pecan groves that line the smooth asphalt road. A first-time visitor is guided to Andersonville by small brown road signs that constantly remind the traveler that they are on the "Andersonville Trail."

Andersonville National Historic Site is part of the National Park System, famous the world over for how well it maintains our national heritage, with well-trimmed lawns and fresh coats of paint. When you drive past the two red brick buildings that make up the site's Visitors Center and Park Headquarters it seems at first glance as if you have entered just another well-tended national cemetery. It is filled with the familiar white marble headstones, American flags, and patriotic statuary typically found in such a place. But on closer examination the visitor discovers that there is something fundamentally different here, something not found at Arlington or any of the other national cemeteries.

In the national cemetery at Andersonville, the marble headstones are so close together they almost touch. The markers sometime appear to be one long headstone as if one grave grew out of the other. The men in these graves were buried completely naked, shoulder to shoulder, under less than three feet of dirt. What you are seeing in the cemetery is the last vestiges of a great American tragedy. These long lines of white marble headstones are, in reality, a mass grave or more accurately, a series of mass graves, containing the remains of nearly 13,000 Union prisoners of war who died of disease and starvation between February 1864 and May 1865.

In only fourteen months the Confederate prisoner of war camp at Andersonville, Georgia became the most terrible "death camp" to exist on American soil. During the horrible summer of 1864, over 33,000 prisoners of war were jammed into a vastly overcrowded and incredibly filthy pine log stockade. Their diet consisted primarily of raw pork meat and corn meal that had been ground up with the cobs and shucks thrown in for extra bulk. To men already weakened by hunger and diarrhea, the rough corn-meal literally tore their bowels apart. The longer the prison stayed open, the longer the burial trenches grew. Death became so common at Andersonville that the prisoners built up a mercantile system around the burying of the dead.

No visitor can come to the Andersonville Historic Site and leave without profound soul searching. Moral, ethical, and factual questions come to mind. How could this terrible thing happen? Who was responsible? Have the guilty been punished?

When something this terrible happens, we seem to crave a villain, someone who will take the blame and by so doing absolve us of our guilt. We must be assured that the terrible events that happened at Andersonville were the work of one lone madman, who was adequately punished for his crime. His punishment reaffirms our own self-concept. It assures us that what happened at Andersonville doesn't prove that there is anything fundamentally wrong with our history, the nature of our society, and our own since of justice, mercy, and basic humanity.

However, things at Andersonville are not that simple. Directly across the highway from the old prison site is the small village of Andersonville, after which the prison draws its unofficial name. Crossing the highway towards what a gray highway sign calls "Historic Andersonville Civil War Village" is like moving from one perspective to another. The small village consists of only a dozen or so aged wood-framed, tin-roofed buildings that have been converted into tourist shops, selling mostly antiques and Civil War souvenirs.

In the direct center of the village is a tall obelisk monument made of light gray granite that has turned yellow over the years by the red-oxide clay soil of the region. The inscriptions on the monument are hard to read, but one word clearly stands out: in large bold letters on the front of the monument is the single word "WIRZ."

The monument honors the memory of Captain Henry Wirz of the Confederate States Army, the commander of "Camp Sumter," the official name for the Confederate prison across the highway. That is the same prison where the men who lie in the long trench graves died of starvation, disease, and by some accounts murder.

Henry Wirz was the first person to be legally executed for atrocities committed during a time of war. Around his neck was hung the bloody albatross of Andersonville Prison. But the very existence of the Wirz monument in the center of the small village suggests that there is something very unusual about the legacy of Andersonville Prison.

The story of Andersonville reveals a rich human drama with amazing people, in unbelievable situations, thrown together under the strangest of circumstances.

For example, there was Captain Wirz, a pathetic Swiss immigrant, who endured a horribly unfair trial, tainted by postwar hysteria, a deep national need for the catharsis of revenge, and a firm belief that someone must be responsible for so horrible a tragedy. With a large crowd in attendance, Henry Wirz was executed in Washington, D.C. on land now occupied by the United States Supreme Court building. With the newly completed capitol dome in the background, a Civil War photographer captured Wirz's final minutes of agony as the ram-rod straight solders around his scaffold chanted "Wirz remember Andersonville, Wirz remember Andersonville."

The story of Andersonville is also the story of a one-legged cripple, driven to order his own execution. It is the story of a young clerk, who braved both his captors and his own government, to see that the names of the dead would not be forgotten. It is about a brave Catholic priest who risked his own life to tend to the sick and dying men in the Andersonville stockade. It is about a determined woman who challenged the most powerful man in the United States in order to preserve the prisoners' cemetery. It is about a New England widow who came south to beautify and hallow that same cemetery.

There are a host of minor characters. They include a wiry little escape artist called "Frenchy," who even won the respect of his captors. A former Confederate officer who put aside the regional differences that had led him to war to assume the duty of protecting the graves of his former enemies. The unknown Georgia slaves who fed and sheltered the escaped Yankee prisoners of war, and many more, known and unknown.

All these people, good and bad, right and wrong, cowards and heroes, villains and saints, had one thing in common: they were touched by a place, a place called Andersonville. It was a small out-of-the-way place that should by all rights be obscure and forgotten. They were not born there, but many of them died there, and they all suffered there. They all had taken an Andersonville Journey.

Wirz Monument

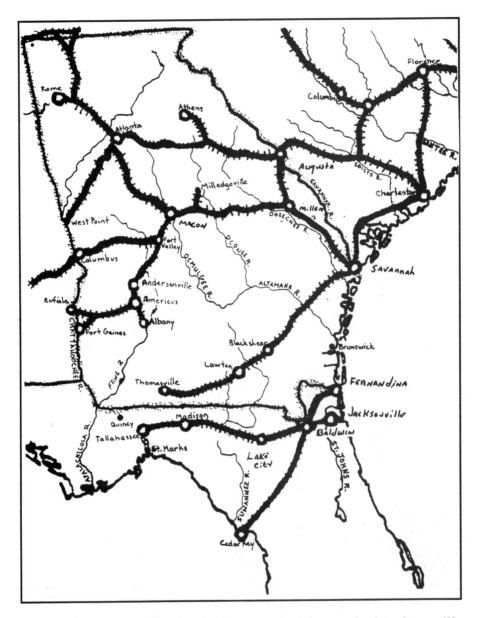

Map of the Major Railroads and River Systems that Serviced Andersonville Prison

Map by Joanne Steele

INTRODUCTION

The Beginnings of a Tragedy

Before the arrival of the railroads to the South, there were few small villages like Andersonville. There was really no need for them. Each Southern plantation was more or less self sufficient with its own blacksmiths, harness makers, carpenters, and even physicians. After the end of the Civil War, when the large plantations were broken up into small sharecropping farms, the familiar little crossroads communities the South is so famous for today grew up to serve the everyday needs of the local farmers.[1]

The only towns that existed in the South before the war were market centers where cotton or tobacco, the South's two primary "cash crops," were brought to be sold at auction. The larger of these market towns, such as Charleston, Savannah, and New Orleans, became full fledged cities. They were located on the Atlantic and Gulf coasts, where major river systems emptied into the sea. Others Southern cities, such as Natchez, Memphis, and Nashville, were situated on major inland waterways, where riverboats picked up the big bales of cotton for shipment down river.

In these Southern market centers, wealthy plantation owners had opulent winter homes and foreign cotton and tobacco merchants staged lavish dinner parties in their own mansions.

The state of Georgia had the elegant and oak-shaded port city of Savannah, where cotton was loaded aboard ocean-going vessels for transportation to the textile mills of Europe and the northern United States. It was the state's most important seaport, and the ultimate destination of almost all cotton grown in the interior of Georgia.

Upriver from Savannah, there were several smaller, more rustic, inland market towns such as Augusta and Macon. Before the railroads were built, these inland market towns were small and primitive places, which served as regional markets for the upcountry, working plantations of central Georgia.

These inland areas of Georgia were not the stereotypical South of large mansions and hooped skirts. Here the soil was red oxide clay instead of the sandy loam of the coastal plain. Plantations were smaller, as were the cotton crops. They had fewer slaves, and a visitor might see the plantation owner and his family working in the fields beside their slaves. The area was also characterized by small dirt farms, where poor whites managed to grub out a living without the ownership of slaves.

One of the major problems in the inland regions of Georgia was the difficulty of getting the large, 500-pound cotton bales from the regional market towns to the coast. The state of Georgia had no organized system of building and maintaining roads. What roads did exist were carved out of the wilderness by local landowners for their own purposes, following trails first laid down by the Creek and Cherokee Indians.

These dirt roads were hazardous traveling. Following a heavy summer rain, the roads would be a sea of choking mud. When the mud dried, the road would be so deeply rutted that it was impossible for a wagon to pass. A teamster had no way of knowing if a bridge would still be standing when he got to it or if a road was blocked by a fallen tree, mud slide, or other obstruction.[2]

River transportation in prewar Georgia was not much better than the dirt roads hacked out of the wilderness. The first riverboats were flat bottomed keelboats, pushed upriver by strong-backed men with sturdy poles. Later, these keelboats were replaced by small paddlewheel steamboats. The rivers which drained south out of the north Georgia mountains could not accommodate the large steamboats commonly found on the Mississippi and Ohio Rivers.

During most of the year, the Georgia rivers were too low to permit even small vessels to move up and down river; at other times they were raging torrents, covering their wide flood plains with swirling dark waters. Even under the best of conditions, the rivers were muddy and treacherous with submerged logs, hidden sandbars, and floating tangles of debris.

When the first railroads were laid through central Georgia in the decade before the Civil War, they were a blessing to the upland farmers. For the first time they had a year-round method of getting their cotton crops to market. The railroads also radically changed the social and economic makeup of the region. Cities like Macon and Albany, which were only small market towns before the railroads came, suddenly became major economic centers.

The railroads created new metropolitan areas in the upland heart of the state. The small farming town of Marthasville had a pre-railroad population of only 2,000 people. However, after it became the spot where four of the state's largest railroads came together to form a hub, its population swelled to over 20,000 people in only three years. The name of the town was changed from Marthasville to Atlanta since it was the southern terminus of the Western and Atlantic Railroad that ran north to Chattanooga.[3]

The railroads allowed new and much larger cotton plantations to grow up on the Macon plateau, reaching as far north as the mountains north of Atlanta, and south to the edges of the Okefenokee Swamp. To accommodate those new cotton plantations, the Georgia Southwestern Railroad pushed its tracks southwest from Macon, towards the small Flint River towns of Americus and Albany. The railroad would eventually connect with the Chattahoochee River at Fort Gaines and Georgetown, across the river from Eufala, Alabama. The small cotton farmers of the region were happy to see the big steam powered locomotives rolling across the countryside, knowing that they no longer had to depend upon the flood and drought-prone Flint River to float their big cotton bales to market.

The Georgia Southwestern, like most other Southern railroads, was designed for only one purpose, the moving of cotton to market. Little or no attention was paid to long-distance passenger traffic or the moving of products from one part of the South to the other.

The railroads of the South were inadequately financed, poorly managed, and burdened with substandard equipment and untrained employees. All of the lines in the South, except one, were less than two hundred miles in length. They were not of a standard gauge, (or track width), which meant that the locomotives and boxcars of one railroad would not necessarily be able to operate on another railroad's track. Even when the railroads were of uniform gauge, they often did not connect. Regional politics and ownership rights kept the railroads apart, sometimes by only a few miles. Persons wanting to move over long distances across the South were forced to change trains at regular intervals and travel by a combination of rails, steamboat, and sometimes horseback or wagon.

All Georgia railroads used the standard five-foot wide track gauge as did the neighboring states of South Carolina, Alabama, Tennessee, and Florida. However, when rail traffic moved into North Carolina, the gauge changed to four feet eight and a half inches. The railroads of Virginia were a frustrating mixture of both gauges of track, which made transportation of men and materials a logistical nightmare.[4]

The locomotives of Southern railroads were fueled exclusively with wood. Northern railroads burned coal, a far more efficient fuel. Coal was easier to acquire in large quantities, transport in special coal cars, and store outdoors in huge piles. Wood was difficult to obtain in large quantities and had to be protected from the weather. Coal also burned cleaner than wood with less waste. Wood-burning locomotives had to be placed out of commission on a regular basis for cleaning the fire box. Even the best of firewood, such as oak, would foul the interior of the fire box with a thick deposit of unburned materials that would build up over time, reducing the efficiency of the engines.

The wood burned in Georgia railroads was obtained from local landowners by contract.[5] It took vast acreage to keep the railroads supplied and the land adjoining the tracks soon became totally deforested of hardwood trees. The vast pine forests of Georgia were of no help to the railroads. Pine wood could not be burned in locomotive engines. Its thick turpentine sap caused debilitating creosote deposits to build up in the fire box and smokestack.

In the decade before the Civil War, a small farming village emerged from the pine forests along a small tributary of the Flint River called Sweetwater Creek. Located only ten miles from the river town of Americus, the small village was named Anderson, after an early local resident. When the Georgia Southwestern Railroad laid its tracks through the small village, the name was changed to Anderson Station. Eventually, it would become known as Andersonville Station, and finally simply Andersonville. In 1860, the town consisted of a post office, a blacksmith shop, two general stores, a stable, a Methodist Church, a one-room schoolhouse, and about a dozen houses owned by local cotton farmers.

The trains passed through Andersonville twice a day but didn't stop except on rare occasions to take on freight. A small freight loading platform was built beside the tracks to ease the burden of loading cotton, but a depot building would not be constructed until after the opening of the Confederate prison. A telegraph line would not connect Andersonville to Macon until after the prison was opened and filled to capacity.

By 1864, in order to supply wood to the railroads, the land around Andersonville had been almost totally deforested. When Confederate authorities first inspected the area looking for a site for a new Confederate prison, they commented that the area contained large stands of healthy pine trees. The perimeter walls of the proposed prison were to be made from rough hewn pine logs, and there were more than enough tall pine trees around Andersonville for that purpose. It seems that it was of little concern to the inspectors that there were few hardwood trees to provide the firewood that would be needed for cooking the prisoners' food and providing heat in the winter months.

This was the first major blunder in creating the tragedy that would become known as Andersonville. There would be many more to follow.

The Confederate states held a virtual monopoly on cotton, the world's most desired raw material. Without those precious white fibers, the industrial revolution in Europe and North America would grind to a halt. However, the South was almost totally dependent on imports for almost every manufactured product from matches to locomotive boilers.

Confederate politicians had laughed when Abraham Lincoln first proposed a naval blockade on the South. They never believed that the small

Union Navy could possibly blockade over 3,000 miles of Southern coast-line. However, within a year the blockade was being felt in the South. After two years it was a stranglehold, and by the time Andersonville Prison was opened in February of 1864, the blockade had become a death grip.

Of the three necessities of life—food, clothing, and shelter—the one that was most in short supply in the South during that fateful summer of 1864 was clothing. Blankets that had been handed out free to Confederate soldiers at the beginning of the war were so scarce by 1864 that carpets and draperies were being cut up to provide warmth for both civilians and soldiers.

Ironically, the "land of cotton" had no textile mills to turn the regions vast amounts of cotton into cloth. Homespun was all that was available. Confederate soldiers had their wounds bandaged with tablecloths, nap-kins, bed sheets, even fancy needlework. Southern homes were devoid of curtains, rugs, bed linens, hand-embroidered tapestries, and anything else that could be turned into a uniform blanket or bandage.[6]

Food became scarcer as the war went on. The capture of New Or-leans in 1862 meant that Louisiana sugar could no longer be had in the Confederacy. The fall of Vicksburg stopped the supply of Texas beef and the leather needed to make shoes. By 1864, shoes were in such short supply they were almost non-existent. Shoes were fashioned from old strips of leather, old horse harnesses and cut up rugs.[7]

Food shortages were made worse by periods of drought, such as the long dry spell that hit southern Alabama in 1862, and flooding when the Mississippi went on a rampage in 1861, and again in 1862.[8]

Food shortages varied in the South, depending upon the proximity of the Confederate Army and local growing conditions. Areas where large numbers of Confederate soldiers could be found, such as southern Vir-ginia, had serious food shortages. Other areas, such as the interior of Ala-bama, Texas, and Florida, which were far removed from the fighting, had only sporadic shortages of food. Because of the confused state of the Con-federate railroad system, areas that had adequate food supplies could not supply other areas where there were shortages.

Georgia was saved from widespread hunger by the good luck of a bumper corn harvest in 1863 and in 1864. However, that does not mean that food was plentiful. The population of Georgia was greatly enlarged by refugees who had fled south from Tennessee, and east from Mississippi after those states were invaded by the Union Army. After Sherman's army began moving south towards Atlanta, both the Union and Confederate armies made great demands upon the civilian food supply.

While the South was a land covered with woodlands, there was a serious shortage of building materials. By 1864, most of the sawmills in the South had been shut down because of broken or worn-out steel saw blades that could not be replaced. There were only two factories in the

South capable of making nails in large numbers, and both were in the hands of a greedy cartel, which hoarded the nails to force the price up. Other basic building materials, such as hammers, saws, files, and crowbars, were all imported and could not be replaced because of the Union blockade. Local blacksmiths could fashion tools, but they were not able to turn out nearly enough to fill the need, and those handmade tools became prohibitively expensive due to the high demand.

The shortages in the South were aggravated by hoarding and speculation. The Confederate government urged plantation owners to forgo the planting of cotton and tobacco and replace them with food crops to feed the Confederate Army. However, large plantation owners, who had most feverishly argued for the war, refused to give up the production of cotton and tobacco, as long as the price paid for these products in Europe was skyrocketing.

Corn which could have been used to feed the Confederate Army was turned into high-priced whiskey. While Confederate soldiers were ragged and hungry, there were warehouses in the South full of salt (badly needed to preserve meat), coffee, leather, soap, cod liver oil, and medicines, all owned by war profiteers.[9] No appeal to patriotism could convince the owners to part with their booty, while the war-inflated prices were still going up. Vital supplies, such as medicines, linens, lumber and lead, were controlled by small cartels of speculators, willing to make every ill-gotten dollar they could.

The Confederate government refused to act on these problems. The Confederate Congress and most of the state legislatures were primarily made up of the wealthy land- and slave-owning gentry. They were also closely allied with, or in some cases actually involved in, the speculation and hoarding. Also, neither the Confederate Congress nor the state legislatures really grasped the seriousness of the problem until it was too late. In 1862 the Confederate Congress failed to act on the problem of speculation and hoarding, saying any such legislation would be premature, since at that time the Union blockade had not fully taken hold. In 1863, having finally realized that speculators were hurting the war effort, the Confederate Congress brought out the old Southern doctrine of "States' Rights," claiming that it was the duty of the individual state legislatures to take action.[10] Some of the state legislatures did take action, but without much success.

Speculation was a national problem in the Confederacy that could not be solved by the actions of the individual state legislatures. In 1864, the Confederate Congress finally passed strong legislation to stop speculation and hoarding, but by that time it was too late, and the damage had been done and the war lost.

In 1863, the Confederate government, after much bickering, finally decided that it had the authority to send out impressment agents to seize, by force if necessary, the supplies needed by the Confederate Army.[11]

However, the impressment agents found a cold welcome in most parts of the South. Large plantation owners and speculators used bribes and political influence to ward off the agents. Smaller farmers used more ingenious means: hams were hung in the top branches of trees, basements had secret rooms and false floors, corncribs and barns held carefully hidden supplies of linens, medicines, and jugs of whiskey. Secret root cellars were dug in remote corners of plowed fields and deep in the woods. Some Southerners even hid supplies in family cemeteries, buried in crates, disguised as fresh graves of non-existent relatives.

By the time Andersonville Prison was opened early in 1864, there were also fundamental changes occurring in the North. The summer before, there had been terrible anti-draft and anti-war riots in Northern cities. Some Northern newspapers were openly calling for peace and advocating a negotiated end to the fighting. The anti-war and anti-draft feelings were running so strong that some seriously doubted if Abraham Lincoln would be reelected in the fall.

The Union Army had also changed during four years of war. Union officers complained bitterly that their ranks were swelled with draftees, bounty jumpers, ex-convicts, and petty criminals fresh from the slums and jails of Northern cities. Luckily, the Union Army also contained a dedicated hard core of brave men, who had been in the army since the beginning of the war and were determined to see the conflict through to final victory. They had reenlisted over and over, knowing full well the horrors of what they had already seen, and what lay ahead. Those men held the army together and provided the courage at Andersonville, as they organized to protect their fellow prisoners, not from the Confederates, but also, from their own fellow soldiers.

The Union prisoners of war sent to Andersonville were a mixture of the best and worst of the Union Army. Some would rob, cheat, and even murder their fellow prisoners; while others would show great courage and humanity, binding together to survive the great tribulations before them.

When people speak of Andersonville there is one recurring question: How could this terrible thing happen? Most are looking for a "smoking gun," some piece of tangible evidence that indeed Confederate officials had deliberately starved to death nearly 13,000 prisoners of war, or that the tragedy of Andersonville was to be blamed on the Union blockade and the North's refusal to exchange prisoners of war. In reality there is no "smoking gun" in the Andersonville story. Many factors had to come together to cause the catastrophe.

Besides all the shortages and transportation problems in the South, the situation at Andersonville was further aggravated by unwise personnel decisions. The Confederate prison system was commanded by a sixty-five, year-old general with a heart condition, and probably a myriad of other ailments common to a man of his age. His subordinate was a foreign-born immigrant, who was also in ill health, tormented by the constant pain of his wounds.

Due to local politics, the prison was located in an unhealthy spot, without an adequate water supply, proper drainage, or waste disposal. The Confederate guard force was ill equipped, poorly trained, and totally undisciplined. All this was combined with the shortages of food, medicines, clothing and tools, caused by the Union blockade and the Confederate railroad system. What resulted from this mixture of events was a time and place where the greatest tragedy of the Civil War occurred.

PART ONE

"May God have mercy on your souls."

Captain Henry Wirz, C.S.A.
Provided by Colonel Heinrich L. Wirz,
Army of Switzerland

Henry Wirz

The man who would pay with his life for what happened at Andersonville was born in 1823 as Heinrich Hartman Wirz in Zurich, Switzerland. Later in life, after he migrated to America, Wirz began to use the name Henry, the Anglo version of the German name Heinrich, to better fit into the social and professional life of his new country.

The young Heinrich Wirz grew up in a well-respected, German-speaking, middle-class, mercantile family. The Wirz family can be dated back to 1422, when the original family coat of arms was recorded in Uerikon, Switzerland. The surname Wirz is a genitive form of the professional title "Wirt" or "des Wirtes", meaning an innkeeper, host, or landlord.

The Wirz family has had two coats of arms in its long history. The current coat of arms is a golden shield with two "pallets gules" or vertical red bands, indicating a willingness to shed blood for one's sovereign. It indicates military strength and fortitude and is usually given as an honor to the defender of a city. Before 1492, the family coat of arms carried a blue fish on a silver field, indicating that one of Henry Wirz's ancestors, a man named Ulrich Wirz, was a "schiffmann" or sailor. He had become a citizen of Zurich in 1401, when he recorded the family's first coat of arms in the city ledger.[1]

The young Wirz was a bright but moody youth with a small body frame and pale skin. He had a better than average education in Switzerland and Italy.[2] His father tried to interest his son in the family mercantile trade, but the boy longed for a career in medicine.

Little is known about Wirz's early childhood, but it appears that during his teenage years his relationship with his family was troublesome. Like most German-speaking people in northern Switzerland, Wirz's family were typical Protestant followers of the teachings of John Calvin.[3] To the dismay and anger of his family, the young Wirz decided to abandon his family's traditional faith and embrace the Catholic religion. This was a serious act of rebellion, and it appears to have produced a deep schism within the family.

There is no documentary evidence that Wirz ever received a degree in medicine while living in Europe. However, he may have been trained as a pharmacist, a similar profession at that time, or he might have worked as an attendant in a bathhouse, when it was believed that hot baths would cure a variety of medical ailments and restore one's youth.

When he was twenty-one years old, Wirz married Emile Oschwald, a woman several years older than he was. The marriage was turbulent and the couple argued frequently, usually about money. Apparently unable to support his new wife, Wirz changed jobs several times and the family went deeply in debt. Despite their troubles, Emile presented Henry with a child and was soon pregnant with a second.

In 1848, Wirz's already troubled life totally went to pieces. After three years of marriage, his pregnant wife took their young son and returned to her family. The second child, a daughter, would not be born until after the separation.

The young Wirz was also in some form of legal difficulty, but exactly what the problems were is still unclear. However, it most certainly involved money, most probably some form of illegal financial dealings.

In the early nineteenth century, as it still is today, Zurich was a center of international finance and banking. Wirz, most likely got in over his head in some of the convoluted financial dealings that characterize the city. However, his problems might have been as simple as too much debt, which was a crime in Switzerland at that time. To the deep disgrace of his family, Wirz was found guilty and exiled by the Swiss government.

Following the lead of thousands of other Europeans, the exiled Heinrich Wirz decided to emigrate to America. With money borrowed from his family, he booked passage on a crowded immigrant packet and sailed to the United States.

Wirz arrived in Boston in 1849, twelve years before the start of the Civil War. Almost penniless, and perhaps using a phony name, he found work as a common laborer in a dirty textile mill in Lawrence, Massachusetts. He found living in America difficult but bearable. Boston was an immigrant town, and German was commonly heard on street corners, restaurants, and taverns. Wirz hated the drudgery of the textile mill, but the long hours and hard work kept him from spending his pay and allowed him to save his money.[4]

After only a few months at the mill, Wirz found employment working as a low-paid assistant to a local German-speaking doctor, a job much more to his liking. It was probably around this time that Wirz began calling himself Henry and dropped the use of his middle name, the too-German-sounding Hartman.

After the end of his apprenticeship, Henry Wirz moved to the frontier town of Cadiz, Kentucky, where he quickly established a practice as a homeopathic physician.[5] Western Kentucky was a rough and tumble place and Cadiz, located on the Cumberland River, was full of all types of shady characters who came and went with the big riverboats. Henry Wirz was simply another stranger in town, along with hundreds of riverboat gamblers, fur trappers, and land speculators.

Coat of Arms of the Wirz Family
Provided by Colonel Heinrich L. Wirz

In the nineteenth century there were no government regulations on the practice of medicine and the licensing of physicians. As far as the state and federal governments were concerned, anyone who desired to do so could hang out a sign and call themselves a doctor. However, to have some credibility with his patients, a physician had to show some indication of formal medical training.

Within the young United States there were dozens of medical schools that ranged from highly respectable institutions to outright diploma mills, fraudulently belching out impressive looking certificates and diplomas to anyone who could pay their fee. Bright young men, who could not afford to pay the high fees demanded by the medical diploma mills, such as Henry Wirz, could also learn their craft by working for a time as an assistant to an established doctor.

Because it was so easy to become a doctor, there were too many of them and the competition for patients was fierce. When business was slow, physicians were often forced to work as barbers or dentists to earn enough to pay their bills.[6]

It was not long after arriving in Cadiz that Henry Wirz found himself the target of a campaign to drive him out of town. Other, more established doctors questioned his medical training, ethics, and experience. They disliked the fact that Wirz was a Catholic, not of British ancestry, but most of all they disliked the fact that he was a homeopathic physician.

Homeopathy was based on the theory that a sick person could be cured if given minute doses of a substance that causes similar symptoms in a healthy person. Homeopathic medicine was much more popular than many of the painful treatments, such as bleeding, and the applying of hot plasters to cause blisters, used by mainstream doctors.

The American Medical Association (AMA) had been formed in 1846, and one of its first acts was to expel all homeopathic physicians from its ranks. It then passed rules saying that any member of the AMA who consulted with a homeopath or other "non-regular" practitioner would lose his membership in the American Medical Association. The AMA waged a powerful campaign against all types of "non-traditional" medicine with volumes of medical essays, hours of lectures, and outright political pressure on local politicians.[7]

Henry Wirz tried to obtain respectability in Cadiz by marrying an illiterate local widow named Elizabeth Wolf. She was a Methodist, who had two daughters already by her first marriage. She quickly became pregnant and presented her new husband with a daughter they named Cora. Evidence indicates that the couple also had a second daughter, who died sometime before the Civil War.

Henry Wirz was ill prepared to deal with the prejudice directed towards him. He had a standoffish personality and could not communicate well in his heavy German accent. Wirz tried to present himself as a refined gentleman with good tastes and manners. However, in the rough and muddy river town of Cadiz, such refinement was for nothing. The gossip and prejudice in Cadiz destroyed Wirz's medical practice. With no patients, he had little choice except to move on.

Ironically, the South, which has developed a reputation for racial bigotry in both popular fiction and historical fact, was the most religiously tolerant region of the United States in the decades before the Civil War. It was Savannah, Georgia that received the first shipload of Jews to come to the New World. The seaport city of Charleston, South Carolina, first gave Jews the right to vote. The first American president to appoint a Jew to his cabinet was Jefferson Davis, who appointed Judiah P. Benjamin, a Sephardic Jew, to be attorney general and later secretary of state for the Confederate States of America.[8]

The Roman Catholic faith was widely practiced in all the Southern states that were formerly Spanish or French territory. In Louisiana, the number of Roman Catholics was so large that local government districts were called "parishes", instead of "counties", like the rest of the United States. Religious tolerance was so strong in Louisiana that it had elected Judiah P. Benjamin to be the first Jewish member of the U.S. Senate.

It was no surprise that Henry Wirz decided to move south to Louisiana, where he hoped he could find acceptance both as a physician and as a Catholic. After a period of time in New Orleans, he eventually obtained a position as a physician to slaves on the Marshall Plantation, near Milliken's Bend, Louisiana.

The end of the slave trade in the early part of the nineteenth century caused the value of healthy slaves to rise dramatically. To protect the vast

amount of personal wealth the slaves represented, large plantation owners often contracted with white physicians to keep their slaves healthy.
This made the South a fertile area for the overabundance of physicians
barely eking out a living in the North.

The standard pay for a white physician treating slaves was three dollars per year for each slave treated.[9] This meant that an energetic doctor
on a large plantation could make as much as three hundred dollars a year.
This was at a par with what a physician in the North, with a reasonably
good practice, could expect to make.

The life Henry Wirz and his family were enjoying on the Marshall
Plantation was shattered by the election of Abraham Lincoln and the coming of the Civil War. Wirz's loyalties were firmly with the South. He had
come to love the region with its warm climate, gentle elegance, and courtly
manners. The South had given Henry Wirz more economic prosperity and
respect than he had known in Massachusetts, Kentucky, or Europe.

Following a deep-rooted Germanic sense of duty, Henry Wirz enlisted as a private in the Madison Infantry of the 4th Louisiana Battalion.

Eventually, Henry Wirz was promoted to sergeant, and the 4th Louisiana would be sent to southeastern Virginia to defend Richmond. Shortly
after the Battle of First Manassas, the Madison Infantry was assigned to
guard a group of Union prisoners of war. It was probably at this time that
Henry Wirz met Provost Marshal General John H. Winder, who was impressed with the young sergeant's handling of the prisoners.

In March of 1862, Federal troops, commanded by General George
B. McClellan, were moved south from Washington by sea to Fortress Monroe, Virginia. They then began a cautious move up the peninsula formed
by the James and York Rivers towards Richmond, in the hope of capturing
the Confederate capital.

In a still controversial move, Confederate forces led by General Joseph E. Johnston withdrew from a strongly fortified position near Yorktown
to do battle closer to Richmond, where their forces could not be outflanked
by Union gunboats. Events transpired so that the two forces fought near an
obscure country crossroads southeast of Richmond, characterized by a
small clump of pine trees.

The violent military encounter near the small crossroads would go
down in history as the Battle of Seven Pines. For two bloody days, May 31
and June 1, 1862, Union and Confederate forces shed one another's blood
in the sandy, low country soil of the Virginia tidewater. During the battle
Sergeant Henry Wirz was badly wounded.

Two Union minie balls struck Wirz's right arm and shoulder. Upon
impact, the two soft lead projectiles flattened out to a size nearly an inch in
diameter. They tore through Wirz's arm ripping away handfuls of bone and
muscle tissue. Wirz lay amid the other dead and wounded until help arrived in the form of two badly overworked stretcher-bearers. They loaded

the Louisiana sergeant into a rickety farm wagon to endure an agonizing ride to the field hospital in Richmond.

Henry Wirz's wounds would never heal. For the rest of his life he would have frequent infections, his arm and shoulder would swell and have to be lanced to allow the accumulated pus and diseased blood to drain. Wirz's existence would be one of constant pain that he would attempt to endure stoically. Never a friendly person to begin with, Henry Wirz now became sullen and bitter with frequent outbursts of violent temper, when he would spew forth caustic profanities in his heavy German accent.[10]

Wirz also suffered from long periods of mental depression and physical weakness when he was unable to rise from his bed, giving rise to rumors that he was addicted to pain-killing drugs.[11] After his wounding, Wirz favored his injured right arm that hung nearly useless at his side. He often wore his arm in a sling, as he did three years later when he walked to the gallows.

In a modern army Wirz would have been discharged as disabled. However, the Confederacy was far too short of men to allow any but the most gravely wounded to leave the service.

The Confederate Army was filled with badly wounded men. General John Bell Hood had lost the use of his arm at Gettysburg and had his leg amputated after the Battle of Chickamauga. The general was so badly maimed that he had to be strapped into his saddle with a specially designed leather harness. But despite his wounds, General Hood went on to command Confederate troops defending Atlanta and at the battles of Franklin and Nashville.

Comparatively, Henry Wirz was in fairly good shape. He was ambulatory, could mount and ride a horse with no assistance, fire a pistol or wield a sword with his remaining good arm. But most importantly, he still had possession of all his mental faculties and was able to perform clerical duties. Despite his physical pain and periods of depression, the Confederate States of America still had use for Henry Wirz.

With the help of high-placed persons in the Confederate Army, most likely by General John H. Winder, Wirz was commissioned a captain and assigned to the provost marshal's office in Richmond.

A month after reporting to his new duty post in Richmond, Wirz was sent to Tuscaloosa, Alabama to search for missing military records. He arranged for his wife and family to join him, and was subsequently given command of the newly opened military prison near Tuscaloosa.[12] Wirz's tenure at Tuscaloosa was brief, less than four months, but it is important to note that while he was in command there were no charges of brutality or mistreatment of prisoners leveled against him. Most veterans of the prison remember it as a decent place to be confined with better than average food and humane treatment.

In December 1862, for reasons still undetermined, Wirz was given a furlough to return to Europe.[13] This is a mysterious period in Wirz's life and exactly what his mission in Europe was is still unknown. However, educated speculation abounds: Some believed Wirz was on an espionage or diplomatic mission. At that time the Confederacy was involved in several secret negotiations with foreign governments, hoping to get military assistance and diplomatic recognition.

The South's greatest hope lay with the French Emperor Napoleon III, who had taken advantage of the American Civil War to send an army into Mexico. Jefferson Davis hoped that history would repeat itself and France would come to the aid of the Confederate States of America, as it had done with the young United States during the Revolutionary War.

Henry Wirz spent the majority of his year abroad in Berlin and Paris. In a Paris photography studio, he stood in his Confederate officer's uniform, his weak right arm anchored with his thumb in his coat flap and his left arm on a chair for support, and had his photograph made. Wirz is wearing a red sash over his shoulder and a French style "kepi" hat that was popular for both sides during the Civil War. A pair of field glasses and a folded map in the chair give the false impression that Wirz was a combat officer commanding troops in the field. Despite his serious wounding, Wirz is still an impressive figure with a full, neatly trimmed beard, projecting an image of dignity and pride. This is the clearest image of Henry Wirz ever taken and the most familiar. Except for a badly damaged and poor quality photograph made at Andersonville, the next time Henry Wirz would stand before a photographer, he would be on a gallows scaffold listening to his death warrant being read.

Wirz must have enjoyed his stay in Europe; it had been productive for him personally even though little good had come out of the trip for the Confederacy. No secret arms deals had been struck and no diplomatic recognition for the Confederacy had been won from any European power.

Wirz is believed to have had surgery done on his wounded arm to remove diseased bone fragments, hoping to give him at least temporary relief from his pain. He probably also visited his family in Switzerland. Wirz must have felt redeemed since he had left Europe in poverty and disgrace. He had returned an officer in the Confederate States Army, wearing an impressive new uniform and bearing on his body the honorable wounds of battle. He would never see his family again.

In January 1864, Henry Wirz boarded a gray-painted Confederate blockade runner to return to the South. Using the cold and foggy January weather as camouflage, the gray blockade runner delivered Wirz and the rest of its passengers and cargo to the windswept North Carolina coast. From coastal North Carolina, Wirz traveled north to Richmond and reported for duty at the provost marshal's office.

It was shortly after he arrived in Richmond that Henry Wirz first heard the word Andersonville. He was ordered to report to the small Georgia town to serve as an assistant in the operation of a new prison to be called

Camp Sumter. It was scheduled to open as soon as construction was completed and prisoners could be transported. The new prison was supposed to house 10,000 Union prisoners of war, relieving the overcrowding in the makeshift warehouse prisons in and around Richmond.[14]

Henry Wirz remained in Richmond the remainder of January and all of February. It was not until mid-March that he and his family finally departed for Andersonville. After enduring a long and tiresome train journey, Henry Wirz and his family arrived at Andersonville on March 27, 1864.

General John H. Winder, C.S.A.

– 2 –

Prisoners of War

The problem of confining large numbers of prisoners of war was first dealt with during the American Civil War. The entire concept of prisoners of war is a relatively modern phenomenon. There has existed, probably since the advent of our species, hostages, captives, and slaves, but not what we know of today as prisoners of war.

The first Americans who could possibly hold the title of prisoners of war were members of George Washington's army captured after the Battle of Long Island. The British modified several warships into floating prison hulks and anchored them in New York Harbor. The British also confined captured American sailors in prison hulks in Plymouth and Portsmouth, England; Halifax, Nova Scotia, and Antigua in the West Indies. The number of Americans confined in these prison hulks were relatively small compared to the thousands held during the Civil War. However, the conditions in the overcrowded, and disease ridden, prison hulks were a bitter foretaste of what was to come.[1]

The American Civil War began with the same amount of mutual respect and gentleman-like behavior that had characterized eighteenth-century warfare, when prisoners were paroled on their honor not to return to battle. When Union Major Robert Anderson surrendered Fort Sumter to Confederate forces, commanded by Confederate General Pierre G. T. Beauregard, his men were allowed to vacate the fort keeping their arms, the U.S. flag, and all the personal items and military equipment they could carry. Anderson was even allowed to fire a 100-gun salute to the American flag before it was lowered from the fort's ramparts.

This mutual respect was understandable since Pierre Beaureguard had been a student of Major Anderson when he was a cadet at West Point and had stayed behind after his graduation to serve as Anderson's assistant, training new cadets in the use of artillery.[2]

Abraham Lincoln had commanded a militia company during the Black Hawk Indian War, but had never seen combat. He was a pragmatic politician, who would do whatever was necessary to save the Union. He cared little for West Point classmate sentimentalities or military etiquette.

Lincoln's greatest fear was that the Civil War would evolve into some type of protracted stalemate with the South gaining diplomatic recognition, and perhaps military aid, from some European power, reminiscent of what had happened during the American Revolution when France came to the aid of the young United States.

Lincoln particularly feared France's ambitious Emperor Napoleon III, who flirted with the Confederacy, and had launched a foreign military adventure in Mexico in violation of the Monroe Doctrine. An alliance with Napoleon III was the dream of Confederate President Jefferson Davis, who openly made overtures to the French.

The Confederate defeat at Gettysburg made foreign intervention in the Civil War much less likely; however, it was still a possibility. Abraham Lincoln was therefore in a hurry to end the war before Napoleon III, or some other foreign potentate, decided to get involved.

Abraham Lincoln could not afford to treat the Confederate States of America as an independent and sovereign nation. To do so would make it appear that the Confederacy was equal, not subordinate, to the government of the United States. This presented a tricky problem when it came to the issue of prisoners of war. How could the U.S. government negotiate prisoner exchanges and paroles without giving the Confederate government the political legitimacy it was so desperately seeking.[3]

The first prisoner of war crisis arose in February of 1862 when Union forces, commanded by Ulysses S. Grant, captured Fort Donaldson, Tennessee, and with it 15,000 Confederate prisoners of war. This was a remarkably large number of prisoners, since there had only been 16,000 officers and men in the entire United States Army only a year before.

In July of the same year, a meeting was held under a flag of truce and a prisoner exchange cartel was negotiated. Representing the Confederacy was Major General D. H. Hill and for the Union was Major General John H. Dix. The Dix-Hill Prisoner of War Cartel was based on a similar agreement negotiated with the British during the War of 1812, ironically, by the father of Confederate General John H. Winder who would become Confederate commissary general of prisoners.

The Dix-Hill Cartel was clumsy and unworkable from the start. Instead of a simple one for one exchange, a complicated ratio system emerged where a commanding general had to be exchanged for an officer of equivalent rank or sixty privates. A major general required forty privates or an officer of equivalent rank. A brigadier general required an equivalent or twenty privates. A colonel, fifteen privates or an equivalent. A lieutenant colonel an equivalent or ten privates, a major an equivalent or eight privates. Captains and lieutenants required only four privates or an officer of equivalent rank.

During the first year of the war, officers were not put under guard but allowed to return to their command, on their honor as officers and gentlemen, that they would not return to combat until an "equivalent" was made. This "equivalent" would be either an officer of equal rank or an agreed upon number of privates. When such a deal was completed, that is when an officer of equivalent rank or the required number of privates were returned to the other side, the officer was considered to be "matched" and was therefore eligible for a return to duty in the field.

Enlisted men were often paroled under terms similar to those made to the officers. However, other enlisted men were held under light guard in outdoor camps and makeshift prisons such as old warehouses and abandoned buildings. The final decision on what to do with prisoners was usually left up to the discretion of the commanding officer. There were seldom any attempts to escape, since all enlisted men were usually "matched" within ten days.

Both the Union and Confederacy had regulations that specified that prisoners of war were to be treated humanely. United States Army Regulations, that dated to before the war, specified that prisoners were to be sent to the rear, and the care of wounded prisoners of war was to be the same as the care given the wounded of the rest of the army. Prisoners were to obey the necessary orders given them and were to receive rations without regard to rank. A prisoner's horse could be taken for the capturing army, but his personal property was to be respected.

Confederate regulations were less clear and made no mention of a prisoner's personal property, but the regulations did say that the quartermaster general shall provide for the safe custody and sustenance of prisoners of war, and that it should be the same in quantity and quality as fed the Confederate Army.

As the Civil War wore on, the system of prisoner exchanges began to break down. The mountains of paperwork and tedious bookkeeping needed to make sure neither side was being shortchanged resulted in discrepancies that could not be negotiated away.

The problems were made more acute when both sides began bickering with each other over alleged violations of the parole agreements. The North claimed to have found paroled Confederate soldiers under arms on the battlefield. The North also decried the dubious Confederate practice of forming paroled enlisted men into labor battalions, that dug earthwork defenses much too close to the front lines to suit Union commanders. The South denied such charges, defended their own practices concerning labor battalions, and submitted their own charges of misconduct in the prisoner exchanges.[4]

The Confederacy, which was short of everything, needed to fight a war and had much more to lose in a breakdown in prisoner exchanges than the North. The South desperately needed its soldiers back and did not have the resources needed to house, feed, and guard large numbers of prisoners of war. But, in an unbelievable display of arrogance, the South finally pushed the issue to the breaking point.

The issue that finally brought an end to prisoner exchanges was the use of Black troops by the North. Confederate officials threatened to execute any white officer found in command of Black soldiers and to sell all captured Black soldiers into slavery. Under no circumstances would the South ever consider exchanging Black soldiers.

There had been a growing opposition to prisoner exchanges in the North for some time. It was evident to Secretary of War Edwin Stanton that the Civil War would last at least through the end of 1864, and that the conflict would not be decided through one huge battle or single campaign, but in a slow, drawn-out war of attrition.

Other critics of the prisoner exchanges, such as General Ulysses S. Grant, argued that every exchanged prisoner only prolonged the war by funneling more troops back into the Confederate Army. Grant was frustrated that Confederate units he had paroled after the siege of Vicksburg had been found in front of his troops at Chattanooga.[5] Grant argued that the war could only be won when the Confederate Army could no longer replace the troops that were killed, wounded, or captured. General William T. Sherman was even more militant. Not only did he oppose prisoner exchanges, he believed that simply defeating the Confederate Army was not enough to win victory. Sherman felt that the war must be taken to the civilian population, that had agitated and started the conflict in the first place. Sherman's army would carry out his ideas in 1864, destroying the South's infrastructure and its very will to wage war.

In July of 1863, Ulysses S. Grant signed an order ending all prisoner exchanges within his command. Only a few days later, Secretary of War Edwin Stanton, a Radical Republican and fervent abolitionist, who was furious over the South's refusal to exchange Black soldiers, ordered a general halt to all prisoner exchanges throughout the Union Army.

However, neither of these orders were absolute. Union commanders still had the authority to parole or exchange prisoners under certain circumstances, such as when it would be dangerous to the command to keep them, or when the Union forces were operating in remote areas where prisoners could not be easily shipped to a prisoner of war camp. Also, these orders did not prohibit Union and Confederate officials from meeting and negotiating ad hoc prisoner exchanges or paroles when both sides felt they were necessary. These became known as "field exchanges" and they occurred until the end of the war, but on a very limited scale, usually in small engagements in remote areas.

As thousands of Union prisoners of war were taken in the heavy fighting of the summer and fall of 1863, the South began to realize the error of
its ways. The burden of caring for all these Union prisoners was more than
it could handle. Confederate officials offered to again begin exchanging
prisoners on a one-for-one basis with no questions about race or rank taken
into consideration. However, the North refused to change its policy, and
the number of Union soldiers in Confederate hands continued to grow at a
staggering rate.

In a desperate effort to change the Union Army's policy, the South
began a campaign of disinformation, blaming the North's decision to use
Black troops as the reason for the breakdown of prisoner exchanges. Northern prisoners of war, held under horrible conditions, were routinely told by
Confederate officers that it was Abraham Lincoln's concern for Black soldiers that was the reason for their misery. Pro-Confederate Northerners
and Confederate agents in Canada also spread the word that Lincoln cared
more for Black troops than for the white soldiers suffering in Confederate
prisons. An examination of the diaries of Union prisoners of war shows that
they largely shared this rhetoric and greatly blamed Abraham Lincoln for
their suffering. Like prisoners of war in the twentieth century, they largely
felt abandoned and forgotten by their own government.

Eventually Confederate leaders had to face the fact that no widespread resumption of prisoner exchanges or paroles would occur anytime
in the near future. They now had to begin to try and deal with the thousands of Union prisoners of war jammed into every inch of space in existing Confederate prisons, and find some place to put the tens of thousands
of new prisoners that were arriving each day.

During the time when prisoner exchanges were taking place, it was
expedient to have prisoner detention areas close to the front lines. This
was especially true in the South because it prevented valuable railroad
resources from having to be used to transport prisoners of war over long
distances. Since the amount of time Union prisoners of war were held was
fairly short, usually a matter of weeks or months at the most, the southern
part of Virginia was the most logical place to hold them.

Old warehouses, that were formerly used to store tobacco and cotton, were quickly changed into temporary prisons. The largest and most
well known were in Richmond, but prisons also existed in the cities of
Danville and Petersburg.

Once the prisoner exchanges were halted, all this changed. Confederate government officials worried about having so many thousands of
enemy troops so near the capital. It was feared that a large Union cavalry
force could sweep down on the Confederate capital and free the imprisoned men. There were also escapes that threw the city into a panic, the
largest of which involved over one hundred Union officers who managed
to tunnel out of Richmond's Libby Prison in February 1865 and flee to the

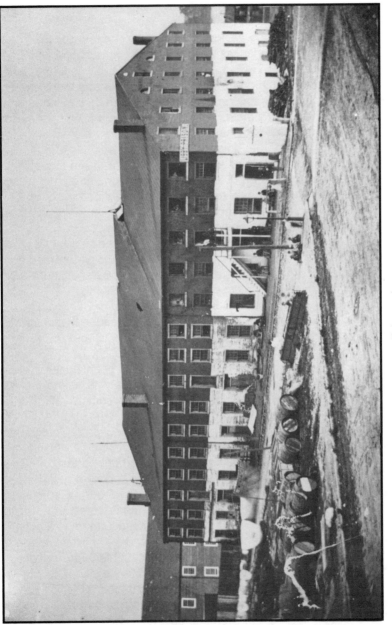

Libby Prison

nearby homes of Union sympathizers who gave them shelter. From these scattered homes, most of the Union officers were able to find their way to the Union lines, using what was left of the old "Underground Railroad," that had been used to aid runaway slaves before the war.[6]

The danger of escape was aggravated by the conditions in the makeshift prisons. The old warehouses were cold in winter, unbearably hot and stuffy in summer, and filled with lice and other vermin. It was feared that a mass escape could result in an orgy of looting, rape, and the murder of civilians as the freed Union prisoners took revenge for their mistreatment.

Another problem was that buildings suitable for holding prisoners of war were becoming harder and harder to find. Landlords scoffed at the low rent paid by the Confederate government and their appeals to patriotism had little effect. Faced with a shortage of old barns and warehouses, the Confederates had opened an outdoor prison on a long stretch of alluvial mud, called Belle Isle, in the James River within sight of the city of Richmond. At Belle Isle, Union prisoners of war shivered in leaky tents and huddled together for warmth against the cold and damp.

In December of 1863, a Union prisoner was found frozen to death in the mud of Belle Isle. News of the death leaked out and was carried north by Union spies and newspaper reporters. The incident shocked the citizens of Richmond, causing widespread anger in the North.[7]

It was Confederate Major General Howell Cobb of Georgia who first proposed to Confederate Secretary of War James Seddon that southwest Georgia might be a good spot for a military prison to relieve the overcrowded situation in Richmond.[8]

Cobb was a distinguished Georgian who had been Speaker of the U.S. House of Representatives and governor of Georgia before the war. He had also been secretary of the treasury in the administration of his good friend James Buchanan. When Lincoln was elected president, Cobb urged Georgia to secede and chaired the 1861 convention in Montgomery, Alabama that established the Confederate States of America. Cobb returned from the convention filled with patriotic vigor and organized the 16th Georgia Infantry. He led his troops in the retreat from Yorktown and in heavy fighting during the Seven Days' campaign. He also led the Georgians at Antietam. On September 9, 1863, Cobb was made commander of the military district of Georgia and Florida with his headquarters in Macon.[9]

In a letter dated November 24, 1863, Secretary of War Seddon ordered General John H. Winder, commander of Confederate prisons, to find a site in southwestern Georgia for a new military prison. The site was to be far enough from the fighting to be out of danger of Union cavalry raids. This would not be easy since the Union anaconda was slowly squeezing the life out of the Southern Confederacy. With each passing day more and more Southern soil was falling to Union troops.[10]

General Winder chose his son, thirty-year-old William Sidney Winder, to travel to Georgia and find a suitable prison site. General Winder suggested to his son that Americus or Fort Valley were the best spots to look, but he gave Sidney permission to travel as far south as Albany.[11]

Sidney Winder's new assignment would involve a lot of careful diplomacy on his part. A deep political rivalry had developed between General Howell Cobb and Georgia's Governor Joseph Brown. The new prison site would have to have the blessing of both men or the project was doomed to failure from the start.

Joseph Brown was to become one of the unsung villains of the Andersonville tragedy. Born in the north Georgia mountains, an area known at the time as "Cherokee Georgia," and raised in typical hill farm poverty, Joe Brown rose to become governor of Georgia. He was a self-made man of strong personal beliefs, little formal education, and an iron will.

Joseph Brown was a fanatical, some might say lunatic, states' rights advocate even by hardcore Confederate standards. He was also a thorn in the side of Confederate President Jefferson Davis with whom he constantly feuded. Brown was shocked when he learned that Jefferson Davis intended to use Georgia troops as part of the Army of Northern Virginia. He declared that soldiers from Georgia would only see service on the soil of their native state. Brown endured overwhelming public criticism from Richmond newspapers stating he was hurting the Confederate cause before giving in and allowing Georgia troops to travel to Virginia. However, he continued to argue against the conscription of Georgia militia units into the Confederate Army and the paying of taxes imposed by the Confederate Congress. Brown fought against the hated conscription by giving exemptions to all Georgians who held public office and then appointing hundreds of his friends, political supporters, and relatives to public jobs. Rural Georgia counties that had previously only had a single sheriff to enforce the law now found that they had scores of new deputies with very little to do. Even though almost all legal activity had been suspended because of the war, Brown appointed a host of new county court clerks, bailiffs, inspectors, and judges to each county.[12]

Joseph Brown's office was in the medieval-looking state capitol building in Milledgeville and it was Sidney Winder's first stop in his visit to Georgia. The irascible Georgia governor looked more like a New England abolitionist than a staunch secessionist. He was pale and thin with a "Quaker style" beard, without a mustache, that flowed gently down to his chest.

Brown was civil to Winder, but his attitude reflected the mood of most Georgians. He opposed the placement of Union prisoners of war in his state. However, Brown was a also a savvy politician who knew that the onus for the placement of Union prisoners of war in Georgia would most likely fall on his arch political rival, General Howell Cobb. Therefore, the Georgia governor would not do anything to block the prison.

Sidney Winder had to thread a fine needle in dealing with these two men, who were deeply suspicious and jealous of each other. After leaving Milledgeville, he traveled directly to Macon to pay his respects to General Cobb.

Brigadier General Howell Cobb was a heavy, barrel-chested man with a long, thick beard. He received Sidney Winder at his home in Macon and suggested at their meeting that the prison be located in the sandy hill country south of Albany, at a place called Blue Springs, but Winder had written orders from his father specifying that the prison be located north of Albany due to the danger of Union cavalry raids from Union forces in Florida. Studying local maps, Sidney Winder had already come to the conclusion that Americus would be the best site for the new prison because of its isolation. The general was amiable and offered Winder support for his mission.

Sidney Winder arrived at Americus on November 28, 1863, and was met by Uriah Harrold, who had served as Confederate commissary agent for the region since the beginning of the war.[13] Harrold was thoroughly familiar with the area and referred Sidney Winder to an area west of Americus called the Plains of Dura.

The Plains, as they were called, had served many times as the site of huge religious revivals, where thousands of believers would gather to sing, pray, and listen to long-winded sermons that went on for hours. These religious revivals occurred frequently during the nineteenth century and often lasted for weeks at a time. Thousands of worshipers would travel by train to Americus and walk the ten miles to the revival site. They often camped for weeks on the Plains, finding the site to have good drainage and better than adequate water supplies for all the worshipers.

However, Sidney Winder felt that the Plains of Dura were too far removed from the railroad, and local citizens had adequately expressed their displeasure at having a prison located in the area.[14]

Another factor was that religious revivals were still being held at the site, so local ministers particularly objected, threatening to take their case to Governor Brown. It was while he was inspecting the Plains that Winder first heard of the small village called Andersonville Station, located ten miles north of Americus. He arranged transportation to Andersonville, leaving behind the Plains of Dura, which would gain its own fame a century later as the home of Jimmy Carter, the 39th president of the United States.

According to census reports, there were about seventy people living in the area of Andersonville Station, most of them single men who farmed and cut wood for the railroad. It was difficult for small "dirt" farmers to find wives due to the grinding poverty and back-breaking hard work that was associated with that type of livelihood.[15]

The small town had everything Sidney Winder was seeking. It was isolated, close to the railroad, and there was an abundance of tall Georgia pine trees to build a stockade.

Winder met with Benjamin Dykes, the town's postmaster and leading merchant, who helped Winder select a site about two miles from the railroad. Dykes steered Winder to a large piece of land owned by him and another citizen of the village. The site was crossed by a small tributary of Sweetwater Creek, that was later given the name Stockade Branch after the prison opened.

Benjamin Dykes strongly lobbied Sidney Winder to choose the Andersonville site. While doing so, Dykes seriously misled Winder about local feelings toward the prison. He gave the young Confederate captain the impression that local citizens supported the prison, and could be counted on to help any way they could. Dykes was hoping to make a small fortune in rent for the prison site land and in what he could sell to the soldiers who would form the guard force. He also cast greedy thoughts toward the Union prisoners, who would likely have coveted Yankee dollars to spend.

Sidney Winder felt that the small creek could supply enough water for the six thousand men he expected to be imprisoned at the site. If Sidney Winder had any way of knowing that the prison population would eventually grow to over thirty thousand prisoners of war, he certainly would have never chosen the Andersonville site. Winder's only apparent dereliction of duty was failing to notice that the region had been almost totally denuded of hardwood trees. They had all been cut down to provide wood for the railroad.

General Winder sent another relative, a second cousin, Captain Richard B. Winder, to help Sidney build the prison. Richard was six years older than his cousin. Like the rest of the Winder clan, he was the scion of a prominent Maryland slave-holding family. He had joined the 39th Virginia Infantry, organized to perform the almost impossible task of defending the eastern peninsula of Virginia and Maryland. The 39th Virginia found little support from the Confederate government who considered the Maryland-Virginia peninsula expendable. When the Maryland-Virginia peninsula was inevitably occupied by Union troops, the 39th Virginia was disbanded. To keep his rank, Richard Winder moved to Richmond and went to work for his cousin, General John H. Winder.[16]

Sidney and Richard Winder were totally perplexed by the fierce opposition in Sumter County to the building of the proposed prison. The obsequious cooperation of Benjamin Dykes had misled them into believing that they could expect help from the local citizens in the form of tools, slaves, and mules to build the prison stockade. However, they were seriously mistaken.

Local slave-owning farmers feared that another John Brown would be imprisoned at Andersonville and that he would lead a mass escape of Union prisoners to ravage the countryside. They refused to provide any slaves or materials to help construct the prison stockade. Even a visit by General Howell Cobb, who gave a powerfully patriotic speech, failed to stir the local citizens to allow Sidney Winder to hire their slaves or rent their mules.

Richard Winder's first priority was to get the stockade built and with it a cookhouse to prepare the prisoner's food. To do this he needed lumber.

He could only pay the official price of $50 per 1,000 lineal feet. While this might have been a fair prewar price, wartime inflation had caused the price of lumber to soar well beyond what Richard Winder was able to pay. Local sawmill operators refused to sell their lumber to Winder, saying that they could get twice what he was offering from civilian customers.[17]

Doing his patriotic duty to assist Richard Winder, Governor Brown also visited Americus. He shook hands with local people he met on the street and met with leading citizens. However, it was a wasted trip, cooperation was not forthcoming. Sumter County farmers steadfastly refused to lend either their slaves or mules to help build the detested prison.

Finally, a frustrated Confederate Secretary of War Seddon, tired of the delays, wrote an order giving Richard Winder permission to commandeer any personnel or materials he might need and pay, the scheduled Confederate rate.[18] With the force of law behind him, Richard and Sidney Winder could now begin work on the new Confederate prison, ironically to be called Camp Sumter after the Georgia County that bitterly opposed its construction.

On January 10, 1864, commandeered slave gangs began felling trees and clearing the site. The crude pine log stockade that would later become known as Andersonville Prison began to take shape on the steep banks of the tiny stream.

Winder's order from Secretary of War Seddon carried a sixty-day limit. In order to have as much work done as possible before the order expired, the slave gangs were worked from daylight to past dark, digging the trenches and setting the upright pine log posts into place.

In an effort to further foster cooperation from Georgia officials, Confederate authorities asked General Howell Cobb to suggest a commander for the new prison. It was generally felt that Sidney Winder, as a captain, did not have enough rank for the task. Cobb suggested Lieutenant Colonel Alexander W. Persons, a native of Fort Valley, Georgia, which was only thirty miles from Andersonville.[19]

Colonel Persons was a twenty-seven-year-old lawyer, who had been originally commissioned to command the 55th Georgia Infantry. It was a mutinous unit of rebellious drunks who had previously been commanded by an incompetent officer who failed to enforce discipline. The 55th Georgia had never seen combat and Colonel Persons had been given the difficult task of whipping the unit into shape for battle.

When Persons took command of the 55th Georgia, they were in southern Kentucky near the Cumberland Gap. He barely had time to introduce himself and issue orders before he returned home on furlough. While Colonel Persons was at home in Fort Valley, his command was surrounded by a superior Union force, which quickly captured the entire 55th Georgia Infantry with little difficulty. Most of the men of the 55th Georgia would spend the rest of the war as prisoners of war at Camp Douglas, Illinois.[20]

The only part of the 55th Georgia not captured were men home on furlough with Colonel Persons and convalescent troops recovering from various illnesses in military hospitals. Howell Cobb believed that Colonel Persons would be able to round up enough of these men to form a unit, too small to go into battle, but large enough to serve as a guard force for the estimated six thousand men expected to arrive at Andersonville.

On February 17, 1864, Richard Winder received notice from Richmond, that the first Union prisoners of war were already on their way to Andersonville. He was panic stricken by the news. Colonel Persons and his band of less than one hundred guards had just arrived. The stockade was only about half finished, and the construction of the cookhouse had only just begun. But, most importantly, no arrangements had been worked out to feed the prisoners. There were also no locks for the gates, no lumber for shelters inside the stockade, and Colonel Person's soldiers were basically unarmed, except for whatever side arms and personal shoulder weapons they might have been carrying when they arrived.[21]

The decision to begin moving the Union prisoners out of Richmond had been caused by the successful escape on February 9 of more than one hundred Union officers from Libby Prison. To make matters worse, one of the Union officers who had escaped was Colonel Abel D. Streight, a notorious Union cavalry raider, who had led a seventeen-day cavalry sweep through northern Alabama until he, and most of his men, had been captured by Confederate forces, commanded by Confederate General Nathan Bedford Forrest. It was feared that Streight would soon return to raid Richmond.[22]

Also, notice had been given to General Winder that southern Virginia could no longer provide enough food to feed the tens of thousands of Union prisoners and continue to feed the Army of Robert E. Lee. Faced with this type of military threat and serious food shortages, there was little choice except to begin moving prisoners to Georgia, regardless of the state of readiness of the new prison.

General Winder's fears about a Union cavalry raid to free prisoners of war was confirmed in the final days of February, when a reckless and dashing Union brigadier general Judson Kilpatrick led a bold cavalry raid on Richmond. He was assisted in his two-pronged assault by an equally daring young colonel, Ulric Dahlgren. The plan of the raid called for Kilpatrick's force of 3,500 cavalrymen to move against the Confederate capital from the north, while Dahlgren's force would come from the west.

It was a mixed combination of rain swollen streams that hampered the movement of the Union cavalry, Confederate bushwhackers, and stronger than anticipated resistance that made the raid a failure.

Colonel Dahlgren was killed in the raid, and bloodstained documents found on his body showed that the purpose of the raid was to free the prisoners of war confined on Belle Isle and in Richmond. Then the prisoners were to be allowed to loot and pillage the city, while Dahlgren's men attempted to capture or assassinate key Confederate government officials, including Jefferson Davis.[23] While the Kilpatrick-Dahlgren raid was a failure, it was successful enough to terrify the Confederate government and begin an accelerated movement of Union prisoners of war out of Richmond.

The movement of prisoners from Richmond to Andersonville was a logistical nightmare. No fewer than nine different rail lines were involved. Two hundred prisoners at a time were crammed into four railroad boxcars, guarded by sixty-one Confederate soldiers.[24] Food supplies, scheduled to meet the trains, were usually late or didn't arrive at all, and the February weather was bitter cold. It was General Winder's goal to ship at least four hundred Union prisoners out of Richmond each day, most of which would be bound for Andersonville.

While the first prisoners were en route to Andersonville, Richard Winder was busy trying to procure enough food to feed the men.

The original plan had been to drive herds of beef cattle up from Florida.[25] There were sufficient supplies of beef in the Florida panhandle where the small town of Quincy, Florida was to be the staging area for the cattle drives.[26] While the supply of cattle was ample, the skilled cattle drivers, called "Crackers" because of the sound of their long rawhide bullwhips, were almost totally unavailable.

Unlike their western counterparts, Florida "Cracker Cowboys" usually did not ride horses. They often walked along with the cattle herds, using their long bullwhips to control the lumbering beasts. Throughout the Florida wilderness the cowboys had erected large split-rail corrals. Cattle drives consisted of driving the cattle from one corral to the next, where they were penned for the night. They also had special mixed breed "cow dogs" to run down strays and hold them by biting into the layer of fat under the animal's neck until a "Cracker Cowboy" could arrive to tie the stray steer with a rope and lead him back to the cattle herd.

The Florida cattle were not the noble "Longhorn" steers found in south Texas. Florida cattle were much smaller, many no larger than a donkey. Florida cowboys were very adept at wrestling the beasts to the ground with their bare hands. One Florida visitor commented that the cattle were as tough as the long, stringy, wire grass they fed on.[27]

Unfortunately, the "Florida Cracker Cowboys" did not receive an exemption from conscription into the Confederate Army. By 1864, there were not enough of them left to drive the beef herds north to Andersonville on a regular basis. Slaves could not be trusted to do this type of work. Being a "Florida Cracker" demanded skills, and a toughness, that could not be picked up with only a few days' training. Some cattle drives did make it north to Andersonville, but not nearly enough to adequately feed the constantly growing prison population.

With few cattle coming from Florida, Richard Winder decided to substitute pork. The woods of the American South were filled with large herds of wild hogs, who could trace their ancestry back to the expedition of the Spanish explorer Hernando de Soto, who had brought the first pigs to the region during his murderous trek across the South during the years 1539 to 1543.

Large numbers of pigs were also raised by Southern farmers. They were easy to keep, requiring little care, and would eat almost anything. Pork made up a large part of the Southern diet, especially in winter, when other foods were in short supply.

While there was pork available from a nearby source, local farmers balked at the miserably low prices the Confederate government was willing to pay. They could make more money by selling their smoked pork to meat speculators in Macon and Savannah.

The prime cuts of pork meat, the hams and shoulders, usually found their way to the tables of Southern civilians. Less favorable parts of the pigs such as the intestines, called chitterlings, the feet, head, tail, and backbone were fed to slaves. The fatty underbelly of the hog, called "sowbelly," was what usually found its way in large quantities to the Confederate Army.

The "sowbelly" pork that eventually made its way to Andersonville was of the poorest quality available. Richard Winder noted that it was more fat and sinew than meat and was often rancid. However, this was the best he could get with what he was allowed to pay for pork by the Confederate government.

Richard Winder also felt that corn would be a good source of food for the prison. The Confederate government did everything it could to encourage Southern farmers to grow as much corn as possible to feed the Confederate Army. However, few farmers were patriotic enough to pass up the huge profits that could be made by converting their corn into whiskey. The Civil War also drove the price of cotton to unprecedented heights, and few farmers would plant corn to sell to the Confederate Army at prewar prices, when they could plant cotton to sell to blockade runners for considerably more money.[28]

The only corn Richard Winder was able to procure was from a mill located south of Americus.[29] It was a crude cornmeal ground from poor quality corn with the cob and shucks thrown in to give it more bulk. Before the war, such a mixture would only be used for animal feed. Now it would be used to feed the Union prisoners of war at Andersonville.

This mixture of rancid, fatty, pork and bulk cornmeal, mixed with water and baked into cornbread, would make up most of the Union prisoner's diet as long as they were at Andersonville.[30] It must be noted, in all fairness, that the diet of Confederate soldiers in the field wasn't all that much better, and that the guards at Andersonville shared the same food as the men they guarded. Also, whenever vegetables, molasses, and beef became available they were fairly distributed to the prisoners.

On February 24, 1864, the first load of Union prisoners of war arrived at the small train depot at Andersonville. With a large crowd of local civilians gathered to gawk at the Yankee prisoners, the men were unloaded and marched under guard from the depot to the still unfinished pine log stockade. Some of the prisoners were seriously ill and had to be carried in makeshift litters.

Upon entering the stockade, the men saw a large area surrounded on only three sides by a pine log wall. There were no shelters of any kind and the ground in the prison compound had only been partially cleared of underbrush. There was still heavy vegetation growing in the stockade, especially on the slopes of the creek bank.[31] A skirmish line of guards closed in the open side of the stockade. Although the guards were only lightly armed, there would be no escapes. The Union prisoners were all veterans of the freezing cold and damp of Belle Isle and were far too exhausted and ill from their journey to even move, much less run away. The prisoners were issued a ration of pork or beef, sweet potatoes, and beans. All food was issued raw to the two hundred prisoners. The cookhouse was still unfinished, and the prison had no pots or pans in which to prepare the food. The prisoners had to scavenge wood to build a fire and use whatever implements they might have brought with them to cook their first meal.[32]

The next day, Captain William Sidney Winder formally turned over control of the prison to Colonel Persons. Sidney Winder would return to Richmond to his previous position, assisting his father, who was busy planning the establishment of new prisons in South Carolina and Alabama. His cousin, Richard Winder, would remain behind to assist Colonel Persons at Andersonville.

In the weeks ahead, Richard Winder would be the busiest man at Andersonville. Under the command system established at the new prison, Colonel Persons would be in charge of all the area surrounding the prison, dealing with local civilians, supervising the guard force, chasing down escaped prisoners, and would have overall responsibility for the prison when communicating with Richmond. Under him would be Captain Richard Winder who would be quartermaster and commissary officer. Richard Winder would have the terrible responsibility of feeding, sheltering, and clothing the Union prisoners of war.

Until another officer arrived, Richard Winder would also have to assume command of the inside of the stockade, called the inner prison. It would be his job to prevent escapes, riots, disruptions, and generally be responsible for the good order and discipline of the men confined within the stockade. General Winder had promised Richard that as soon as possible he would send another officer to relieve him from having to do both jobs. The man General Winder had already chosen for the job of commander of the inner prison would be a Confederate officer of Swiss descent, recently returned from Europe, named Henry Wirz.[33]

During the time Andersonville Prison was in operation, the small Georgia Southwestern Railroad that serviced the town was taxed to its limit. Trains passed through Andersonville twice a day. Those coming from Macon would usually be bringing new prisoners for the stockade, while trains going north from Albany would be carrying badly needed food, cloth-ing, and ammunition for the Confederate Army.

Colonel Persons was constantly attempting to get an available train to transport lumber and building materials to Andersonville. According to his testimony at the trail of Henry Wirz, he stayed in constant communica-tion with the superintendent of the Georgia Southwestern Railroad. Colo-nel Persons claimed to have only been able to get a train every ten or twenty days, and whenever he could get a train, he used it to ship lumber, what he considered the most badly needed building material at Andersonville. The entire time Colonel Persons was at Andersonville, he only managed to get five or six trains. Each train had only six to eight carloads of lumber, making for a grand total of fifty carloads of lumber.

With the lumber he was able to get, Colonel Persons was able to complete the bakehouse, but built little else. After the war when testifying against Henry Wirz, and no doubt trying to save his own neck, Colonel Persons claimed that he saw fifty or sixty houses built outside the stockade from lumber he claimed he acquired, while Union prisoners of war were suffering without shelters.

One of Winder's greatest concerns was the health of the workers building the stockade. Any type of medical emergency could halt the work indefinitely. At his request, General Winder sent a twenty-five-year-old regu-lar army surgeon, Isaiah White, to Andersonville. Isaiah White was a close associate of General Winder, and like most of his cronies, he was also from the eastern peninsula of Virginia. He had an unusual amount of stamina and was quick to take decisive action when it was warranted.

Until the first train load of prisoners arrived, he had busied himself treating the Black laborers working to build the stockade. He immediately saw that many of them were seriously ill, mostly from pneumonia. Chief Surgeon White quickly established a small hospital on high ground in the extreme northeast corner of the stockade. It began with only a single white army tent and a bed of pine straw.[34] This would be Andersonville's first hospital.

One of the first Union prisoners admitted to the hospital was thirty-four-year-old Adam Swarner of the 2nd New York Cavalry. Swarner had arrived with the first load of prisoners from Belle Isle and was near death when he was unloaded from the train. Swarner's body was ravaged by chills and fever and a quick listen to his chest showed that Swarner's lungs were filled with fluid. Chief Surgeon White ordered Swarner put on the bed of pine straw inside the tent. Despite what little White could do, Adam Swarner died on February 27, 1864.

Colonel Persons and Richard Winder chose a burial site for Swarner on high ground just north of the prison stockade. The Union cavalryman was buried in a hastily made wooden coffin, fashioned from rifle cases that had arrived on the same train with him from Richmond. Richard Winder recorded the death in his records. Anticipating other deaths, he designated

Swarner's final resting place as grave number one.[35] Within a month, the cemetery would grow to over twenty graves, and that would be only the beginning. Before the prison would close, fourteen months later, over twelve thousand Union prisoners of war would lay beneath the red-clay soil of the Andersonville Prison cemetery.

On March 3, 1864, Chief Surgeon White diagnosed a Tennessee prisoner with smallpox. He knew that the disease would spread like wildfire if it was not quickly contained. He immediately ordered that a second hospital be built on the edge of the woods south of the stockade, far removed from the other prisoners. All prisoners who showed any sign of the disease were quickly moved to the hospital.

Surgeon White's quick actions are credited with preventing a major outbreak of the disease. However, at the trial of Henry Wirz, White's next actions were called into question. He ordered that all prisoners who could not show signs of a "healthy" smallpox scar were to be immediately vaccinated against the disease.[36] Many of these vaccinations became badly infected in the unsanitary conditions of the stockade, and as a result some limbs had to be amputated to stop the spread of the infections. Later, prisoners would write and testify about being subjected to horrible medical experiments at the hands of quack Confederate doctors.

During the three days Adam Swarner lay dying in the single tent hospital, prisoners were arriving from Richmond at the rate of five hundred men a day.

The prisoners quickly cleaned all undergrowth from the stockade, seeking firewood and building materials for shelters. Latrines, called sinks, were established near the prison wall next to the creek, and the water in the small creek was dammed up on the opposite side to provide a small pool of water for drinking and cooking. By March 1 the stockade was basically completed, but the prison population was continuing to grow.

On February 20, 1864, the only full-scale Civil War battle to be fought in the state of Florida took place near an otherwise obscure railroad depot called Olustee Station, near an equally obscure lake named Ocean Pond. As was the custom, the North would name the battle after the nearest body of water, in this case Ocean Pond, and the South would name it after the nearest settlement or town, Olustee.

Hoping to sweep across the state of Florida and capture the strategic bridges over the Suwannee River, Union forces, commanded by Brigadier General Truman Seymour, moved down the tracks of the Florida, Atlantic and Gulf Railroad, not expecting to encounter a significant Confederate force in the sparsely inhabited region of pine forests and small dirt farms. Unknown to the Union troops, a powerful Confederate force of nearly 5,000 men awaited them about 50 miles southwest of Jacksonville, just east of Olustee Station. The Confederate forces had anchored their northern flank on the south shore of Ocean Pond and their south flank on the railroad tracks and a tangled cypress swamp.

The first shots were fired late in the morning of February 20, as the Union troops probed the Confederate positions to determine the size of the force before them. By dark, the Union forces were in full retreat back to Jacksonville. General Seymour had lost over a third of his force and it was only a strategic blunder on the part of the Confederates that allowed him to escape to the safety of Jacksonville with what was left of his expedition.

The Battle of Olustee eliminated any serious threat of a Union cavalry raid on Andersonville from Florida. However, it created another problem. One of the objectives of General Seymour's raid on Florida was to destroy the plantations near Tallahassee and recruit liberated slaves for the Union Army. To help in this recruiting, General Seymour had taken with him some of the largest and most well-known Black regiments in the Union Army. His force included the 8th and 12th U.S. Colored Infantry, the First North Carolina Colored Infantry, and the 54th Massachusetts Infantry, that had distinguished itself the previous summer in an heroic, but failed attack, on Battery Wagner near Charleston, South Carolina.

Most of the men captured at Olustee were wounded. They were transported by rail to Tallahassee, where they received medical care. As soon as the Yankee prisoners were well enough to be moved, they were sent by rail to the Apalachicola River and put on a small river steamer that sailed up the Apalachicola and Chattahoochee Rivers to Fort Gaines. From there, the prisoners were transported by rail to the Confederate prison at Andersonville.

Colonel Persons and Richard Winder were flabbergasted when they learned of the arrival of the Black troops from Olustee. They had been given the impression that no Black prisoners would be sent to Andersonville. They were terrified of the thought of Black prisoners of war.

Nothing terrified Southern whites as much as the sight of Blacks in uniform under arms. These proud Black soldiers showed none of the signs of humility and servility so common in slaves and free Blacks living in the South. The news of the Black soldier's arrival swept through the surrounding countryside. Rumors of possible slave rebellions and of Union secret agents recruiting Blacks for the Union Army were rampant throughout Sumter County. The sheriff of Sumter County ordered that no local Blacks were to approach the prison.[37]

Approximately one hundred Black soldiers were ever sent to Andersonville, the largest group coming from Olustee. The Black troops voluntarily segregated themselves from the white prisoners, living in their own little enclave near the South Gate. The captured Black soldiers were formed into labor details and forced to do hard manual labor, expanding the stockade and later digging earthwork defenses. They largely replaced the gangs of Black slaves that had been reclaimed by their white masters after Confederate Secretary of War Seddon's impressment order expired the first week in March. It must be noted that Black troops were primarily used for fatigue details in the Union Army before their capture. However, testimony at the trial of Henry Wirz showed that many of the Black soldiers were subjected to brutal floggings, indicating that many probably resisted having to work for the Confederates.[38]

A far more serious problem was presented with the white officers who commanded the Black regiments. While the sight of Black soldiers might have caused fear, the sight of their Caucasian officers created an almost unbelievable level of anger and revulsion. To Southern whites they were the worst form of traitors. Confederate authorities refused to recognize such men as officers and sent them to prisons set aside for enlisted men.

The Confederates originally vowed to hang any white man caught in command of Black soldiers for the crime of inciting servile rebellion. However, such a threat was never carried out, probably out of fear of Union retaliation against Confederate officers in Union prisons.

One of the white officers captured at Olustee, was Major Archibald Boyle, commander of the 12th U.S. Colored Troops. He arrived at Andersonville on March 14, near death from wounds he had received at Olustee. His Union officer's uniform made him a conspicuous target for Confederate wrath. The Confederate medical officer on duty at the depot refused to send Boyle to the hospital despite his severe wounds. Major Boyle was placed in the stockade with the rest of his Black soldiers, who tended his wounds as best they could.

Boyle's wound was badly infected and full of gangrene. With the help of other Union prisoners, he managed to get into the hospital. However, while Major Boyle was being treated by a Union prisoner of war assigned to work in the hospital, Chief Surgeon Isaiah White happened by and noticed Boyle's officer's uniform. Swearing an oath, Isaiah White ordered the steward to stop treating Boyle and "send him out there with his niggers." The steward refused to obey White's orders and continued dressing Major Boyle's wound. Boyle was later sent out of the hospital, but somehow managed to get his wounds treated.

About a month later, Boyle was again smuggled into the prison hospital, where he had another acrimonious encounter, this time with the chief hospital steward, a man named Robinson. The chief steward had also noticed Boyle's officer's uniform and asked him if he was a major in a Black regiment. Boyle answered that "he was an officer in the United States Military Service." The chief steward then, according to Boyle's testimony, ordered him out of the hospital. When Boyle asked the young steward who he was, he replied that it was none of his business. Boyle then refused to leave feeling that a mere steward had no right to order him out. The chief steward then left and summoned the hospital orderly treating Boyle. He reportedly ordered the man to remove the major from the hospital or he would "shoot him and ball and chain the orderly." With this ultimatum, Major Boyle left the hospital area.

Major Boyle continued to recover with the help of his fellow Union prisoners. Apparently, Union prisoners assigned to work in the hospital were able to smuggle him clean bandages and medications. Later, after the arrival of Henry Wirz, Major Boyle made two formal demands that his rank be respected. Captain Wirz, who had by that time assumed command, begged off, protesting that he was only a subordinate of General Winder. Later, captured Confederate documents showed that Wirz had tried to get Major Boyle transferred to an officer's prison or exchanged.

Major Boyle would survive his captivity and testify at the trial of Henry Wirz. His testimony indicates that Captain Wirz was sympathetic to his plight and did what he could to help. However, strong objections by the prosecution prevented Major Boyle from testifying to that fact.[39]

By the end of March the population of the prison had already reached ten thousand inmates, and conditions in the now muddy stockade were beginning to rapidly deteriorate. The entire prison compound was surrounded by upright pine logs, seventeen feet high, embedded six to eight feet into the ground, enclosing an area of sixteen and one-half acres.[40] The bark had been removed and the logs squared with a broad axe. Along the run of the wall, at regular intervals, were roughly built one-man sentry towers, the prisoners contemptuously called "pigeon roosts."[41]

The prison compound had two gateways, both on the west side facing the town of Andersonville and the railroad depot. The gate north of the small creek that divided the compound was appropriately called the North Gate, the entrance south of the creek was the South Gate. They were built like square pens sticking out from the run of the wall. Each gate had two sets of double wooded doors, one set on the inside and another on the outside. The inside gate was never opened unless the outside gate was closed and vice versa. There were no padlocks, only a stout oak log laid across the double gates secured the gateway. Each gate was flanked by two sentry towers with armed guards, observing the comings and goings. A small gate shack was constructed outside the gate, and Confederate sentries checked each person entering and exiting the stockade.

Inside the stockade running eastward from the gates were two muddy footpaths that the prisoners called "Broadway" at the North Gate and "South Street" at the South Gate. The winding trail leading down to the creek was appropriately known as "Water Street."[42]

A fourth street, called "Market Street," wasn't even a muddy path like the other two "streets," but was just an area near the North Gate that became the prison's main business district. It has been estimated that at least 200 private entrepreneurial activities went on inside the stockade under the eyes of the guards on the tower flanking the North Gate. Union prisoners of war operated barber shops, launders, watch repair, sewing and clothing alteration, and a host of other businesses. They also peddled homemade pipes, eating utensils, buttons, suspenders, pants, shirts, hats, and anything else that could be made or procured under the circumstances. The stockade also included a wide assortment of quack doctors, faith healers, prison evangelists, fortune tellers, card sharks, and raconteurs. Testimony at the Wirz trial indicated there was at least one type of entrepreneur for every twenty-five to thirty prisoners.[43]

The Union prisoners found they had something their Confederate guards, and Southern civilians, were desperate to get their hands on: Federal "greenback" currency. By 1864, Confederate money was virtually worthless and even blockade runners and government officials were refusing to accept it. With their Federal dollars the Union prisoners of war could purchase virtually anything they wanted from their Confederate guards and the crowds of civilians, who were always hanging around the prison grounds.[44]

It was common practice during the Civil War for soldiers to carry with them a wide variety of personal items. These included small Bibles, pocket knives, stationary, watches, rings, religious jewelry, and tintype photos of family members.[45] Soldiers being soldiers, they also carried a number of items that would not meet with the approval of their parents or family minister. These items included playing cards, dice, flasks of whiskey, and a type of early pornography, (that wouldn't raise an eyebrow today), called "French Postcards."

The prisoners found that their guards would trade for relatively minor items the Union prisoners took for granted. One such item were the buttons on the Union soldier's uniforms. These brass buttons with an embossed eagle were highly coveted by the Confederates. Called "hen buttons" by the prisoners, they were traded for fresh vegetables, eggs, eating utensils, pots and pans.

This trade became so heavy that Richard Winder and Colonel Persons feared that a mass escape might occur, should dishonest Confederate guards smuggle in digging utensils or firearms. To stem this illegal trade, it was decided that the prisoners should be kept a safe distance from the perimeter wall. To keep the prisoners back, a small fence was built inside the stockade, ten feet from the run of the pine log wall. It consisted only of a row of evenly spaced upright fence posts about four feet high, topped by a single plank board. This would become known as the dreaded "deadline." It was unclear who gave the order for its construction. But, since the small fence was erected shortly after the arrival of Henry Wirz, he was blamed. However, it was probably Colonel Persons or Richard Winder who gave the order for its construction.

No matter who ordered it erected, the "deadline" was not a concept unique to Andersonville. Civilian prisons had long had such a structure to keep prisoners from approaching the wall. Other military prisons, in both the North and South, also had "deadlines." Sentries at Andersonville were given strict orders to shoot anyone who crossed the deadline and Wirz's trial was filled with horror stories of prisoners being shot dead for crossing or coming close to the deadline.[46]

Prisoners at Andersonville had no shelters provided to them by their Confederate captors. It would not be until August, after the stockade had been in operation more than six months, that a handful of wooden barracks would be built on the north end of the stockade. These flimsy structures could only shelter a small percentage of the thousands of prisoners inside the Andersonville stockade.

Some of the prisoners who arrived at Andersonville still had their pup tents. They were extremely lucky. Other prisoners had to use their own ingenuity to fashion shelters out of scrap wood, pine branches, blankets, oil cloths, or anything else that could be bought, borrowed or stolen. The prisoners called these flimsy shelters their "she-bangs." The most desperate prisoners had to fashion crude bricks out of the sandy, red clay that floored the stockade. The wet clay was put into homemade molds to harden, then dried in the sun. Once enough bricks were made, the prisoners could fashion a damp hovel. Prisoners who had nothing with which to fashion a she-bang could only dig a grave-like hole out of the ground, often by hand. Other prisoners burrowed out caves in the side of the creek banks, where they huddled like animals in a hole. Life for the prisoners at Andersonville was already becoming a miserable existence, and it would get worse.

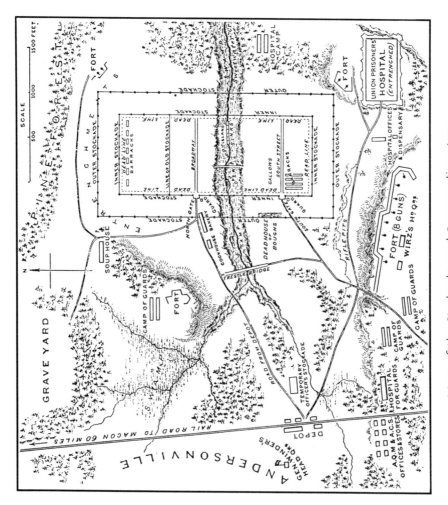

Map of the Stockade and Surrounding Area

The Raiders

Captain Henry Wirz had arrived by train at Andersonville on March 27, 1864. The day after his arrival, he formally assumed his duties as commander of the inner prison.[1] Henry Wirz would officially be responsible for the discipline of the prisoners, preventing escapes, tracking down and capturing escapees, and generally maintaining good order and discipline among the Union prisoners of war. He had no responsibility for their medical care, or how they were fed, clothed, or housed. Those responsibilities had been given to Colonel Alexander W. Persons, Chief Surgeon Isaiah White, and Captain Richard B. Winder.

Colonel Persons had provided Henry Wirz a small clapboard shack to use as an office. It had been built on a small rise of earth beyond the southwest corner of the stockade. From his new office, Wirz could clearly see the train tracks, as well as overlook the two prison gates, noting the comings and goings of guards, prisoners, and sutlers. In the manner of a good country doctor, Wirz nailed a wooden shingle outside of his office, indicating his name, rank, and position.

Wirz would manage to also acquire decent lodgings for his family, boarding with a family in the village of Andersonville. Due to his rank and position as third in command of the prison, he could have been given much more comfortable and respectable accommodations than the small clapboard shacks and field tents where the other Confederate soldiers would live while they were at Andersonville. All the Confederate officers and enlisted men lived in regal splendor compared to the miserable existence of the Union prisoners of war inside the stockade.

A meticulous records keeper, Wirz had a pair of paroled Union prisoners assigned to keep a daily record of the name, regiment, grave number and cause of death of the Union prisoners of war who had died in the stockade. After the war ended these records would prove invaluable in writing the history of Andersonville Prison.[2]

The already complicated command structure at Andersonville was made even more confused by the arrival of Major Elias Griswold, who showed up at the prison only a few days after Henry Wirz. He also had orders from General Winder to take command of the inner prison, the same duties Wirz had just been sent to assume.

This was a major confusion, typical of the Confederate War Department and the workings of General Winder's office. Griswold had been provost marshal of Richmond and had commanded the Confederate prison at Tuscaloosa. He was more experienced than Henry Wirz, had a higher rank, and apparently did not have the wide range of physical and personality problems from which Wirz suffered. It is interesting to speculate if things would have been different if Major Griswold had received the command of the inner prison instead of Wirz. However, shortly after Griswold arrived, a telegram came from Richmond sorting out the problem. Major Griswold would return to Richmond, leaving Henry Wirz to command the inner prison.

Every day, large crowds of off-duty guards and local civilians would gather along the train tracks to greet the big locomotives bringing the Union prisoners to Camp Sumter. Some came simply to gawk at the dreaded Yankees, but most came to trade with the newly arrived prisoners. They hoped to swap fruits, vegetables, blankets, firewood, tobacco, molasses, and the most coveted item of all, whiskey, in exchange for Yankee "greenback" dollars. By this time Confederate currency was virtually worthless, and one Yankee dollar could purchase as much as seven or eight Confederate dollars.

Many of the new prisoners were known as "Hundred Day Men," newly enlisted soldiers who had signed on for a three-month enlistment in exchange for a sizable enlistment bounty paid in cash money by their local states and the Federal government. These prisoners were often sporting new uniforms, shoes, jewelry, and dashing kepi hats.

The custom of allowing men to enlist for only one hundred days began during the Indian wars of the colonial and early national periods of American history. Small farmers on the frontier refused to enlist in local militias to fight in the Indian wars for longer than a hundred days, fearing that their families would be left to starve if they were not at home to help with the planting and harvesting of crops. Military campaigns organized against the Indians would always begin in the late fall, usually late October, with the clear understanding that the fighting would be over before the time for spring plowing.

During the Civil War it was ridiculous to sign on soldiers for only one hundred days. By the time the men were uniformed, trained, and transported to the South, their enlistments were nearly over. However, traditions in the military die slowly and the Federal government desperately needed recruits. Once the men were with their units, large cash bounties, appeals to patriotism, unit loyalty, and a strong desire to see the war end in a Union victory would induce most of the soldiers to reenlist.

Henry Wirz issued an order banning local civilians, and off-duty soldiers, from gathering at the railroad tracks.[3] This order did not make Wirz very popular with the guards and prisoners, not to mention the local civilians. However, he did continue to allow local civilians to gather on the high ground on the south side of the stockade to look down into the stockade at the prisoners.

Wirz knew that he could not possibly hope to stop all trade between the guards, civilians, and prisoners, so he sought to control it. Wirz appointed an officially licensed sutler, James Selman Jr., a former clerk for Richard Winder, to supervise the trade between the prisoners and local civilians and guards.

Selman built a sutler's store in the stockade out of scrap lumber and stocked it with all types of merchandise. The sutler's shack is clearly visible in some of the photographs taken inside the stockade. The clapboard sutler's shack was located near the center of the stockade, and until the barracks were built in September 1864, it was the largest building inside the stockade. Selman's commissary building stands out conspicuously in the primitive photographs and illustrations, standing high above the rows of small she-bangs.

Reportedly, it had rows of shelves where Selman stored seasonal items such as flour, salt, peas, rice, onions, potatoes, and grapes. Things that would not spoil were stored in bulk in a basement, dug out under the shack. One particular item was a barrel of "saleratus", a type of sodium bicarbonate used to cure intestinal disorders and for leavening bread.[4]

Wirz's problems with the illegal trade among prisoners, guards, and civilians were made even worse by the arrival of a new group of prisoners called the Plymouth Pilgrims. These men had been part of the Union garrison manning the forts around the tidewater city of Plymouth, North Carolina.

Since the coastal regions of North Carolina had first fallen to Union forces in 1862, the men garrisoning the coastal forts, built by Union Army engineers, had enjoyed comfortable quarters, good rations, and had not seen combat in over a year and a half. It was not difficult for officers to get these men to reenlist, especially since each time they did so they got a generous reenlistment bonus from the Federal government, their home states, and sometimes even their local communities.

Unknown to the Union soldiers at Plymouth, Confederate forces were building an ironclad ram, named the CSS *Albemarle*, in a shipyard and dry dock on the Roanoke River, upstream from Plymouth. Robert E. Lee had diverted part of his Army of Northern Virginia into eastern North Carolina in an attempt to drive Union forces out of the coastal cities of Plymouth and New Bern, North Carolina, and thus provide a port for Confederate blockade runners.

The *Albemarle* sailed down the Roanoke River, bypassing the forts at Plymouth and New Bern and positioning itself between the coastal forts and the wooden Union gunboats waiting offshore. The Union forces had been taken completely by surprise. The position of the Confederate ironclad cut off the men in the earthwork forts around Plymouth and New Bern and from resupply and reinforcement from the Union warships offshore.

The *Albemarle* patrolled the coastal shoals, sinking one Union gunboat and keeping the others out of range of its guns, while Confederate ground troops attacked the forts at Plymouth from the land side. The Confederate attack against New Bern fizzled, but after three days of Confederate artillery bombardment, the commanding officer at Plymouth surrendered his garrison. All total, the Confederates captured four full regiments and parts of three others, as well as a battery of artillery, making a grand total of over three thousand men.[5]

The Plymouth Pilgrims were an affluent-looking group of prisoners. Three of the captured regiments at Plymouth had just reenlisted in January and had used part of their bounty to purchase new uniforms that they had planned to wear home on their thirty-day reenlistment furlough.

When the Plymouth Pilgrims finally arrived at the Andersonville stockade late in the afternoon of April 30, 1864, the soldiers' pockets were stuffed with thousands of dollars in United States currency. It has been estimated that the Plymouth Pilgrims introduced into the Andersonville stockade anywhere from one hundred thousand to one million dollars.[6] One Andersonville prisoner would write after the war that upon seeing the well-dressed soldiers, he had said to a fellow prisoner, "Helloa! I'm blanked if the Johnnies haven't caught a regiment of brigadier generals somewhere."[7]

The arrival of the Plymouth Pilgrims caused a wave of greed to sweep over the stockade. Many of the other Union prisoners of war saw the new arrivals as a bunch of "fresh fish" to be relieved of their cash. All manner of gambling devices were pulled out, and games of chance sprang up all over the compound. Men who had a good location for their she-bangs would rent out space to the Plymouth Pilgrims for large sums of money. The price of everything in the stockade doubled and tripled. Simple items such as ordinary tent poles were selling at a rate of ten dollars for three poles.[8]

News of the arrival of the Plymouth Pilgrims also spread rapidly among the civilian population. Peddlers from Americus and Macon descended on the small town of Andersonville, wanting to exchange whatever they could sell to the newly arrived prisoners for their precious Yankee "greenback" dollars. Off-duty Confederate guards defied Captain Wirz's orders by gathering at the prison's gates to openly trade with the Plymouth Pilgrims. Any Confederate soldier who entered the stockade to remove the dead, take the daily count, or issue the rations did so with his pockets bulging with boiled eggs, turnips, apples, and small bottles of homemade whiskey.

The trade with the new prisoners became so intense it began to affect the burying of the dead. When the Plymouth Pilgrims arrived at Andersonville the death rate was climbing at such an alarming rate that just getting the dead buried was a major task.

Outside the stockade was a small brush arbor shelter the prisoners called the "dead house." Shortly after dawn, the corpses were collected from all over the stockade, as well as the prison hospital, to be laid out in the "dead house." From the "dead house" details of prisoners would load the bodies in wagons and move them to the prison cemetery where they would dig the long trenches and bury the corpses.

This burial detail offered ample opportunity to trade with Confederate guards and civilians. When the wagon load of corpses arrived at the prisoners' cemetery, they were always met by a large crowd of Confederate guards and civilians wanting to trade. It was such a profitable venture the prisoners worked out a system to ensure everyone was given fair access to the prison cemetery.

The rule worked out was that the man who cared for the dying man during his last days, his mess mate and friend, would be given the opportunity to escort the body to the cemetery. He was allowed to choose two other prisoners to act as stretcher-bearers and to help with the digging. These positions could be sold to the highest bidder, bringing the dead man's friend and nurse much needed cash.

The burying of the dead often went on until late afternoon. But, the earlier a prisoner got to the cemetery in the morning, the better the selection of goods available. As the day wore on, the civilians and guards would complete their business, finish selling whatever they had and drift away. The standard rate for a stretcher-bearer to go out with the first burial detail was three dollars. As the day went on the rate would rapidly drop to one dollar, and by late afternoon to as little as fifty cents or a quarter.[9]

Shortly after Andersonville began receiving prisoners, troubles began to arise with a group of rowdy thugs, that became known as the Andersonville Raiders. They were a group of street-wise, petty criminals most of whom had enlisted in the Union Army only for the enlistment bounties. Most had become "bounty jumpers," deserting at the earliest opportunity, only to return home to enlist again using an assumed name. Bounty jumpers had little or no taste for combat, and if they were not able to desert, would surrender with little or no provocation.

After being sent to Confederate prisons, the captured bounty jumpers would form themselves into tight-knit gangs that preyed on other prisoners. Most of these gangs consisted of between twenty and fifty men and each gang was named after the ruffian chosen to be their leader, followed by the word "Raiders." They bore such names as "Curtis Raiders,"

"Sarsfield's Raiders," and "Delancy's Raiders." It has been estimated that fewer than five hundred of the thousands of prisoners in the Andersonville stockade were Raiders. However, the gangs were well armed with a wide variety of homemade weapons and presented a united front when challenged, ready to fight any and all comers.[10]

Their favorite targets were newly arrived prisoners, such as the Plymouth Pilgrims, with fresh uniforms, money, and jewelry. Usually the gang members would pretend to befriend the new arrival, only to brutally beat and rob the poor man as soon as dark fell. The Confederate guards in the sentry towers might have heard the man's cries for help, but because of the poor nighttime visibility, they could do little or nothing to help. The other prisoners tended to their own business, unable to challenge the well-armed and organized Raider gangs.

After darkness fell the Raiders would prowl the camp looking for new victims. They would be quickly attracted to a prisoner with a good she-bang, blankets, canteens and, hopefully, a stash of food, jewelry and money. Men who were weakened by illness were also particularly vulnerable. The cowardly Raiders sought victims who were unable to fight back. The Raiders would attack the she-bang, beat the occupant senseless, then take anything the poor man had, leaving him naked and bleeding on the bare ground. Men who had nothing left to steal would be forced to fetch and serve the raiders, who grew bolder with each passing day.[11]

Not everyone took the Raiders' abuse without resistance. Some combat-hardened veterans banned together into self-defense groups. One of the strongest became known as the "Regulators" and was led by a strong-willed, former street brawler known as "Limber Jim." However, while these self-defense groups were willing to fight to defend themselves, that was all they would do. The Raiders were too well armed and their strongholds too well defended to be challenged even by the Regulators. Some prisoners talked of forming a government inside the prison, but others shunned the idea, feeling, or perhaps hoping that their stay at Andersonville would be so brief it would not be necessary.

The matter of the Andersonville Raiders came to a head when they began to threaten the prison sutler and attacked some of the small merchants who plied their trade on Market Street. This threatened the lives of nearly all the Union prisoners at Andersonville. There was not hardly a man in the stockade who didn't in some way depend upon trade and barter to survive.

On the steamy, hot morning of June 29, 1864, a delegation of prisoners, led by Limber Jim and the Regulators, went to the North Gate and politely, but firmly, demanded to see Captain Wirz. After some haggling, Wirz agreed to meet with the prisoners. One of the men had been born in Europe and spoke to Wirz in his native German.

The prisoners asked Captain Wirz to supply them with pistols with which to arrest the Raiders. The delegation explained that the Raiders had built up a supply of powerful slingshots, capable of hurling rocks and other missiles that could knock a man senseless from a considerable distance away.[12] The Raiders also had managed to smuggle large Bowie knives into the stockade. With these deadly razor sharp blades, they could slice a man to ribbons in a matter of seconds. Without firearms to counter the slingshots and Bowie knives, the Regulators could do almost nothing to challenge the Raiders' power over the stockade. The prisoners gave their word that the firearms would be returned once the Raiders were in custody.

Wirz appeared to have been genuinely moved by the stories told by the delegation of prisoners. However, the task of cowering the Raiders caused Captain Wirz much concern. He knew he would certainly be court-martialled for supplying prisoners with firearms for any reason. Especially, if other prisoners, or some of his guards, were killed or injured. Something else had to be worked out.

While he clearly wanted to help the prisoners, Captain Wirz had other concerns even more pressing than the Raiders. The population of the prison was nearly up to 30,000 prisoners, food was short, the hospital was full to overflowing, and the death rate was growing at an alarming pace. To make matters even worse, there had been a radical shake up in the command structure of the prison.[13]

In May, Union forces, under General William Tecumseh Sherman, had begun moving south from Chattanooga. Their target was clearly the city of Atlanta, the most important railroad hub in Georgia. Even Georgia's isolationist and obstructionist Governor Joseph Brown saw the serious-ness of the situation and ordered every available man drafted into service to halt the Union advance. Except, of course, the large group of political supporters and old friends whom he had given exemptions from military service. Despite the threat to Atlanta, Brown still refused to allow the large numbers of sheriff's deputies, bailiffs, jailers, court clerks, and judges whom he had appointed to sometimes non-existent positions to be conscripted.

In May, an order was received from Confederate Secretary of War Seddon ordering the 55th Georgia Volunteers to move from Andersonville to join the Confederate forces north of Atlanta. Colonel Persons and his men would be gone before the end of June.

Andersonville would also lose the services of Richard Winder, the prison's beleaguered quartermaster and commissary officer, who had done so much to help get the prison in operation.

In February of 1864, the Confederate Congress passed a law reliev-ing the quartermaster's department from the responsibility of feeding pris-oners of war, shifting that responsibility to the commissary department. From this point onward, the Confederate commissary office in Columbus, Georgia would be responsible for providing rations for the prisoners. Lieuten-ant James H. Wright, formerly the quartermaster of the 55th Georgia, was appointed to be commissary officer, and Richard Winder was relieved of the thankless responsibility for feeding the growing prison population.

However, this was a typical ill thought out Confederate bureaucratic blunder. Richard Winder had carefully cultivated supplies of food for the prison from a variety of sources, including beef from Florida, cornmeal from Americus, and vegetables from a variety of small farms and plantations around Andersonville. Lieutenant Wright would be a poor substitute for Captain Winder. Due to the bungelsome purchasing policies of the Confederate commissary department, Lieutenant Wright could do little but requisition cornmeal and salt pork from Confederate storehouses in Columbus and Macon.

In May, after weeks of simply hanging around Andersonville doing what he could to help, Richard Winder was given the dual responsibility of being quartermaster (actually commissary officer, although the duties were nearly identical, the only change was in how the food and other supplies were obtained and from whom) at the officer's prison at Macon, as well as at Andersonville.

This reassignment was Richard Winder's golden opportunity to flee the filth and misery of Andersonville. Although there were thousands of prisoners at Andersonville, and only 170 officers at Macon, Richard Winder immediately moved his headquarters to Macon, leaving his clerk James Duncan behind at Andersonville. Richard Winder would remain in Macon until September, when he would be named chief quartermaster at the new prison at Millen, Georgia.[14]

The first week in June, General John H. Winder, who had for some time been showing signs of strain due to his age, ill health, and the pressures of dealing with the growing prisoner of war quagmire, was bumped upstairs being given command of all Confederate prisons east of the Mississippi River.[15]

General Winder's new position involved no increase in rank, and it meant moving his headquarters from Richmond, where he was generally disliked, to Andersonville. He had requested permission to live in Americus so he could bring his family with him, but the request was denied. He was ordered to live at Camp Sumter. It seemed as if the Confederate government felt that just his physical presence at Andersonville could solve all the prison's problems.

Henry Wirz had complained for some time about how his lack of rank hampered him in obtaining cooperation from other Confederate agencies, especially since the departure of Colonel Persons, the only field grade officer at Andersonville. Wirz wrote several letters to various persons complaining that his duties would be easier if he were promoted. In later works of fiction about the Andersonville tragedy, these requests for promotion would be twisted to portray Wirz as a scheming ego-maniac obsessed with rank and position. In reality, Wirz was simply tired of always talking up to people who should have been answering to him. Instead of ordering food and supplies, he was in reality begging for it. His low subaltern rank meant he got little respect from clerks, commissary agents, and government officials in Richmond and Columbus.

Obviously, Wirz was hoping for a promotion when he wrote letters protesting that someone above the rank of captain should be in charge of the prison. Instead, he received the sixty-five-year-old General Winder, who had cultivated powerful enemies in the Confederate War Department and in Richmond social society, where his high-handed actions in ferreting out Yankee spies had earned him the nickname "the dictator of Richmond."

It was General Winder's plan to open at least a half dozen new prisons in remote areas of Georgia to relieve the overcrowding at Andersonville and eventually close all the existing prisons in Richmond. Technically, General Winder would be in command of Andersonville, replacing Colonel Persons, but, in reality, he would be gone much of the time, working to establish new prisons and supervising the affairs of Confederate prisons in Alabama, Georgia, and the Carolinas, leaving Captain Wirz in charge.

To make matters worse, General Howell Cobb had replaced Colonel Person's 55th Georgia with two regiments of the Georgia Reserves. These two regiments had been quickly assembled by General Cobb from local farmers and merchants, who had the bad luck of not being able to have acquired one of Governor Brown's famous exemptions from military service. The Georgia Reserves were primarily made up of middle-aged men, teenage boys, and semi-invalid convalescent troops. The Georgia Reserves contained boys as young as twelve and a few men as old as seventy. Luckily, the Georgia Reserves also had just enough reliable and disciplined veterans to keep the unit from being totally useless.

The Georgia Reserves had no uniforms and many of the men had shown up for duty without shoes. There were not enough firearms to go around and many of the reserves had to be armed with Bowie knives and hand pikes. Those that had firearms often carried their own personal weapons. These armaments consisted of old smoothbore shotguns, intended for bird hunting, not warfare, and even some Revolutionary War vintage smoothbore flintlocks not accurate beyond fifty yards.[16]

This pathetic gaggle of graying men and teenage boys, wearing only civilian clothing and armed with only the most primitive of firearms, bowie knives, and hand pikes, were not likely to strike fear into the hearts of the notorious Andersonville Raiders. However, Captain Wirz knew he had to do something.

Working with the Regulators, Henry Wirz slowly developed a plan of action. He carefully picked a detail of his best armed and uniformed soldiers to enter the stockade and arrest the Raiders.[17] He also doubled the guards on the sentry towers and brought up some pieces of field artillery, loaded with grape shot, to prevent a rush on the gates.

Wirz's armed detail of Georgia Reserves were met at the gate by an assembled group of Regulators, led by a determined and angry Limber

Jim. They were ready to point out the Raiders and help arrest them. Henry Wirz had refused the Regulators' requests for pistols, but he did allow them to arm themselves with clubs and carry ropes to secure the Raiders after they were arrested.

When Wirz and his men entered the stockade, the Raiders, forewarned by informants of the approaching attempt to arrest them, reacted quickly. Some tried to avoid arrest by dispersing into the general prison population. However, they were easy to spot, looking well fed and neatly manicured, in a sea of pale and gaunt faces. The Raiders were also conspicuous because of their fresh clean uniforms and jewelry. Other Raiders retreated to well-guarded, almost fortified, strongholds in the far corners of the stockade, where they had stockpiled food, water, and weapons.

The Raiders did not surrender meekly. There was a series of jarring fist fights as the dispersed Raiders were confronted one at a time by the Regulators and their former victims eager for revenge. Soon the entire compound was one huge brawl, as one Raider after another was beaten into submission and delivered to the prison gates to be put in chains and guarded by Captain Wirz's armed soldiers.

With the rest of the Union prisoners cheering them on, Captain Wirz's soldiers charged into the Raiders' strongholds with unloaded firearms and fixed bayonets. The Regulators assisted the Confederate soldiers by running down and beating into submission any Raider trying to sneak away. The once fearsome bullies were quickly reduced to whimpering cowards, crying and begging for mercy.

Wirz could not remove all five hundred of the Raiders. He had no place to segregate such a large number of prisoners nor the guards to watch them. When the day's brawling was over, only one hundred and twenty-five of the Raiders had been removed from the stockade. The Regulators, who had overseen the removal, assured Captain Wirz that all the Raiders' ringleaders were in custody. The Regulators felt that the Raiders who remained in the stockade could be contained by the the other prisoners, now that they did not have their leaders and their stockpile of weapons that the Regulators had seized during the sweep.

Many of the Union prisoners had joined the Raiders only as an act of self-preservation, feeling it would be better to be a Raider than one of their victims. Most of these men really had little desire to mistreat their fellow prisoners. Now that the ringleaders were in custody, and their cache of weapons gone, their biggest problem would be to avoid their former victims who would certainly want to exact some revenge.

It had taken almost the entire day for Captain Wirz's soldiers to subdue the Raiders, and hard fought fist fights continued to erupt for hours after Wirz's men had left the stockade. Apparently, many of the prisoners saw this as an ample opportunity to settle old scores, and they continued to exact revenge against known Raiders who had escaped the sweep.

When the wagons showed up at the North Gate with the prisoners' food for the day, Captain Wirz decided that there was too much confusion and violence inside the stockade to expect the prisoners to line up in their squads to draw their rations. He feared a general riot if he opened the gates to allow the wagons to enter the stockade. If a general riot were to erupt, Wirz had no way of putting it down, short of firing artillery into the stockade, something he didn't want to do.

The first artillery had been sent to Andersonville from Florida in early February. Under the command of Captain Charles E. Dyke, the collection of old mismatched field pieces became known as the Florida Battery or Dyke's Battery. Most of the original guns were unserviceable, but after the Battle of Olustee, Captain Dyke had managed to acquire two good pieces of captured Federal artillery.

This artillery was Henry Wirz's strongest weapon against a mass escape or riot. Wirz had once posted notices at the two prison gates threatening to fire into the stockade, when he had been notified by informants of a plan by some prisoners to rush the gates. However, the planned mass escape was never carried out, and Wirz was not forced to use his artillery.

During his tour of duty at Andersonville, Captain Wirz never did anything more dangerous with the Florida Battery than fire blank shots as a warning, and only once fired an artillery round over the stockade to restore order after a section of the wall collapsed during a thunderstorm. Henry Wirz seemed to have no desire to kill unarmed prisoners of war with his artillery, and would do anything to avoid doing so, including not feeding the prisoners while the stockade was in a state of confusion and turmoil. Having to choose between the lesser of two evils, Wirz decided not to risk feeding the prisoners the day of the assault on the Raiders.

The well-planned and executed sweep to remove the Raiders' leaders had occurred on the Fourth of July, a fact hardly noticed in all the confusion and fighting going on in the stockade. However, nearly a year and a half later, at the trial of Henry Wirz's, the prosecution would accuse him of refusing to feed the prisoners that day in order to keep them from celebrating Independence Day.[18] Nothing could have been further from the truth.

After their removal from the stockade, a dozen of the top leaders of the Raiders were confined in chains under the pine trees next to the Confederate guard's camp. The rest were marched to Castle Reed, a small stockade near the town, originally used to house Union officers mistakenly sent to Andersonville shortly after the prison opened.

Wirz's soldiers would have to put in extra hours of guard duty to supervise the stockade, Castle Reed, and the Raiders under the trees. On top of these duties the Georgia Reserves would also have to meet the trains twice a day and escort the newly arrived prisoners to the stockade, as well as to supervise the burial details and the daily feeding of the prisoners.

Captain Wirz had already learned that the guards could be as much trouble as the prisoners. In April the men of the 55th Georgia had staged a major mutiny because of overwork and poor rations. The old men of the Georgia Reserves were much less physically able to stand the extra hours of guard duty, and the teenage boys used the situation to become more rebellious than they already were. To maintain order and discipline in his guard force, Captain Wirz would have to resolve the problem of the Raiders quickly.

Captain Wirz established a court-martial board that would be made up entirely of Union prisoners of war. A second group of prisoners would act as jurors. With the help of the Regulators, Wirz was extremely vigilant to ensure that no suspected Raiders would be on the court-martial board or the jury. He wanted the trial to be fair, but at the same time he wanted to keep his involvement in the proceeding to a minimum. He gave strict orders that his men would only provide security to prevent any prisoner from using these proceedings to escape, and maintain order. Wirz was worried about how this whole affair would be interpreted at war's end. He wanted all the responsibility for actions taken against the Raiders to fall on the prisoner's court and not himself.

He met with the group of Raiders, allowing them to pick men from the prison population to act as defense attorneys. Some of the prisoners in the stockade had legal training, but mostly the Raiders chose prison ministers, who had an eloquent gift of oratory to plead their case. They reasoned that an impassioned plea for mercy might be more useful than a good knowledge of the law.

The Raiders' trial would be held outdoors under the shade of the pine trees near the Confederate camp. The evidence against the accused was overwhelming. Witness after witness told horrible stories of having been victimized by the Raiders. As the evidence against them mounted, the accused Raider leaders became sullen and arrogant, pledging reprisals against those who testified against them.

When the trials were completed, all the accused Raiders were found guilty. Under the circumstances, the prisoners' court showed great restraint in dealing with the convicted men. Only six of the 125 arrested men were sentenced to hang. The rest were sentenced to lesser punishments, everything from receiving a flogging, to being hung by the thumbs, to something as mild as having their heads shaved.

Captain Wirz ordered that his soldiers would take no part in the upcoming executions. He wanted all the blame for what was about to happen to fall upon the Union prisoners of war, not upon him or his men.

Soldiers during the Civil War were used to executions. Men were routinely shot for desertion, cowardice, and offenses as minor as sleeping on guard duty. Almost all military executions took place before the troops as an example to the other soldiers. However, Henry Wirz had no way of knowing how the prisoners would react to seeing their own kind executed while they were prisoners of war in the custody of the Confederate Army.

Wirz had decided that he would simply return the six Raiders to the stockade, and then whatever happened, would happen. However, the Regulators had requested lumber to build a gallows, and Wirz really had no choice except to honor the request, since he had already gone this far. Wirz would also have to provide an armed guard detail for the gallows until after the execution. He didn't fear that the prisoners would tear down the gallows to halt the hanging, but rather to steal the badly needed wood to build she-bangs and for firewood.

Henry Wirz worried that he might be violating the rules of war by allowing the executions to take place, but he also worried that to forbid the hangings would cause a riot or that the confusion surrounding the executions would be used as a cover for a mass escape.

Only two weeks before the assault on the Raiders took place, Henry Wirz had learned of a mass escape plot, where paroled prisoners working outside the stockade would disarm the guards, throw open the gates, and free all the prisoners inside the stockade. Wirz was able to prevent the mass escape by arresting the ringleaders, and then posting a notice inside the gate threatening to fire his artillery into the stockade in the event of any future mass uprising. That foiled the mass escape plot. However, several paroled prisoners who lived outside the stockade did manage to escape during the episode and the whole affair was leaked to the civilian population. This terrified the local civilian population and did nothing to improve relations with Governor Brown.[19]

Wirz had another problem with the executions, a deeply personal one. He was an ethnocentric man who hated punishing his own kind. Five of the six condemned Raiders were Roman Catholics. This filled the deeply religious Wirz with worry and remorse. He went to considerable trouble to procure the services of a priest to administer the last rites and be present at the executions. After the Civil War, Henry Wirz would be portrayed as a heartless brute. However, the way he dealt with the situation of the Raiders shows that he deeply disliked the taking of human life and wanted to do the correct and humane thing.

On the hot sweltering afternoon of July 11, 1864, Henry Wirz rode into the crowded stockade, followed closely by a Catholic priest and the six condemned Raiders, who were under heavy guard by a detail of the Georgia Reserves.[20]

With the coming of hot weather, Henry Wirz seldom wore his gray wool Confederate uniform, preferring a much cooler and more comfortable outfit, that consisted only of a heavily starched and ironed shirt and trousers made of coarse, but strong, white duck cloth.

A supply of the same white duck cloth was provided to the prisoners to sew new clothing to replace their blue wool Union Army uniforms that quickly rotted away within the constantly wet stockade. The white duck cloth was strong and comfortable, very resistant to rot, but impossible to keep clean inside the dirty stockade. The white duck cloth quickly took on a dingy gray color from exposure to the black pine tar smoke and the muddy dirt floor of the compound. As summer wore on, more and more prisoners were wearing the homemade dirty gray uniforms. By August, a novice looking into the stockade would see a sea of gray shirts and pants. He might have mistakenly thought the prison was made up of Confederate rather than Union prisoners of war.

Henry Wirz had entered the stockade riding a lumbering white mare instead of his usual brownish-red roan horse. The combination of the white mare and Wirz's freshly washed and ironed, white duck outfit caused one Union prisoner to write the appellation "Death on a Pale Horse."[21]

The morning of the executions, the Regulators had risen early to erect the crude gallows to be used in the execution. During the construction they were protected by Wirz's sentries. It was a crude and pitiful looking structure. The uprights were barely high enough so that the condemned men's feet would clear the ground when the trap was sprung. The platform on which they would stand was narrow, being only two or three planks wide. The trap was about the same width as the platform and was supported by a pine log brace, that would be knocked out of place by one of the Regulators when the time came. The condemned men would have to climb up to the platform on a rickety pine wood ladder that didn't appear very steady.

While the scaffold was crude, it was sturdy enough to be adequate. What worried both Henry Wirz and the Regulators most were the ropes. They were the best that could be found, but that wasn't saying much. They were worn and frayed, and Wirz worried that they might break under the strain of the men's weight. The six condemned Raiders were heavy and strong.

As word of the upcoming executions spread through the surrounding countryside, a large crowd of local civilians began to gather on the high ground to the south of the stockade. As the morning wore on, the crowd continued to grow in size, even though they could barely see the small gallows from their position beyond the pine log walls. The civilians were joined by a collection of assorted camp personal: quartermaster clerks, sutlers, teamsters, and laborers, standing on their tiptoes or sitting on horseback in order to stare at the execution proceedings.

Every able-bodied member of the Georgia Reserves was on duty, manning the pigeon roosts atop the walls and the rifle pits outside the prison walls. A small detachment of cavalry, probably from Macon, stood at the ready near the crowd of civilians, and the Florida Battery had moved its guns forward to the crest of the high ground and trained them down into the stockade.

The size of the crowd of civilians was estimated at over a thousand, and as the day wore on, some wandered in front of the artillery pieces trying to get a better view, and had to be pushed back by the Confederate guards. One Andersonville prisoner wrote there were an unusually large number of Black faces in the crowd of civilians gathered on the high ground. This would indicate that many local masters had brought their slaves to view the execution, hoping perhaps that the sight of Yankees being hung would restore a little fear into the slaves, who were becoming more bold and defiant with each advance of the Union Army.

Before he officially turned the Raiders over to their fate, Henry Wirz made a brief speech. "Boys I have taken these men out and now I return them to you, having taken good care of them. I now commit them to you. You can do with them as you see fit." Then turning to the condemned Raiders he said, "May God have mercy on your souls." Wirz then turned and ordered his soldiers to leave the stockade.[22]

One of the condemned men was Charles Curtis, formerly of the 5th Rhode Island Artillery, and leader of Curtis' Raiders. For Curtis, this was the moment he had been waiting for. He watched with close attention as Wirz and his armed guards disappeared through the South Gate. The rope, which was tied to the Raiders' hands, was as worn and old as the rope which made up the dangling nooses. Curtis had duly noted it while he was being tied, and from that time onward had been silently struggling against his rope bonds. As Wirz was making his speech, Curtis had finally managed to break the bonds and get his hands free.

Just as the Raiders were ordered to mount the scaffold, Curtis made his move. The burly Raider broke free and began throwing wild punches, knocking one of the Regulators down. He then rushed into the crowd of prisoners, dodging blows and pushing and punching his way through the throng of prisoners.

Some of the prisoners cried out that Curtis had a knife and the crowd of nearly thirty thousand Union prisoners parted, letting him through. Several prisoners bravely stepped forth to try and stop Curtis, and were knocked flat for their efforts. Curtis was trying to reach a group of his former gang members, who had been returned to the stockade after their trials, and had taken refuge in a far corner of the stockade.

The former Raiders had spent the morning taunting and yelling curses at the other prisoners, as the scaffold was being built. They vowed that the planned executions would never take place. When they saw Curtis break free, they began cheering and urging him to join them. However, once it was determined that Curtis did not have a knife the Regulators were able to block his path and keep him from joining his friends.

In apparent frustration, Curtis decided to run into the swampy area that flanked the creek, maybe believing that the Regulators would not follow. Curtis plowed into the marshy ground and immediately sank up to his knees in the mixture of soft mud and human sewage. Just before he reached the far side, Curtis collapsed in exhaustion. The Regulators had ran across the small bridge that crossed the creek and headed him off. In a few minutes, the Regulators were on Curtis and had pulled him free from the muck. Curtis begged his captors for water and it was given to him. The members of Curtis' gang were chest fallen that their leader had not managed to escape. They continued to yell obscenities at the Regulators, but did nothing to try and rescue their former leader.

The Regulators jerked Curtis to his feet and began leading him back to the gallows. As Curtis passed through the crowd of bedraggled prisoners for the second time, he was greeted with insults and curses. Curtis answered with foul insults of his own until he seemed to tire of the exercise and became morose and quiet.

When Curtis made his break for freedom, another of the condemned Raiders also braced himself to flee, but Limber Jim stepped forward with a large Bowie knife and threatened to disembowel the man on the spot.[23]

Wirz was terrified by what was happening. From outside the stockade he could only hear the noise of a terrible commotion, and was certain that this was the beginning of the mass escape he so feared. Wirz rode toward the Florida Battery yelling for the men to fire.[24] However, the artillerymen who could see better as to what was happening from their elevated position held their fire. However, the gunners drew tight the lanyard cords of their fully loaded guns, ready to fire in a split second, should the crowd of prisoners turn from the muddy swamp where Curtis had fled, and begin running towards the gates or one of the walls.

As Curtis was being led back to the gallows from his aborted escape attempt, the other condemned Raiders were begging the Catholic priest, Father Peter Whelan, to appeal to the other prisoners to spare their lives. Father Whelan walked to the front of the gallows and made an eloquent plea to the assembled prisoners of war for the lives of the Raiders. However, he was shouted down with cries of derision from the men, who had suffered too much and lived in fear of the Raiders' brutality for too long.

While the fugitive Curtis was being returned to the gallows, the other Regulators decided that the execution had already been delayed too long, and the order was given to get on with it. Following standard custom, each of the condemned Raiders was given a chance to speak. The first to be offered the chance was Cary Sullivan of the 72nd New York Infantry; he had nothing to say. Sullivan, like most of the Raiders, had several aliases, and was also known as W. Rickson, which is the name he was buried under. The next Raider was a sailor, Andrew Munn from New York, who described himself as a poor Irish lad.[25] He said he came to the prison four months earlier an honest man, but starvation and evil companions made him what he was. Munn spoke of his mother and sisters in New York. He said he cared nothing about himself, but the sure knowledge that news of his ignominious death would be carried home to his family, made him want to curse God that he had ever been born.[26]

Patrick Delaney, of the 83rd Pennsylvania Infantry, made no plea of innocence or asked for any forgiveness. He spoke boldly saying that he would rather be dead than live the way most of the prisoners were expected to live in Andersonville. He proclaimed that if allowed to steal he could get enough to eat, but since he could no longer steal, he would just as soon be dead. Then he surprised everyone by saying that his name really wasn't Delaney, that it was a phony name he made up to draw a second enlistment bounty. He proudly proclaimed that no one at Andersonville knew his real name, and therefore he had no fear of his family finding out about his dishonorable fate.

William Collins, of the 88th Pennsylvania Infantry, and John Sarsfield, of the 144th New York, also made pleas for their families. Collins claimed he was innocent of murder and for the sake of his family asked to be spared. Sarsfield echoed Munn and blamed all his problems on evil companions.

The last man to speak was Charles Curtis. Since his failed escape attempt, Curtis had been returned to the gallows, reeking of sweat and filth. He sat on the ground trying to catch his breath as his hands were rebound. Delaney berated him from the scaffold, "Come on up now, show yourself a man, and die game." Limber Jim, whose brother had reportedly been killed by Curtis, stood over Curtis with his Bowie knife drawn, ready to react should Curtis try to flee again. Slowly Curtis arose, and with much difficulty he mounted the scaffold. With each step Curtis seemed to regain his old stamina and defiance. When allowed to speak, Curtis growled that he "didn't give a damn," and he just wanted to get it over with "and not make such a fuss over such a small matter."[27]

After the men had made their final statement, Father Whelan began to pray, only to be interrupted by Delaney, who began shouting instructions to his friends who had now drawn in close to view the hanging. Delaney was telling them what to do with his stash of stolen property. When Father Whelan could stand it no more, he said, "My son, let the things of this earth go and turn your attention towards Heaven." Delaney ignored the priest and continued to yell to his friends such things as give my watch to this person, my ring to that person and so on. Finally, one of the Regulators pulled a watch from his pocket and gave Delaney two more minutes to talk. With this warning, even the tough-talking Delaney seemed to be filled with melancholy. He replied, "Well good bye boys, if I've hurt any of you, I hope you will forgive me." He then looked to a man in the crowd he had assaulted and robbed only three weeks before and asked his forgiveness. The other prisoner was not in a forgiving mood and replied with a profane oath.

With the talking done, white flour sacks were placed over the condemned men's heads, the hemp rope nooses were adjusted around each

The Execution of the Raiders

man's neck, and upon a signal, two of the Regulators kicked out the brace supporting the trap door, and the Raiders fell.

The execution was a botched and messy affair. Munn and Delaney died quickly as the rope jerked their necks at just the right angle to cause it to break cleanly. The other four men twisted and jerked violently. The six ropes strained and made loud creaking noises, as the men struggled and swung back and forth. John Sarsfield began drawing his knees up to his chest and then thrusting his legs downward in a vain effort to break his own neck. Each downward thrust was weaker and more pathetic than the last as Sarsfield slowly strangled to death.

William Collins slowly twisted and swayed until unexpectedly his rope broke. Collins fell to the ground with a thud and then reeled forward landing on his face. The Regulators pulled Collins to his feet and jerked off his hood. Collins was bleeding profusely from the nose and mouth. The once tough Raider, who would heartlessly steal a blanket from a sick man on a cold night, was crying and whimpering like a little boy. It took some time for one of the prisoners to splice the two broken ends of the rope back together. Collins looked up and saw Sarsfield's death agony and the twisting bodies of the other men as life slowly left their bodies.

Collins used these precious moments to plead one more time for his life. Father Whelan also asked that Collins be spared, but the crowd of prisoners would not hear of it. He was led back up the ladder for the second time and positioned on the small platform. Beneath him the trap door was dangling and the corpses of the other men were still moving. A small board was positioned where the trap had been, and Collins was pushed out on it, much like a man about to walk the plank. While Collins was still whimpering and begging for mercy, the hood and noose were replaced, and then the small board was tipped over. Collins joined the other Raiders in their death agony.

Within fifteen minutes all the Raiders had stopped moving. The Regulators checked each corpse closely to make sure the man was indeed dead. With the hanging finished, the crowd of civilians on the high ground, overlooking the stockade, began to drift away. Wirz ordered his men to stand their ground until the bodies were removed. The bodies continued to dangle for about an hour, then they were cut down, stripped of their clothes, and carted off naked to the prisoners' cemetery.

The prisoners requested that the Raiders not be buried with the rest of the Union prisoners of war. Captain Wirz agreed and ordered that the executed men be buried separate from the other prisoners. A site was chosen that was, at the time, far removed from the trenches where the other prisoners were interred.

It was the custom at the time to bury cowards and executed criminals face down. It is unknown if the men chosen to be the grave diggers for the Raiders paid them that last final measure of disrespect, but based on the rest of the day's events it is highly likely.

When the Raiders' grave site was chosen that hot July day in 1864, no one could foresee that before the prison closed only eight months later, the prisoners' burial trenches would extend far beyond where the Raiders were buried.

Today the Raiders' graves lie almost directly in the center of Andersonville National Cemetery, close to a circular driveway that surrounds the cemetery's main flagpole. At some time during the last one hundred years since the Raiders execution, a magnolia tree was planted between the Raiders' graves and the flagpole. The tree was allowed to grow large and bushy, with the limbs reaching from the ground up. This bush-like magnolia tree shields the Raiders' graves from being seen from the main flagpole, which has been the site of yearly religious and patriotic ceremonies.

Every year on Memorial Day, each grave in the cemetery is marked with a small American flag. Every grave, that is, except the six belonging to the Raiders. These graves are left bare, discreetly out of view behind the overgrown magnolia tree. Federal regulations pertaining to the operations of national cemeteries specify that the graves of soldiers who did not die under honorable circumstances are not to be decorated with flags on holidays.

After the execution of the Raiders, Andersonville Prison was far from being crime free, with plenty of petty thievery, fist fights, vendettas, assaults, and even murders. However, the power of the Raiders was broken and the Regulators, who became a defacto police force, made sure that no other gangs formed. The wholesale terrorism was over, and just in time, for the days ahead would be long and hard.

The Graves of the Raiders, Circa 1867

Andersonville National Historic Site

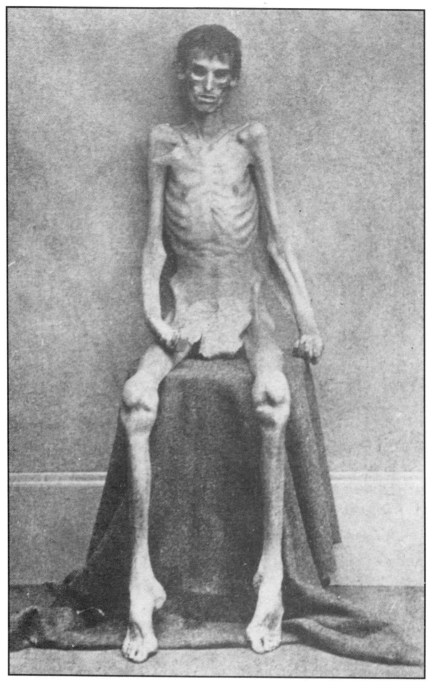

A Union Prisoner of War, Confined at Andersonville

Food and Water

The gruesome end of the Raiders did little to improve the basic living conditions inside the prison. As the stifling heat and humidity of the Georgia summer descended upon the overcrowded stockade, the death rate among the prisoners rose to exceed three hundred a day. According to the best records available to historians, approximately twenty-eight percent of the prisoners assigned to Andersonville died.[1] However, this figure is probably much too low. Thousands of prisoners who transferred out of Andersonville were near death when they were moved, and probably either died on the way home, or soon afterwards. Other prisoners died weeks, months, or years later from medical conditions directly related to their incarceration at Andersonville.

The vast majority of the deaths at Andersonville were directly attributable to the prisoner's diet and the unsanitary and overcrowded living conditions inside the stockade. By June 8, 1864, the population of the prison was over 23,000 prisoners of war, more than twice the number the prison was built to hold, and still growing at an alarming rate.[2]

That same month, Colonel Persons in one of his last official acts supervised the enlargement of the stockade by ten acres. He originally wanted to build a second stockade near Sweetwater Creek, but was unable to find the necessary hardware to fashion hinges for the gates. Forced by necessity, Persons did the next best thing and knocked down the north wall, using the logs he salvaged, along with more that were freshly cut, and enlarged the stockade in that direction.

This addition to the stockade was functional but not as well built as the rest of the prison. Colonel Persons had no broad axes or adzes to square the logs and remove the bark. He also did not have the authority to impress local slaves so he had to depend upon paroled Union prisoners to do the work. These men hesitated on ethical grounds to enlarge the prison to hold more of their comrades. But, Colonel Persons was able to convince them that the enlargement of the prison would only save the lives of their fellow prisoners by creating more habitable living space inside the stockade. He also issued to the men who worked on enlarging the stockade double rations.[3]

After the enlargement was finished, the new area was widely coveted as a spot for a she-bang. It was high ground, well drained, and still covered with grass and undergrowth. Veteran prisoners and men who had worked on the enlargement were given first choices for living areas inside the stockade addition.

Shortly after the end of the Civil War, photographs would be taken of the decaying prison pen. The images were shot from the north side, clearly showing upright pine logs, round in shape, with their bark left on. These photographs would create a confusion as to whether the logs that made up the stockade were square or round, with the bark left on or removed. The issue would not be cleared up until the twentieth century, when an archaeological dig would unearth the remains of some of the original square pine logs with the bark removed.

The Union prisoners of war were not issued any type of food containers or eating utensils, other than what they had brought with them or could fashion from materials found inside the stockade. Some lucky prisoners had regular mess kits. The remaining prisoners had to fashion dinnerware out of canteen halves, old boards, shingles, or twisted pieces of tin or stovepipe. Prisoners made spoons from roots, sticks, barrel hoops, and even oyster shells. Many of the prisoners were forced by necessity to eat their rations out of their shoes or their dirty kepi caps.[4]

According to Confederate records, each Andersonville prisoner was to be issued either a one-third pound piece of pork or a one-pound serving of beef, as well as a one and one-quarter pound serving of ground cornmeal. When it was available, the men were also issued sweet potatoes, onions, peas, beans, molasses, or a tablespoon full of salt.[5]

Under Confederate law, prisoners of war were to be issued the same rations as Confederate soldiers. It was a law the Confederacy took very seriously and made every effort to enforce. Records show that the members of the Georgia Reserves, serving at Andersonville, were issued the same rations as the prisoners. However, the guards could forage for additional food and firewood and were allowed to return home periodically on furlough and arranged for their families to send them additional food. The guards also had the luxury of occasionally traveling to Americus or Macon to purchase what they needed.

The prisoners were allowed to write brief one-page letters to their families that were censored by either Captain Wirz or General Winder before mailing. They could also receive packages from home, but very few packages made it all the way across the war-ravaged Confederacy to Andersonville without the contents being pilfered or stolen outright.[6]

When the prison first opened, all food was issued raw and the men were expected to cook it themselves. This was the way rations were issued to armies in the field, and the Union prisoners of war were used to cooking their own food. Soon after arriving at Andersonville, Richard Winder started to work planning to build a bakehouse. Winder envisioned that the bakehouse would turn the raw cornmeal into freshly baked bread. However, shortages of laborers and lumber kept hampering him. He was also unable to procure the necessary cook pots and bake pans needed to put the bakehouse into operation. By the first of April, the bakehouse was still not in operation.

In the meantime, prisoners fashioned small ovens out of the red Georgia clay and baked their own cornbread. Others would mix the cornmeal in with the grease from the pork or beef ration and cook it over an open fire, wrapped around the end of a stick, or flattened out in an old canteen half or other piece of salvaged sheet metal.

The ration of cornmeal and meat issued each day was received from the commissary warehouse in Columbus, Georgia, sixty miles to the northwest of Andersonville. A commissary officer, Captain James Armstrong, was sent to Andersonville to coordinate the operation. The amount of cornmeal that arrived from Columbus each day was based on the prison's population the day before. The Union prisoners were counted early each morning, and the figures were then sent to Columbus. At Columbus, commissary officials would carefully measure out the cornmeal and then transport the bagged cornmeal and salted meat to Andersonville by train. There was no telegraph at Andersonville so the message had to be relayed through Macon, which took some time.

The measured ration that arrived at Andersonville never took into consideration the number of prisoners who had arrived by train from Richmond since the previous morning's count. At first the discrepancy was minor, but soon hundreds of prisoners were arriving each day without warning. In order to feed everyone, Confederate officials at Andersonville were forced to cut the ration of cornmeal to make up the difference. The Union prisoners complained bitterly when they were issued short rations by their Confederate captors, although the same thing happened on a regular basis at other Confederate prisons. As the prison population continued to grow, and the number of prisoners arriving each day grew larger and larger, short rations became a regular occurrence.[7]

The cornmeal fed to the prisoners was "unbolted", meaning that the bran and the kernel were not separated. Simply put the cob was ground up with the corn. Normally the cornmeal could be sifted out with bolting cloth, but like most everything else, bolting cloth could not be found, despite the

best efforts of Colonel Persons, Richard Winder, and Henry Wirz to procure it. Some prisoners fashioned homemade sifters by punching holes in
jar lids, tin plates, canteen halves or even thin strips of wood.[8]

The unbolted cornmeal was largely indigestible, and it produced all
types of intestinal disorders, the most common of which was diarrhea. To
men already weak from hunger, the rough cornmeal acted like tiny razor
blades in their lower intestines. Many Andersonville survivors claimed that
they still suffered from intestinal distress decades after being released from
the prison.

The beef and pork, issued to the men, were often rancid and contained more fat than meat. The same problems with supply that affected
the cornmeal also affected the meat, but was made more acute because
of spoilage. The meat was always issued raw, and the prisoners were expected to cook it. No plans were ever made to issue the men cooked meat.

When the first prisoners arrived at Andersonville the floor of the stockade was covered with dead limbs and underbrush, that could be turned
into firewood. However, by the first of March, the prison floor had been
completely cleared of anything that would burn. Some prisoners found
firewood by digging up roots, but soon even the old roots were gone, and
there was no more firewood inside the stockade. Without firewood the
prisoners were forced to eat their meat ration raw, or not eat it at all. Without firewood, all they could do with their cornmeal was mix it with water to
form a type of cold mush.

Captain Wirz sent out details of prisoners to cut firewood. At first
these wood details found dead limbs and hardwood within sight of the
prison. They also picked sweet blackberries in the dense briar thickets that
floored the Georgia woods. But, as the prison's population continued to
grow, they were forced to cut down pine trees and to venture deeper and
deeper into the surrounding woods.

The smooth-talking Yankee prisoners assigned to these wood details
began to grow overly friendly with their teenage Confederate guards and
soon began to use the wood details as an opportunity to slip off into the
woods and escape. Seldom were any shots fired, the guards always claimed
to have been distracted by other men on the wood detail, or some might
have just simply chosen to look the other way. The escapees were not
reported until the detail returned at the end of the day, ensuring they were
a safe distance away.

Henry Wirz countered by requiring that all prisoners sent out on wood
detail take an oath not to escape. However, on June 17, the entire wood
detail escaped when they overpowered and disarmed their guards. An
embarrassed and frustrated Wirz responded by not letting wood details go
out the next day. From that point onward, a pattern was set up of sending
out wood details every other day. Each time the wood detail went out,
some prisoners would always escape, and the angry Captain Wirz would
retaliate by not allowing the details out the next day.[9]

A frustrated and angry Henry Wirz decided to increase the number of guards on the wood detail to a ratio of one armed guard for every three prisoners. This put a deep strain on his already overworked guard force and caused an increase in desertions by the Confederate guards. Ironically, the wood details gave the guards a perfect opportunity to desert their posts and go home.

Eventually, Wirz realized there was little or nothing he could do and relented on his threats not to allow the wood details to go out. By mid-summer conditions in the stockade were so horrible, no one could really blame a prisoner for trying to escape. Cutting off the wood detail for even one day simply caused too much suffering in the stockade to justify it. To make matters worse, as the prison population grew, so did the number of prisoners and guards needed to harvest enough firewood for so many men. Also, the wood details had to venture farther and farther from the stockade to find the necessary wood, and by this time it was mostly all pine that was being brought back to the stockade.

The situation became so bad that Georgia Governor Joseph Brown complained to General Cobb and the Confederate War Department about bands of renegade guards and runaway prisoners roaming the countryside, stealing from civilians and disturbing the peace. General Winder responded to Governor Brown's complaint personally. He argued that the outside work details performed useful services for the prisoners and relieved overcrowding in the stockade.[10]

The second leading cause of death inside the stockade was the lack of clean water for drinking, washing, and waste removal. When the prison site was first chosen by Sidney Winder, the small tributary of Sweetwater Creek provided adequate water for the six thousand Union prisoners of war who were expected. However, there was simply no way the small creek could accommodate the twenty thousand prisoners, who had been crammed into the pine log stockade by the beginning of summer.

While the stockade was being built, gangs of Black laborers had piled up dirt changing the natural channel of the creek, causing it to flow farther south than it normally would. This change in course eroded a wide flood plain, that grew bigger as the stockade filled up with prisoners. By the beginning of summer, almost one-third of the space inside the stockade was a muddy, uninhabitable swamp. Within the swampy area, just to the north of the prison's latrines, called the sinks, was formed a low peninsula of land that was just dry enough to build several dozen she-bangs. The prisoners quickly dubbed this area "Island Number Ten," after the heavily fortified island near New Madrid, Missouri, that was captured by Union forces in 1862.

Sidney Winder had thought up a plan to build two dams inside the stockade. The first, near the west wall, would hold a pool of water to be used for drinking. This water would flow over a spillway into another pool that was to be used for bathing. The bathing water would also create a

Photograph by A. J. Riddle, Showing the Sinks and the Area Known As "Island Number Ten"

U.S. Army Military Historical Institute

reservoir of water that would be released periodically to flush the offal from the latrines on the other side of the stockade.

Only the first dam was ever built. The rush of prisoners to the prison, and the expiration of the Confederate Secretary of War's emergency order impressing local slaves to work on the prison, meant that the second dam could never be built. Sidney, and later Richard Winder, had to use every available laborer to erect the stockades' walls, not being able to spare men to finish the second dam. The prisoners might have helped build the dam, but Captain Wirz forbid any type of digging tools from entering the stockade, fearing they would be used to dig escape tunnels. Even if the prisoners had the digging tools, they did not have the wood and hinges needed to construct the dam's sluice gates and spillways. It is also doubtful if there was ever enough water flow in the small creek to make the two-dam water system, envisioned by Sidney Winder, feasible. At the trial of Henry Wirz, witnesses blamed the dam that created the pool of water for drinking for blocking the flow of water through the creek, and allowing the area around the sinks to become clogged with human waste. In the testimony it was portrayed as another deliberate attempt by Confederate officials to make the prison as miserable a place as possible.

The worst thing about the water situation at Andersonville was that the water was already polluted before it ever reached the prison. The Confederate guards' camp was built upstream from the prison, and cooking grease, ashes, and sewage from the guards' camp would be washed into the stream by rainwater, to eventually flow into the stockade. When the prison's cookhouse was finally completed, it was sited on the banks of the creek, just upstream from where it flowed into the prison. Prisoners reported that the water had a thick, green, grease scum on it, and men who drank freely would get terribly sick with their faces swelling up to a point where they can't see.[11]

Many prisoners attempted to dig their own wells or fashion cisterns to collect rainwater. Captain Wirz was suspicious of all wells, suspecting they were the beginnings of escape tunnels, and he was usually right. The men had to scrape through the red clay with wooden boards, metal canteen halves, and their bare hands until they reached water. The water that the Union prisoners often dug for days to reach was usually so full of sulfur deposits and red mud, that it wasn't much better than the water found in the creek. Even if a good clean well was dug, it was almost impossible to keep it clean, since the summer thunderstorms would wash dirt and cook fire ashes into the wells despite whatever covering or dikes the prisoners could fashion. When the water in the wells became unfit to drink, they were quickly turned into latrines that tended to overflow during a hard rain, flooding the surrounding area with sewage.

Men weak with diarrhea, who could not make it to the sinks, would scrape out shallow latrines all over the prison. The hard thunderstorms of the Georgia summer would fill these small latrines with rain water and wash all the human waste down into the creek, where it would flood the swamp, creating a wide, sewage filled lake. When the waters receded, the muddy swamp was covered with large gobs of offal that was feasted on by swarms of large green and black blowflies, that laid eggs that later would become a sea of working maggots.

Photograph by A. J. Riddle, Showing the Deadline

U.S. Army Military History Institute

Reforms and Providence Springs

When General Winder arrived at Andersonville in June, he immediately set about trying to correct some of the problems at the prison. Winder obviously had better leadership skills, and his rank earned him more respect than Captain Wirz because he managed to get much more done.

General Winder had paroled Union prisoners of war tear down the cookhouse and relocate it on a high plateau north of the stockade. He also rebuilt the sinks and ordered a general cleanup of the Confederate guards' camp. General Winder imposed a higher level of discipline on the guards, holding them responsible for any prisoners under their care who escaped. General Winder found that his general's rank opened doors that had been closed to Colonel Persons and Captain Wirz. He was able to cut through the bureaucracy surrounding the commissary system and get more cornmeal and meat rations sent from Columbus, greatly improving the amount of quality of the rations issued to the prisoners.

General Winder developed a better relationship with local farmers, most of whom found Captain Wirz to be moody and temperamental. From these farmers, General Winder was able to procure some fresh vegetables that he issued to the prisoners. Although the soil around the stockade was very infertile, shortly after he had arrived, Henry Wirz had ordered the beginning of small garden plots around the stockade. Paroled prisoners were able to produce some turnips, carrots, onions, and peas from the small patches of red-clay soil.

However, everything General Winder did was only a drop in the bucket of misery that was Andersonville. By the first of August over thirty-two thousand prisoners were jammed into the muddy, sewage-filled stockade. It was the fifth largest city in the Confederacy, and a prisoner was dying every five minutes.

The burial details were hauling over three hundred prisoners a day to the cemetery. Already the burial trenches had extended far beyond where the Raiders' graves, who had been buried only a few weeks before.

After the Civil War, General Winder would be greatly vilified by those who testified at the trial of Henry Wirz. The old general, who had done more than any other person to improve living conditions for the prisoners, was depicted as a sadistic brute who bragged that his prisons were "killing more Yankees than twenty regiments of Robert E. Lee's army."[1] This cruel remark certainly didn't fit General Winder's personality, and he probably never said it. If he did, he was probably simply stating a fact as he understood it.

General John H. Winder was an almost stereotypical Southern gentleman of the old school. He had been born into a distinguished, socially and politically powerful, Maryland family. He was raised the child of wealth and was taught all the manners and social graces of a typical, upper-class, tidewater family. Winder was also instilled with a deep sense of duty and honor, which he assiduously observed for the rest of his life.

His father, General William Henry Winder, was commander of the American forces that were sent to defend the new United States capital city of Washington during the War of 1812. During late summer of 1814, a large British army landed on the western shore of the Patuxent River at Benedict, Maryland, and began moving on Washington. Winder choose to make his stand near the small town of Bladensburg, Maryland, and was badly defeated by a superior British force on August 24, 1814. This defeat allowed the British to enter Washington and burn all the government buildings, including the capitol building and the executive mansion, later to be known as the White House.

Ironically, Winder's father had also negotiated a prisoner-of-war exchange agreement with the British that became the model for the Dix-Hill Cartel, that governed the exchange of prisoners during the Civil War until it was suspended in 1863.

The young John Winder was a fourteen-year-old cadet at West Point, at the time of his father's defeat. Already a harsh military school, where the weak and different were tormented unmercifully, the military academy became an almost unbearable place for John Winder, who was hounded continuously about his father's disgraceful defeat. During his entire undistinguished military career, John Winder was still haunted by his father's failure. For most of his career, John Winder served in the Quartermaster and Commissary Corps, unable to show his courage in battle or advance in rank. During the Seminole and Mexican Wars he finally saw action and was breveted, or temporarily promoted, for gallantry. After the war was over, Winder was reduced in rank back to captain; he had just been given the permanent rank of major when he resigned to accept a commission as a colonel of the First North Carolina State Troops. Later, he was promoted to brigadier general by Jefferson Davis and was given the job of provost marshal of Richmond.

John Winder was sixty years old when he assumed his new duty post with the Confederate States of America. He had a penchant for nepotism and appointed as many relatives as possible as subordinates. Duty under General Winder in Richmond meant that the lucky officer could avoid combat and enjoy the social life of the Confederate capital city.

Soon after he assumed his new duties, General Winder was badly duped by a well-organized group of female Union spies. They would invite the jolly old general to dinner and then ply him with wine and flattery to get information.[2] This unfortunate episode gave General Winder the undeserved reputation of being stupid. In reality, General Winder was simply a man from a different time, when gentlemen and ladies did not engage in espionage. The episode with the Union spies changed Winder's personality. He became cynical and suspicious, explaining why he preferred relatives as subordinates rather than strangers. Exactly why he took a liking to Henry Wirz and felt he could trust this Swiss-born man remains a mystery.

Winder was particularly hard on anyone he suspected might be a Union agent. Spying for him was a dishonorable occupation, not engaged in by gentlemen of honor. Winder's harshness with suspected spies and his tendency to feud with subordinates and other officers gave him an equally undeserved reputation of being hard and sadistic.

In reality, General Winder was a very gentle, loving, family man. He denounced cruelty and wrote numerous letters to Confederate officials complaining about conditions in the prisons. He investigated charges of brutality against guards and punished those he found guilty.[3]

In February of 1865, he had just arrived at the Confederate prison at Florence, South Carolina, where he was planning to discipline three officers charged with mistreating prisoners. While he was walking from the train depot to the prison, he suddenly had a massive heart attack and died. He was 65 years old.

If he had lived, John Winder would have undoubtedly been brought to trial for the conditions at Andersonville. However, with his death, Captain Henry Wirz was left holding the bag.

Just as Winder's reforms had begun to improve conditions in the prison, at least a little, the process was brought to a halt, by of all things, the Union Army. As Union General William T. Sherman's army was closing in on Atlanta, General Winder began to fear a Union cavalry raid on Andersonville. The general clearly remembered the failed Kilpatrick-Dahlgren raid on Richmond earlier in the year and the havoc it caused. He fully realized that the poorly armed and trained Georgia Reserves would be no match for Sherman's cavalry.

A young Confederate officer Captain James Dunwoody Jones served as drillmaster and ordnance officer at Andersonville during the spring and summer of 1864, when conditions were at their worst. After the war he wrote about his experiences. One of Jones' duties was to inspect the arms of the men going on duty. Once he reported that: "I found that the 500 muskets carried by men going on sentry duty, not over 100 could have been fired." He reported his finding to Captain Wirz, who seemed unsurprised by the news.[4]

General Winder decided to form the Black prisoners of war into labor brigades, issue them double rations, and begin a program of fortification. The Black prisoners seemed to readily accept this hard labor for the Confederates with little complaint, since this was the same type of duty usually performed by Black soldiers in the Union Army. It was truly tragic that this building of earthworks had to be taken, since it took both prisoners and guards away from the wood details and the small gardens that had been started around the stockade.

During the summer of 1864, General Sherman and Major General George Stoneman put together an ill-defined plan to liberate the Federal prisoners being held at Macon and Andersonville. General Sherman liked to keep his cavalry busy destroying the Confederate railroad system. However, General Stoneman balked at such mundane duty and craved glory. He dreamed of carrying out bold cavalry raids, such as those performed by Confederate Generals J. E. B. Stuart and Nathan Bedford Forrest. He beseeched Sherman to turn him loose to ride boldly through Georgia, freeing Union prisoners of war. Just exactly what General Stoneman was planning to do with 33,000 sick and starving Union prisoners of war once he had liberated them apparently never came up during the meetings to plan the raid.

A cavalry raid was a risky maneuver, especially for Union forces who were unfamiliar with the Southern landscape and unpredictable weather patterns. The cavalry was the eyes and ears of an army. Their primary function was reconnaissance. Their secondary function was to harass the enemy with destructive raids and skirmishes. However, Union cavalry commanders found that raids through the South could be risky business. Many things could go wrong. Rivers, reported to be shallow, and narrow streams were often transformed into a swirling muddy torrent by overnight rains making them impassable. Military objectives reported to be lightly guarded by store clerks and old men, might in reality be heavily fortified with determined fighters manning the ramparts. General Stoneman's raid was proof of the old adage that what could go wrong, will go wrong.

General Stoneman decided that his first objective would be the officers' prison in Macon. Stoneman's troopers found nothing to be as they expected. He ran head first into Confederate General Joe Wheeler's Confederate cavalry. Wheeler was thoroughly familiar with the terrain around Macon and he out maneuvered and out fought Stoneman. Eventually, Stoneman's force was surrounded and forced to surrender. He soon found himself a prisoner of war among the very men he intended to liberate.

After Stoneman's fiasco, Sherman made no further attempt to liberate Andersonville. However, during his famous "March to the Sea" Sherman's foragers encountered escaped Andersonville prisoners. They recounted to Sherman's soldiers all the horrors they had seen and endured.[5] Sherman often used these escaped prisoners to explain the zeal his men felt when they were wreaking havoc upon the South. Sherman never explained why he made no effort to liberate them other than Stoneman's fiasco of a raid.

In February, when the prison first began to receive prisoners of war from Richmond, the pine log stockade at Andersonville became a curiosity to the civilian populations of Sumter and Macon counties. Much to the anger of the Union prisoners inside the stockade, many local civilians, including women and children, climbed to the top of the sentry towers to gape at the dreaded Yankees. The prisoners justly felt that this was an invasion of their privacy, since many of the men were nearly naked and others were using the sinks.

During the warm and pleasant days of May, when Colonel Persons was still at the prison and was anxious to build good relations with the local civilian population, he arranged for some of the local ladies to put on an outdoor dinner for the guards. The members of the 55th Georgia Infantry, who were shortly to depart the prison, showed their appreciation by putting on a display of close order drill, and even staged a sham battle to show how they could, if necessary, defend the community from Yankee attack. The festivities concluded with a dance. The prisoners in the stockade could clearly hear the music, even though Colonel Persons had arranged for the party to be a full mile from the prison. One prisoner commented in his diary that the band played very poorly.[6]

By the time the terrible dog days of August had arrived, local curiosity seekers had ceased to venture near the prison. By this time the stench of the place was so bad it could be smelled miles away. Inside the stockade the air was foul and stagnant. The pine log walls acted as a barrier to keep out fresh air and cooling breezes. Everywhere there was the smell of human waste, and a smoky mist hung over the floor of the prison compound, especially in the swampy area around the creek.

Despite the horrible conditions inside the stockade, there was to be one more invasion of the prisoner's privacy. A Macon photographer, Andrew Jackson Riddle, had arranged with General Winder to travel to Andersonville and photograph the prison. Riddle, like General Winder, was a native of Maryland, and probably used this old-home connection to get the General to approve his visit. Riddle had also promised to take a portrait photograph of the General in his best dress uniform. This uniform was one of General Winder's great vanities. It had been custom made for him at considerable cost while he was in Richmond. He only wore it on special occasions, and loved being photographed in it.

Riddle had been living in Georgia for more than ten years, making a humble living taking daguerreotype images of local government leaders and wealthy citizens. Riddle craved the opportunity to make a name for himself as a Civil War photographer, like his famous Northern counterparts Matthew Brady and Alexander Gardner, who had seen their work reproduced in such well-read publications as *Harper's Weekly* and *Frank Leslie's Illustrated Newspaper.*

At the time of the Civil War, photographers had to develop their negative plates immediately after exposure, so each photographer had to be followed by a portable darkroom. Matthew Brady and Alexander Gardner carried their big cameras and darkroom equipment in a specially made wagon. Riddle was hampered by a lack of mules and wagons and could only transport his bulky equipment by train. How A. J. Riddle managed to move his bulky and heavy equipment around Andersonville is unknown, but General Winder most likely loaned him one of the prison's few wagons and assigned a detail of paroled prisoners and guards to assist him.

Riddle probably waited until mid-day, when the sun was at its brightest, to climb to the top of one of the sentry towers and begin to photograph the inside of the stockade. Riddle's camera caught the full horror of the sinks, which he photographed several times from different angles. The photographs of the sinks show several prisoners squatting with their pants down, having a bowel movement. One shot of the sinks also caught the muddy horror of the area the prisoners called "Island Number Ten." A photograph taken from the opposite side of the prison, shows a crowd of prisoners gathered around the sutler's wagon, staring up at the camera in bewilderment. Another shot caught a clear view of the snake-like deadline, also catching, perhaps by accident, the top of the pine log walls clearly showing the log's square shape.

After Riddle finished taking photographs from a variety of sentry towers he moved to the prison cemetery, by this time it was probably late in the afternoon. One photograph shows the rows of trenches with small headboard markers made from what appear to be wooden roof shingles. The photograph is apparently of Section K, the oldest portion of the cemetery which contained the grave of Adam Swarner. Riddle's most memorable shot was taken on the other side of the road in Section E. This widely reproduced photograph shows a detail of paroled prisoners and their Confederate guards, preparing to bury a loaded wagon full of dead prisoners. Two diggers stand, almost nonchalantly, inside a freshly dug and neatly squared burial trench, while others stand on the freshly dug mounds of earth flanking the trench. One body appears to have already been laid in the trench, next to a crudely made empty litter.

Riddle's photographs are of an inferior quality compared to those of Brady and Gardner. He probably had considerable trouble getting the proper chemicals to develop his negatives, and his equipment was most likely prewar in manufacture. However, he leaves us with our only known visual record of Andersonville prison.

After taking this last photograph, A. J. Riddle packed up his equipment and departed from Andersonville on the next train back to Macon. He was probably happy to be leaving such a horrible place.[7]

During most of the month of August, Henry Wirz was absent from the prison due to illness, and his duties were assumed by Lieutenant Samuel B. Davis. Wirz was ravaged by fever, and his illness was so serious there were rumors circulating within the prison that he had died. General Winder ordered him sent to a hospital in Augusta, where Wirz apparently recovered enough to return to duty sometime before the end of the month.

However, he was horribly weak from his ordeal and had a bed put in his office. He seldom emerged from his office issuing orders to Lieutenant Davis while laying prostrate in his bed. General Winder praised his subordinate, saying that his illness "was directly related to overwork for want of assistance." General Winder claimed that Wirz seriously jeopardized his health by remaining at his post weeks after he should have been relieved due to illness.[8]

During this same period of time, while Wirz was ill, more important improvements were being made under General Winder's direction. After much trouble, the general finally found enough lumber to begin building barracks inside the stockade. However, shortly after work began, he had to scale back construction due to a shortage of nails, which at that time were still being made by hand in blacksmith shops. What finally arose on the north end of the stockade was a strange looking structure, with a roof, a floor, but no walls. One visitor claimed that it looked more like an animal shelter than a barracks. However, each barracks could give shelter to 270 men laying shoulder to shoulder. The first barracks was finished by August 18 and two more would be done by the end of the month.[9]

During July, General Winder ordered both Sidney and Richard Winder to return to Andersonville to help out, but Sidney's stay would be brief. His father would shortly send him off to scout for a suitable location to build a new prison. As commander of all Confederate prisons east of the Mississippi, General Winder had the legal authority to open new prisons. By this time General Winder had correctly concluded that the conditions at Andersonville were not correctable and that the only answer was to begin moving prisoners to a new location as soon as possible.

Early in August, Sidney Winder reported to his father that he had located a new prison site just north of the small town of Millen, Georgia, on the Augusta and Savannah Railroad. This time Sidney Winder was taking no chances on the prison becoming overcrowded. Camp Lawton, as the new prison at Millen would be called, would be able to accommodate up to fifteen to twenty thousand prisoners with no overcrowding. Like Andersonville, it would be a pine log stockade, but with the hardwood trees left standing to provide shade. Sidney Winder also made sure there would be more than enough fresh water. The prison site was crossed by a wide and deep stream of good clean water. The site at Millen also had no swamp; the area within the stockade was all high, well drained, and grassy. While there was still the problem of no lumber or nails to build shelters, Sidney Winder had managed to find enough tents to get the prison operating.

On August 7, 1864, General Winder notified Adjutant General Cooper that the new prison site at Millen had been selected and asked that he please send the necessary authority to impress slaves, teams and wagons, lumber and saw mills.[10]

Little did John and Sidney Winder realize that their new prison would lay directly in the path of General Sherman's army, as it made its way across Georgia after the fall of Atlanta. The large prison Sidney Winder worked so hard to get built and put into operation, would have to be abandoned in November, only a few weeks after it had opened. The rapid advance of Sherman's marauding army moving southeast from Atlanta would require that the prison be closed, and all prisoners transferred in less than three days.[11]

In late July, General Winder had issued a public appeal to the citizens of Macon, Randolph, Schley, Terrell, Baker, Calhoun, Lee, Sumter, and Dougherty counties, asking for enough slave labor to complete the fortifications needed to defend Andersonville from a Union cavalry raid. General Winder estimated that the labor of 2,000 slaves, properly equipped with spades and axes, along with fifty teams and wagons, could complete the work in ten days. He argued that it would be better for a planter to lose all his slaves for only a few days, than for only a part of his labor force to be siphoned off for a longer period of time.[12]

Only a few weeks after General Winder had sent out his public plea for slaves and equipment to build up the fortifications around Andersonville, he received help from an unexpected source. The notorious Union cavalry general Judson Kilpatrick, who had led the raid to free the prisoners of war in Richmond earlier in the year, was now assigned to Sherman's army. In mid-August he broke free from Sherman's army to stage another of his notorious ill-thoughtout raids. Kilpatrick moved south from Atlanta, attacking the Macon and Western Railroads at Fairburn, Georgia. Typically, Kilpatrick's raid was a miserable failure; he was out fought by Confederate General Joe Wheeler's cavalry at every turn. However, his raid threw the central Georgia counties into a panic, and clearly showed the danger to Andersonville.

At almost the same time, Yankee cavalry raiders had struck deep into north central Florida, attacking the railroads near Gainesville, Florida, interrupting the flow of food supplies north into the heart of the Confederacy.

Earlier in July, Major General Lowell H. Rousseau had raided into Alabama, destroying much of the Montgomery and West Point Railroad and seizing over 42,000 pounds of food supplies, mostly bacon, flour and sugar, ironically destined to feed the men in Andersonville. General Winder's dream of building a shoe factory at the prison was forever destroyed when General Rousseau's men seized six railroad freight cars filled with leather.[13]

Unlike the previous February, when Sidney Winder could not get any cooperation from local civilians, now the danger was obvious and civilian cooperation was forthcoming. No one wanted to see the Union cavalry release over thirty thousand Union prisoners of war on the Georgia countryside.

General Winder was never able to get the 2,000 slaves he requested, but he was able to gather enough axes and shovels to begin the extensive program of building defensive structures around the prison with only 500 slaves. A West Point trained engineer, General Winder knew how to set up fields of fire and build earthen embankments that would last. The remains of many of the earthworks built that summer can still be seen today at the Andersonville Prison site.

General Winder decided to circle the stockade with a series of lunettes to hold artillery capable of putting down enfilade fire along the run of the stockade wall. However, General Winder did not have enough cannon to arm all the lunettes with artillery, so they were built to hold riflemen. The main point of resistance would be two forts, both on the west side of the stockade overlooking the two gates. The fort on the north side was to be only a three gun redoubt, but the one to the south, before Captain Wirz's headquarters, was to be much larger, holding twelve pieces of artillery plus positions for riflemen. It was called the "Star Fort," although it bore little resemblance to a star, unless the star had been mashed all out of recognition.

The sight of all the digging outside of the stockade totally delighted the prisoners. To them it was all the proof they needed that Sherman's army was closing in fast on Andersonville, and that their misery would soon end. They took great delight in tormenting the guards in the sentry towers with catcalls and taunts about the futility of trying to halt the mighty Union army with pitiful piles of dirt.

On August 9, 1864, one of the most important events in the history of Andersonville occurred. Afternoon and evening thunderstorms are common in the South during the summer, but the dark clouds that built up to the west of Andersonville that day were more ominous than usual. It had been raining earlier in the day, but around three o'clock in the afternoon it turned into a torrential downpour. General Winder commented in his report that he had never seen such a rain in many years. At the peak of the storm a loud creaking noise was heard. Several prisoners stuck their heads out of their she-bangs just in time to see a large section of the western wall, its loose dirt foundations washed away by the rain, collapse like a bunch of sticks.

A huge cheer went up throughout the prison, terrifying the guards in the sentry towers. General Winder was immediately summoned and he rushed his ragged guard force forward to plug the breach in the wall. He also ordered one of the cannon to fire a warning shot over the stockade, the only time the artillery was fired in anger.

All these precautions were really unnecessary since the soaking wet prisoners had no intention of making a mass escape. They were just as surprised by the collapse of the wall as the Confederates. General Winder was so upset he wired Richmond asking for more guards and begging Confederate officials to halt the shipment of new prisoners to Andersonville until the wall was repaired.[14]

Luckily for General Winder, he already had a force of Black laborers at Andersonville digging the fortifications. He quickly put them to work repairing the one hundred foot section of the collapsed wall. The work crews labored for three days and two nights to get the wall repaired. All during that time the members of the Georgia Reserves were on duty guarding the breach. General Winder would later write: "Never in my life have I spent such so anxious a time. If we had not had a large Negro force working on the defenses, I think it would have been impossible to save the place."[15]

The prisoners seemed to have been amused by their captors fear and anxiety. They used the occasion to taunt their guards, saying that Generals Grant and Sherman were poking holes bigger than that in the Confederacy every day.

After the damage was repaired, General Winder set about erecting a second wall to circle the stockade. This wall was to be of equal height as the first, but with a much larger perimeter. The muddy area between the two log walls would become known as the "covered way." The construction of the second wall would only further tax the resources available to General Winder. Men who could have been put to work growing vegetables and cutting firewood were instead put to work felling pine trees and digging trenches.

In the days after the collapse of the log wall, the pouring rains continued. The tiny creek rose to a depth of over five feet, flooding the bridge and isolating the northern and southern parts of the compound. The prisoners were able to drink their fill of the fresh rainwater, wash clothes, and bathe. The rains also washed away much of the filth that had accumulated inside the stockade, completely flushing away the waste around the sinks.

The cloudy skies gave blessed relief from the sun, but prisoners complained that at night the damp air chilled them to the bone. Many of the men had absolutely no body fat left on their skeletal frames, and were quickly chilled by even a modest drop in temperatures. Most of the she-bangs were completely washed away and had to be rebuilt by men too sick and weak to do the work. What little firewood to be found inside the stockade had also been washed into the creek with the she-bangs, and the wood brought in by the outside details was soaking wet. When the hot summer sun returned a few days later, the pitiful prisoners had no shelters and were eating nothing but raw food.

On August 12, 1864, three days after the collapse of the wall, and following another particularly hard afternoon rain, a group of prisoners noticed something that made them leap for joy. Next to the log wall, just below the North Gate, a small trickle of water was gurgling from the ground. Within a few minutes a small pool of water had formed. It was a spring! A spring of water coming from an aquifer deep within the earth, unpolluted by the filth and sewage in the stockade.

Unfortunately, the small pool of water was inside the feared deadline. Since the prison had been in operation, several Union prisoners of war had been shot and killed by the guards for simply leaning over the railing or crossing the deadline to retrieve a lost object. To cross the deadline meant certain death. One of the prisoners solved the problem by tying a tin cup to the end of a tent pole and dipping out a cup of the precious liquid. It was cool, clear and absolutely delicious. After months of the foul water from the creek and the many wells and cisterns in the stockade, the water from the spring was a taste of heaven. The Regulators posted guards on the spring to make sure the water was taken away only in small amounts and there was no hoarding or selling of the water to prisoners too sick or weak to make it to the spring.[16]

The small spring was almost instantaneously named "Providence Springs." It was an apt name, since its waters probably saved thousands of lives. To many of the prisoners Providence Springs was proof that God had not forsaken them. The discovery of the spring created a type of religious revival within the prison. The prisoners clearly saw the spring as a sign that a merciful God had heard their cries for help and answered. Prison ministers arose to proclaim the spring a "miracle"; prayers of thanksgiving were issued from every throat and even some of the most hardened veterans were moved to tears. Prayer services and hymn singing seemed to break out spontaneously. The men who survived Andersonville would spend the rest of their lives telling anyone who would listen about the miracle of Providence Springs, insisting that only divine intervention, coming as a result of prayers offered to heaven, could have been responsible for the spring appearing almost like magic from the previously barren and dry ground. Some of the more religious of the prisoners compared Providence Springs to the "heaven-wrought miracle as when Moses' enchanted rod smote the parched earth in Sinai's desert waste, and the living waters gushed forth."[17]

The answer to the appearance of Providence Springs might be much more simple. Long time residences of the area claim that the spring had always been there. The spring site was located exactly where workers had piled up dirt during the building of the stockade wall, changing the natural course of Sweetwater Creek. The small spring probably existed unnoticed, until it was buried beneath piles of earth, only to be later freed by the torrential downpours of that hot Georgia summer.

PART TWO

"The duties I had to perform here were
arduous and unpleasant."

Captain Wirz, on Horseback, Leading a Prisoner under Double Guard
Library of Congress

The Transfer and Release

The agony of the prisoners confined in the Andersonville stockade did not end in a bright, glorious flash of liberation, but in a slow agonizing series of transfers to other prisons that took over six months to complete.

Since the founding of the colony of Georgia in 1733, no single year could equal 1864 for tumultuous events. Ever since the Civil War began, Georgia had been filling up with refugees from other parts of the South that had fallen to the Union army. The Georgians had at first displayed their famous hospitality to these fellow Southerners in need. However, by 1864, they had begun to strain the resources of the state, causing severe hardships. Housing was so scarce, people were living in abandoned railroad cars, and under bridges. Only an unusually good farm crop year prevented widespread hunger. Georgians, who had been overly generous at the beginning of the war, were now misers, hiding everything edible and in short supply, not just from the Yankee invaders but also from Confederate foragers, out-of-state refugees, and their own neighbors.[1]

By June of 1864, Sherman's forces had reached as far south as Marietta. More than one-third of the state was now in Union hands. The failure of Confederate forces to halt Sherman's advance towards Atlanta convinced General John H. Winder that the time had come to draw up contingency plans to evacuate Andersonville prisoners. He had obtained permission from Richmond to disperse the prisoners as he saw fit, and now he began to actively seek other sites to build new prisons.

General Winder was looking for sites where a prison could be quickly opened and would not be in the probable line of the Union army's advance. He argued fiercely with Governor Joe Brown who claimed that Winder was being overly pessimistic and spreading defeatism with his highhanded plans. Brown advocated simply enlarging the stockade at Andersonville to accommodate the thousands of new prisoners being taken every day in the fighting above Atlanta and not to worry about the advance of Sherman's army because surely the Confederate troops would soon repulse the invaders.

General Winder was little persuaded by Brown's argument. He reopened the Confederate prison at Cahaba, Alabama. This small prison, located near Selma, had been closed earlier in the war, except as a transfer point for prisoners of war captured in Mississippi being moved east. While the small prison at Cahaba was far removed from Sherman's suspected line of march, there was a great deal of difficulty getting prisoners moved there because the lack of railroads in the area.[2]

All through July and August, as the death rate in the filthy Andersonville stockade was reaching its zenith, General Winder was working feverishly, planning mass transfers from Andersonville to other Confederate prisons and working to have new prisons opened. All this meant wading through a morass of paperwork and logistical planning. This time, local opposition to the building of new prisons was mostly ignored. Even the irascible Governor Brown could not halt General Winder's plans to transfer the Union prisoners out of Andersonville and open new prisons in Georgia.

On September 2, 1864, the city of Atlanta fell to General Sherman's army. With the capture of Jonesborough, the Confederate supply line between Atlanta and Macon was severed, and the new Confederate commander, John Bell Hood, had no choice except to abandon the city. Hood's Confederate forces flanked the city and began to attack Union forces along Sherman's rail link with Chattanooga. After setbacks in north Georgia, Hood began marching across Alabama to threaten the Union held city of Nashville. With the departure of Hood's forces, all of Georgia was now at the mercy of Sherman's army.

The fall of Atlanta panicked the entire state of Georgia. To have Union soldiers in Atlanta was something that would have seemed impossible only a year before. From the state capital in Milledgeville, Georgia, officials had to quickly get their wits about them and plan for Sherman's next move. No one knew for certain where he would strike next. Most felt his target would be Charleston, while others believed that he would march across Alabama and Mississippi to unite with Union forces in Louisiana. Still others felt that Sherman would march to Savannah, the nearest seaport. But, no one knew for sure.

To Georgia officials, dispersing their Union prisoner of war population was now a top priority. Every available railroad boxcar was pressed into service moving prisoners out of Andersonville. Every available man, no matter how old or in firmed, was impressed into service guarding the Union prisoners of war during the transfers. The first prisoners transferred were moved to existing Confederate prisons in North and South Carolina.

Prisoner Came Too Near the Deadline

The Light Security at the New Prisons Opened to Relieve the Overcrowding at Andersonville. Contrary to This Illustration's Caption, the Shooting of Prisoners at the New Prisons Was a Very Rare Occurrence.

The Capture, the Prison Pen and Escape

Later transfers were to new prisons opened near Blackshear, Thomasville, and the large prison at Millen, Georgia.

Once the transfers began, the prison population of Andersonville dropped dramatically. By the end of November, three months after the transfers began, the pine log stockade held only 1,359 prisoners of war, compared to the 33,000 men who had jammed into the eighteen acre stockade the previous August.

The new prisons, opened in Blackshear and Thomasville, were virtually defenseless. They were little more than open spaces circled by a few picket posts and a some hastily erected earthworks, which housed a few mismatched pieces of artillery of small caliber. The guard force was mostly of the same type as had guarded Andersonville prisoners, young boys, convalescents, and old men. Only the new prison at Millen, which had been started during the summer under the guidance of Sidney Winder, had a log wall stockade. All the rest had only wooden stakes driven in the ground to mark the farthermost reaches where a prisoner could wander without the danger of being shot by a guard.

The living conditions in these new prisons were a great relief for the suffering Union prisoners of war. All the new prison sites had been selected with the hard learned lessons of Andersonville in mind. They had abundant sources of safe and clean water for drinking, cooking, and bathing. Tents and lean-to type shelters were built to house the prisoners. In an important concession to prisoner comfort, large shade trees were left standing inside the prison compounds, even though they often blocked the view of the guards. The food was Spartan but adequate.

Local Southern citizens often came to the new prisons to gawk at the Yankee prisoners. Because the new prisons had no high log walls, it was easy for conversations to begin between the Yankee prisoners and local citizens. Many formed friendships and returned to bring the Union prisoners extra food, blankets, medicines and clothes. Generally it was a relaxed atmosphere with much fraternization going on. The commanders of the guard force at the new prisons were understanding and allowed the Union prisoners to accept the gifts from local civilians. Everyone seemed to sense that the war was nearing an end, and it was time to restore broken friendships between fellow countrymen.

Back at Andersonville, Captain Wirz was grateful to have so many prisoners transferred out of the muddy stockade. However, his problems were far from over. Fearing Union cavalry raids from Florida, Confederate officials transferred 3,500 prisoners from the newly opened prison near Thomasville, Georgia, back to Andersonville on Christmas Eve. They were greeted by the 1,359 prisoners left behind after the transfers began. This brought the population of the prison back up to nearly 5,000 men on Christmas Day of 1864.[3]

Captain Wirz had done little since the transfers began to improve conditions in the prison. In fact, things had actually deteriorated. In the cold winter months, food was increasingly scarce than in the summer when local vegetable gardens were in production. The damp cold of the Georgia winter made the prisoners' lives miserable. Almost all the prisoners were shoeless, most were dressed in rags, and some were completely naked. Most prisoners had jammed into the wooden barracks that gave some protection from the elements. Others fashioned she-bangs out of the shelters abandoned by the transferred prisoners. A pitiful few, mostly deranged men shunned by their comrades, dug caves in the creekbanks where they burrowed like rats.

The cold, wet weather of the Georgia winter caused Wirz's wounded shoulder to throb violently with pain. He withdrew into his quarters and was seldom seen around the compound. The Confederate guards at Andersonville were almost as shoeless and as ragged as the prisoners. Perched atop their "pigeon roost" sentry towers, they had little protection from the cold winds and bone-chilling rains. With Captain Wirz too ill to supervise the prison, stealing, desertion, and insubordination among the young guards were rampant. By New Year's Day 1865, discipline had almost completely broken down. Prisoners were escaping in large numbers, primarily due to negligence by the guards.

Once the deserters and escaped prisoners were beyond the reach of Captain Wirz's search parties, escape was a good possibility. Most deserters would simply head home, while the escaped prisoners of war would strive to reach the Union lines. They had plenty of help from runaway slaves and the host of strange characters populating the Georgia woods that summer.

The woodlands of Georgia were filled with a weird assortment of strange individuals the final year of the Civil War. They were a strange mixture of runaway slaves, Confederate deserters, civilians fleeing conscript officers, pro-Union Georgians, war refugees with no place to go, along with assorted bands of thieves, vagabonds, bushwhackers, and assorted good-for-nothings. The famous author Joel Chandler Harris, who was a teenage boy in Georgia during the Civil War, wrote later in life of a strange sight he beheld while walking in the woods near his home. He approached a clearing and beheld a group of runaway slaves and Confederate deserters, preparing their evening meal next to an abandoned cabin.[4]

Each group of Andersonville prisoners that reached the Union lines had a vast repertoire of horror stories about conditions in Andersonville. These men were quickly interviewed by war correspondents hungry for news to send back to their papers. If the stories told by the escaped prisoners were not harrowing enough, the reporter never failed to embellish them. When the reports reached the Northern newspapers, adept artists further added to the horror of the escaped prisoner's accounts with imaginative art work.

Those escaped prisoners who made it to the Union lines described Captain Wirz as some type of madman, foolishly attempting to maintain discipline by riding around the prison followed by a pack of vicious dogs.

They also claimed that he would often pull his pistol and threaten to starve the whole camp by cutting off their rations. They also said that Wirz punished prisoners by staking them spread-eagled on the cold, wet ground completely naked. How many of these reports are true and how many are embellished hearsay is subject to considerable debate. Prison records show that of the nearly 5,000 men confined in the prison after Christmas Eve 1864, nearly 700 died and were buried in the prison cemetery before the prison closed in early May.

In January of 1865, probably as a result of a letter smuggled out of the prison by bribed guards, two woman identified only as Mrs. Spaulding and Ann Williams showed up at the prison to visit two Andersonville prisoners. Captain Wirz maintained in a report that these two women had sexual intercourse with at least seven prisoners and an unknown number of guards. Wirz claimed that the two women were not prostitutes and had steadfastly refused to accept any money for their sexual favors.[5]

In late March, prisoner exchanges between the North and South, that had been suspended since 1863, were quietly resumed. On January 21, 1865, General Grant sent a letter to Secretary of War Edwin Stanton, informing him that representatives of the Union and the Confederacy would be meeting to arrange prisoner exchanges towards a possible resumption of the Dix-Hill Cartel. The representatives met at a camp on the Big Black River near Vicksburg, Mississippi. After a month of negotiations, they finally reached an agreement. The final terms of the agreement were signed on March 16, 1865 by Union Brigadier General Morgan L. Smith and Confederate Colonel N. G. Watts.[6]

The agreement called for the establishment of two neutral areas under joint Union and Confederate occupation. For Union prisoners of war who served in the western armies, the exchange point would be Camp Fisk, located between two bridges over the Big Black River near Vicksburg. For soldiers who served in the eastern armies, the exchange point would be Baldwin, Florida, a small railroad crossroads near Jacksonville.[7]

Confederate authorities were anxious to get rid of their prisoners of war, that had been a tremendous drain on the diminished food and manpower resources of the South. The sooner the prisons could be closed and the prisoners of war delivered to the exchange points the better. The quickest way to move the prisoners to the exchange points was by train. However, this would not be as easy as it would seem.

Even in the best of times, the confused hodgepodge of independent lines that was the Confederate railroad system made the transportation of released prisoners of war a logistical nightmare. To add to the confusion, much of the Southern railroad system had been either destroyed by the war or had their tracks cannibalized to provide rails and crossties for damaged tracks in other places. The entire Confederacy did not have a single factory, or rolling mill, capable of making iron rails or locomotives to re-place those that were missing or destroyed.[8]

Because of the problems with the Confederate railroad system, the released prisoners had to follow a long and tiresome, zigzag route to the exchange points. They sometimes had to travel hundreds of miles out of their way to make the necessary rail connections. At other points the rail-roads simply ran out of tracks, and the released prisoners had to embark on long overland treks, walking to the next railroad junction.

Because of the serious shortage of locomotives and boxcars avail-able for the prisoner transfers, the trains were always filled to overflowing with hundreds of prisoners. The prisoners were jammed aboard the trains in boxcars, that were never intended to carry passengers, with a minimum of sanitary facilities, for a long, agonizingly slow, stop-and-go journey to the exchange points. Some prisoners had to ride on open flat cars ex-posed to the elements. Prisoners were fed and given water on an irregular basis, and no medical services were provided for the prisoners who were sick or wounded.

The prisoners often languished for hours or even days at rural rail-road stations, waiting for trains that had been delayed or would never come. While they suffered through these delays, the men were at the mercy of local civilians. There was a great difference in the treatment of the prison-ers, depending upon the attitude of the local civilians and the resources available in a given area to feed and shelter the men being transferred. Some prisoners of war reported kind treatment from local civilians, others talked of indifference and neglect, but seldom was there outright cruelty or brutality.

Without a doubt the worst part of the journey came when the prison-ers had to march overland to bridge the gaps in the Southern railroad system. The two longest and most notorious treks were from Selma to Montgomery, Alabama for those heading for the exchange point near Vicksburg, and the thirty-five-mile trek between Thomasville, Georgia and Madison, Florida for those in the eastern armies. The railroad from Jack-son, Mississippi to the final exchange point near Vicksburg had also been destroyed during the fighting for Vicksburg, meaning the prison-ers heading for the western exchange point had to walk the last few miles to freedom.

Due to the shortage of mules and horses in the South, the released prisoners of war had to walk every step of the way. Those too weak or sick to walk were carried on jury-rigged litters or pushed along in small two-wheeled carts that the prisoners referred to as a "hop, skip, and jerk." Sometimes the Confederate officials in charge of moving the prisoners commandeered local Blacks to carry the sick prisoners, other times they did not.[9]

Local hospitals and doctors' offices along the transfer route were filled to overflowing with sick prisoners, most of which would eventually die. Many Southerners sincerely felt sorry for the ragged prisoners of war and tried to aid the cadaverous-looking men by bringing them food, water, and medicines. Many small community cemeteries would become the final resting place of former Andersonville inmates.

Along the narrow dirt roads that connected the small farming communities where the railroads stopped and began again, there were few civilians to help. The released prisoners trudged down these dusty dirt roads, enduring midday heat and spring rains. At night they bivouacked in roadside pastures, warding off the nightly chill with small campfires. There were reports of sick prisoners being left along the side of the road to die by comrades, who were themselves too emaciated to carry them any farther. Local farmers would eventually get around to burying the abandoned prisoners of war in shallow, anonymous graves. No records were kept of how many prisoners died on their odyssey from Andersonville to the exchange points, but the numbers must have been substantial.

Once the prisoners were back in Federal hands, their chances of survival greatly increased. Doctors and nurses of the U.S. Sanitary Commission were available to care for and feed the sick and starved ex-prisoners of war. In the exchange camps good food and medicines were in plentiful supply, and the dedication of the doctors and nurses was legendary.

Once the ex-prisoners reached the exchange points they were either sent to local military hospitals or "parole camps" where they waited until transportation could be arranged to take them home. From the parole camp near Vicksburg, released prisoners of war were loaded aboard Mississippi riverboats to be transported to the North. Almost all the released prisoners' enlistments had expired while they were in captivity. However, some men, with an absolutely unbelievable sense of duty, asked to be returned to their units. Others simply wanted to go home.

Those released prisoners sent to the exchange point at Baldwin, Florida made a short rail journey to Fernandina, where they boarded ocean-going vessels that transported them to Camp Parole, Maryland. From there they would either be admitted to a hospital, transported to their homes, or returned to their units.

Almost all former Andersonville prisoners required at least some medical attention. Most had to be hospitalized. Hundreds were beyond saving and later died. Others required disfiguring amputations to remove diseased feet, legs, arms, hands, and eyes.[10] Many men died weeks, months, or later from medical conditions directly related to their captivity in Andersonville. These men, like the men who perished on the trip to the exchange points, were not listed among the nearly 13,000 men who died while the prison was in operation.

It was during the process of returning the prisoners home that one of the most tragic events of the Civil War occurred. On the night of April 27,

1865, the side-wheeled river steamer *Sultana* was plowing northward through the dark, cold waters of the Mississippi River, fighting a strong spring flood current. The *Sultana* had traveled down river two weeks earlier carrying the news of Abraham Lincoln's assassination.

Following the assassination of Abraham Lincoln, Secretary of War Edwin Stanton, fearing that a large conspiracy existed against the Federal government, had banned all telegraph communication concerning the death of Lincoln to areas of the former Confederate States of America. As the *Sultana* moved down river it was the first river steamer to carry the news of the terrible events in Washington to the river towns of the lower Mississippi. New Orleans' newspapers credited the *Sultana* as their source of information when they printed the news of the Lincoln assassination.[11]

After completing its southward journey, the *Sultana* began moving back upriver transporting cargo and taking on passengers. When the *Sultana* docked at Vicksburg over 2,000 released prisoners of war jammed onto the vessel's decks. Most of the ex-prisoners were sick, crippled, or greatly weakened from the ordeal of imprisonment. Records show that most of the released prisoners aboard the *Sultana* were from Andersonville or the small prison at Cahaba, Alabama.

As it pulled away from the dock at Vicksburg, the *Sultana* was seriously overloaded. It began moving upriver at a speed much too fast for the vessel's three overworked boilers. After refueling near Memphis, one of the *Sultana*'s boilers began to leak. The ship's commander Captain J. Cass Mason didn't want to turn back to Memphis because he knew how anxious his passengers were to get home. He hoped to reach Cairo, Illinois, the *Sultana*'s next stop, where the ex-prisoners of war could get proper medical attention and find rail transportation to their homes.[12]

The night was inky black, and the water was smooth as the *Sultana* moved upriver, pushing hard against the darkness. Below deck, the thousands of former prisoners of war slept fitfully, awaiting the morning when they would arise to see the green coast of Illinois, the first pro-Union state they had beheld since their captivity.

Sometime after two o'clock in the morning, the quietness of the cool spring night was shattered by a terrific explosion. One of the *Sultana*'s straining boilers had exploded. Within a few minutes, the *Sultana*'s other two boilers also exploded, hurling passengers and crewmen into the pitch blackness of the Mississippi River. Witnesses reported that after the *Sultana*'s explosion, it literally rained bodies and wreckage up and down the river. Those still alive when they hit the water were so badly scalded by the steam that they hardly lived more then a few minutes in the cold and muddy waters. Aboard the burning *Sultana* there were screams of terror as men leaped for their lives into the blackness of the river. Former prisoners who were unable to walk begged their comrades to throw them into the river so they would not burn to death. There were stories of brave nurses of the U.S. Sanitary Commission who gave their lives attempting to save the patients under their care.

When it was over, 1,400 crewmen and passengers were dead or missing. For weeks, bodies were being recovered from the river. Some corpses floated over ninety miles downstream before they were retrieved for a quick burial.

The *Sultana* explosion caused the greatest loss of life of any single vessel flying the American flag in either peace or war. More people died in the *Sultana* explosion and sinking than would die in the much more famous RMS *Titanic* disaster in the next century.[13]

Image of Andersonville Prison, Showing an Escaped Prisoner Being Chased By Dogs. The Wagon, Carrying the Dead to the Cemetery, Is Labeled "Dead 12, 877."

— 7 —

The Arrest of Henry Wirz

The last train bearing released Union prisoners of war from Andersonville pulled into the small train depot at Baldwin, Florida on May 4, 1865.[1] The prisoners delivered that day were some of the last Union troops to be sent to Andersonville. Most had been captured at the Battles of Franklin and Nashville, fought the previous December. Since they had been at Andersonville only a short period of time, they were still in fairly good physical condition, compared to the thousands of half-starved and sick men who came before them.

After the prisoner releases began, the South followed the North's example and released disabled and seriously ill prisoners first. This was done both for humanitarian reasons and to ensure that the released prisoners of war would not be quickly returned to combat.

The same day the last train from Andersonville was delivering it human cargo to the exchange point at Baldwin, a small U.S. army detachment was en route to Andersonville by train from its base at Macon, Georgia. They had orders to arrest Henry Wirz for the deliberate murder of Union prisoners of war.

The detachment was commanded by Captain N. E. Noyes, who had received his orders the day before from Brevet Major General James H. Wilson, the commanding officer of the Union garrison at Macon, Georgia.

In the final months of the Civil War, General Wilson had become a well-respected Union cavalry commander. After the Battles of Franklin and Nashville, he had reequipped and reorganized a 13,000-man cavalry corps, and in March of 1865, moved it south into Alabama to do battle with the famous Confederate General Nathan Bedford Forrest. In a spirited raid, Wilson's forces crushed all Confederate resistance and captured the city of Selma, Alabama. General Wilson's force then swept across Alabama and into Georgia.

On April 20, Wilson's cavalry rode into Macon, where he learned of the war's end. General Wilson set up his headquarters in the Lanier Hotel in downtown Macon, and became the commanding officer of all Union forces in Georgia.

At the same time as Captain Noyes' troopers were en route to Andersonville, most of the rest of General Wilson's cavalry were riding through the Georgia countryside, looking for former Confederate President Jefferson Davis.

After the fall of Richmond, Jefferson Davis, along with his cabinet and most of the Confederate treasury, had fled south hoping to reach the Florida coast where Davis planned to sail for Texas.

Jefferson Davis had an unrealistic dream of trying to keep the Southern cause alive by reaching the army of Brigadier General Edmund Kirby Smith in Texas. Jefferson Davis believed that if he could reach Kirby Smith's army, he could continue fighting the Civil War on the Texas frontier, while being resupplied from Mexico.

This was not Captain Noyes first trip to Andersonville. He had traveled through the small community only four days before carrying dispatches to Union forces in Eufaula, Alabama. When his train stopped to take on wood and water, Captain Noyes got out to walk around. He saw a group of Union prisoners of war sitting by the railroad tracks waiting to be transported to Macon. He claimed he also saw Confederate officials ordering the Confederate guards to hastily sign paroles that would protect them from prosecution for offenses committed at Andersonville. At the trial of Henry Wirz, Noyes claimed that Henry Wirz was personally supervising the signings and to have heard him say to the Confederate guards: "sign these paroles, or you will die here anyway."[2]

Noyes immediately recognized the parole agreement as the one signed between Confederate General Joseph E. Johnston and Union General William T. Sherman in North Carolina. Noyes knew that the agreement had already been repudiated by the president and the cabinet because that was the business of the dispatches he was carrying to Alabama.

Henry Wirz was mistakenly believing that he was protected by the terms of surrender signed by Confederate General Joseph E. Johnson on April 18, 1865. Part of the terms of the surrender agreement was a "general pardon" for everyone under Johnson's command which included Henry Wirz. Later, defenders of Henry Wirz would claim that this surrender made Wirz's trial and execution illegal.

However, a closer examination of the surrender and its terms indicates that it had no effect on the Wirz case. Joseph Johnston had surrendered to Union General William T. Sherman nine days after Robert E. Lee's surrender at Appomattox Court House, Virginia. Johnston and

Sherman had met at Bennett's Farm House near Durham, North Carolina to negotiate the surrender. The normally tenacious Sherman offered Johnson very liberal terms, including a "general pardon" as well as other controversial provisions such as allowing all duly elected Confederate office holders the right to keep their positions and the observation of Southern "property rights".

When Secretary of War Edwin Stanton read the terms of the surrender in Washington, he was furious. That evening at a cabinet meeting Stanton argued that Sherman had greatly exceeded his authority and had crossed the line from military to civilian matters by granting a general pardon and allowing Confederate office holders to maintain their positions. Stanton claimed that the provision respecting Southern "property rights" could be interpreted as allowing slavery to continue.

After a brief discussion, the cabinet unanimously voted to reject the surrender terms. Stanton ordered General Ulysses Grant to North Carolina to negotiate a new surrender agreement. The new surrender was almost identical to that signed between Lee and Grant at Appomattox Court House. This second surrender agreement was signed on April 26, 1865, ten days before Captain Noyes arrived at Andersonville. It contained no "general pardon" to protect Captain Wirz from prosecution. Since the first surrender was never approved by the president and the cabinet, it was never legal.

When he returned to Macon, Captain Noyes immediately reported the events to General Wilson, who ordered him to return to Andersonville and arrest Wirz.

By the time Noyes and his detachment returned to Andersonville, the Confederate camp was deserted except for a small bedraggled group of young boys and old men who apparently didn't have the money to get home. The prison stockade was totally deserted and its gates were standing wide open. Inside was a sea of mud speckled with the remains of long dead campfires and abandoned she-bangs. Noyes found a pitiful group of 250 Union prisoners of war still housed in the prison hospital. They apparently had not been exchanged because it was believed that they would not survive the journey to Macon. A small cadre of Confederate doctors had remained behind to care for them until they were well enough to travel.

Captain Noyes located Henry Wirz at his home with his wife and two daughters. Even though the war was over and he had no further official duties, Henry Wirz had remained at Andersonville, seemingly paralyzed by indecision over what to do next. It seemed to have violated his Teutonic sense of duty to simply abandon his post. Also, like a lot of his guards, Wirz didn't have the financial resources to leave.

To Captain Noyes, Henry Wirz certainly didn't look the part of a sadistic brute. He was a small, slightly round shouldered man, with sickly white skin and a full thick beard. His wife was pleasant and friendly, yet she appeared to be a woman prone to hysteria and fears. The children were neatly dressed in clean but well-worn and patched clothes. They appeared to have been well raised by their mother who taught them the proper manners and to read daily from the family Bible.

According to Captain Wirz's daughter Cora, who was ten years old at the time, Captain Noyes was warmly received in the Wirz home and joined the family for their evening meal of cornbread and bacon.

Writing years later about the circumstances of her father's arrest, Cora Wirz said that her mother had a strong womanly instinct and did not like Captain Noyes' nervous silence during the meal. She had an ominous feeling of dread ever since his arrival. When Captain Noyes broke the silence to say that Wirz must return with him to Macon, Elizabeth Wirz became hysterical. She had a deep concern for her husband's safety. Although forbidden to go near the prison, Elizabeth knew full well the conditions there and had witnessed the growth of the prison cemetery. She knew that somebody would eventually be held accountable for all the death and suffering that had occurred at Andersonville and she feared that it would be her husband. Captain Wirz, on the other hand, was stoic and showed no fear. He put on a brave, non-concerned face and did his best to reassure his weeping, near hysterical, wife.[3]

The next day as the group was preparing to depart for Macon, Henry Wirz passed to Captain Noyes a letter addressed to General Wilson in Macon. In the letter, Wirz said that he was a citizen of Switzerland and planned to return to Europe as soon as possible. Wirz insisted that "the duties I had to perform here were arduous and unpleasant, and I am satisfied that no man can or will justly blame me for things that happened here, and which were beyond my power to control."[4]

This letter indicated that Henry Wirz had spent the night thinking about what lay in store for him in the hands of the Union army. Captain Noyes reassured Wirz, saying that his orders were to seize all Confederate records and ledgers at Andersonville and that General Wilson only wanted to question him.

As the train was pulling away from the small depot at Andersonville, Henry Wirz peered out the window to see his wife and children pitifully sobbing in the smoke and steam beside the railroad tracks. The family had absolutely no money and they had no idea what would become of them without the family breadwinner. It is hard to estimate Wirz's thoughts at that moment, but he probably realized that his future was bleak despite the belated reassurances of Captain Noyes. Whether he realized it at the time or not, Henry Wirz had seen Andersonville for the last time but he certainly had not heard the last of it.

The train carrying Henry Wirz arrived in Macon only a few hours after it departed Andersonville. Wirz was taken under armed escort to General Wilson's headquarters in the Lanier Hotel.

According to Cora Wirz's account of her father's arrest, General Wilson interrogated Wirz and examined the records seized from his office. Cora stated that the General found everything in order and told Wirz that he could return home. She claimed that her father was at the Macon train station when a detail of soldiers came to take him into custody.[5]

During the trial of Henry Wirz, both General Wilson and Captain Noyes had to defend themselves against defense claims that they had promised Wirz safe passage if he cooperated in turning over all Confederate records in his custody. Both Captain Noyes (who had been promoted to major by the time of the trial) and General Wilson denied that any promises had been made to Wirz. However, both men vacillated in their testimony. Noyes admitted that personally it had been a very difficult task to arrest Wirz. He testified: "It is a very hard thing to take a man from his family and particularly so in that case, Mrs. Wirz and one of the daughters at least were crying and having considerable trouble." Noyes admitted that to pacify the crying women and her daughters, he had told the family that "they need not distress themselves at all." He also told the family that if General Wilson was satisfied "that he had done no more than his duty, and had simply acted in accordance with his orders, he would probably be released."[6]

General Wilson testified that upon questioning Wirz, he had admitted that he had no money, and if he were released, he really had no place to go. He asked General Wilson to provide him and his family with financial help and safe conduct, or better yet, an armed guard to protect him and his family from possible violence. Wirz had a great fear that released Andersonville prisoners would take revenge upon him and his family. Therefore, he felt that his only recourse was to return to Europe as soon as possible.

Although he sympathized with Wirz's plight, especially as it applied to his family, Wilson steadfastly maintained that he issued Wirz no promise of safe conduct, other than that he would not be killed or handled roughly. Wilson also testified that no one under his command had the authority to issue Henry Wirz any type of safe conduct or parole. It appears that both Noyes and Wilson expected to encounter a sadistic devil in Henry Wirz, but instead they found a confused and fearful man for whom they both could feel only pity.

Henry Wirz remained at Macon under guard until May 20, while General Wilson awaited orders on what to do with him. In the meantime, General Wilson had other problems. He had dispatched more than 15,000 cavalry troopers searching every possible hiding place from Atlanta to the Florida coast looking for Jefferson Davis. On May 10 the Jefferson Davis party was finally cornered near Irwinville, Georgia, and the former Confederate president was quietly taken into custody. Three days later, Jefferson Davis along with his wife and children arrived in Macon under heavy guard.

Macon quickly filled with newspaper reporters eager to hear the details of the capture of Henry Wirz and Jefferson Davis. General Wilson

SMITH AND CHURCHILL.   BENJAMIN T. DAUGHERTY (Fig. 1), Co. K. THIRTY-FIRST ILLINOIS.

BENJAMIN T. DAUGHERTY (Fig. 2).

JOHN H. MATTHEWS,
CORPORAL COMPANY F, FOURTH PENNSYLVANIA.

JOHN W. JANUARY, CORPORAL CO. B, FOURTH ILLINOIS.   CALVIN BATES (FIG. 1), CORPORAL CO. E, TWENTIETH MAINE.   CALVIN BATES (FIG. 2).

Widely Read Features, Such As This One Published in *Harper's Weekly* on June 17, 1865, Inflamed Public Opinion Against Wirz

Western Reserve Historical Society

had successfully conducted the most famous manhunt since the capture of John Wilkes Booth. However, he was anxious to get rid of his two famous prisoners and quickly made arrangements for them to be moved north.

Jefferson Davis would travel north on the more comfortable "sea route." He and his family would travel by rail to Augusta, Georgia by way of Atlanta, then by river boat to Savannah, and finally to Fortress Monroe, Virginia by coastal steamer.

Wirz would take the longer, more uncomfortable "land route" to Washington. To avoid broken rails and the war devastation done to Southern Virginia and the Shenandoah Valley, Wirz would travel north from Macon by rail through Chattanooga to Nashville. At Nashville, he would board a river steamer to take him in a long roundabout river route to Pittsburgh, then finally by rail to Washington.

Captain Noyes was chosen by General Wilson to command the guard detachment assigned to escort Wirz to Washington. He would also transport leather trunks filled with all the Confederate records and documents found at Andersonville.

When the northbound train carrying Henry Wirz stopped for fuel and water in Atlanta, Captain Noyes had a serious problem with unruly crowds that had gathered at the depot to see the man who was already being called "the fiend of Andersonville." At Chattanooga, Captain Noyes turned Wirz over to the U.S. army provost marshal for safekeeping, while the rest of the escort retired to hotels to await rail connections. Captain Noyes testified at Wirz's trial that when he delivered his prisoner to the provost marshal, Wirz was neatly dressed in his Confederate uniform. When he returned the next day to pick up Henry Wirz, he discovered that his prisoner had been badly beaten, and his uniform was torn and ripped. Captain Noyes was angered by the incident and vowed not to again part with Henry Wirz until he reached Washington.

At every stop, the armed detachment guarding Wirz had to use the threat of force to protect their prisoner from drunken mobs who wanted to lynch him. The most serious incident occurred at Nashville, where a determined mob attempted to halt Wirz from boarding a steamboat. Several times Captain Noyes and his men risked their lives to protect Henry Wirz from the unruly crowds, who would have torn him to pieces if they had not been stopped.

The harassment of Henry Wirz continued until the group reached Louisville, Kentucky. There Wirz had friends who lent him a black suit and beaver hat to replace his damaged Confederate uniform. Captain Noyes had also ordered Wirz to shave off his beard. With this done, Wirz's appearance was so dramatically changed that no one recognized him until the group reached Washington.[7]

During the last two years of the Civil War, rumors and exaggerated news reports had circulated in the North about the horrible conditions in the

Confederate prisons. However, it wasn't until the prisoners actually began coming home that the true nature of their suffering was fully known. The widely read news magazine *Harper's Weekly* carried the first illustrations made from photographs taken of the released prisoners.[8] The whole nation was shocked at what they saw. The illustrations showed men sitting on hospital beds with feet so rotten with infection, they were swollen into huge blobs. Some men had no feet at all, just bloody stumps at the ankles. Others were virtually living skeletons.

The illustrations that appeared in *Harper's Weekly* were not embellished tales told by escaped prisoners, neither were they wild rumors. A new invention, the camera, in the hands of such skilled men as Matthew Brady and Alexander Gardner had fully recorded the horror of the Civil War. The photographs taken of the recently released prisoners from

A Victim of Andersonville, Too Weak From Hunger to Hold Up His Head, Is Assisted By a Physician

Library of Congress

Andersonville stand as mute testimony to the agony they endured. The images taken of the emaciated prisoners of war, sparked an anger in Americans that demanded vengeance. Justly or not, the lightning rod for that vengeance was to be Henry Wirz.

When Henry Wirz finally arrived at Washington, he was taken to the Old Capitol Prison, located directly east of the capitol building on land that is now occupied by the U.S. Supreme Court building. It was originally a hotel that had been opened early in the nineteenth century to accommodate visitors to the newly established capital of the United States. When British troops burned the public buildings of Washington during the War of 1812, the hotel was spared because it was privately owned. The capitol building across the street was not as lucky, it was completely gutted by fire. While the burned capitol building was being restored, the government occupied the hotel across the street, turning it into a temporary capitol building. When the government returned to the capitol building, the whitewashed, red-brick structure across the street was used mostly for extra office space and storage areas. It became known around Washington as the "Old Capitol Building."

At the beginning of the Civil War, the War Department decided to turn the Old Capitol Building into a military prison. Despite its generally deteriorating condition, it would be used to house suspected spies and politicians from border states with mixed or pro-Southern loyalties. At first persons confined in the Old Capitol Prison lived under conditions that were only a little more severe than house arrest. Later, carpenters attempted to improve the security of the old hotel by nailing boards over the lower windows, reinforcing existing doors, installing locks, building elevated guard posts, and enclosing the courtyard with a high wooden fence.

Even with all these renovations, the Old Capitol Prison was not a very secure facility. The only way escapes could be prevented was by having vigilant Union sentries closely patrolling the exterior of the prison. Union soldiers walking their posts on the sidewalks in front of the prison, had a particularly hard time since large crowds of civilians sometimes gathered outside the prison. Usually, the crowds were mostly curious and only wanted to stare at the prisoners. Sometimes, the prisoners inside the building would yell insults at the crowd and sing rowdy pro-Confederate songs. Other times the prisoners wanted to converse with friends or relatives on the street below. Eventually, the sentries were given strict orders to shoot any prisoner that attempted to stick his head or arms out the windows. They were also given orders to keep the crowd away from the prison's windows and doors making sure no one passed anything into the prison, or accepted anything tossed from the windows by the inmates.[9]

None of those arrested in the conspiracy to assassinate Abraham Lincoln were confined in the Old Capitol Prison. They had been held aboard ironclad warships at anchor in the Potomac River and at the Washington Arsenal, a much more secure red, brick building in the southwestern part of the city.

Henry Wirz was confined in what was once a hotel room on the top floor of the Old Capitol Prison. His room had two windows, a coal-fed fireplace, two wooden chairs, an army cot with a mosquito net covering, bookshelves, and a broom to tidy up with. While Wirz was spared being chained like the Lincoln conspirators before him, he was confined to his room under the watchful eye of an armed sentry, ordered to never let him out of his sight.[10]

While Henry Wirz was being held in the Old Capitol Prison awaiting trial, several Washington area entrepreneurs sold carte de visite photographs, an early form of souvenir postcard, supposedly showing Henry Wirz as a humpbacked, dwarfish-looking man in an ill-fitting civilian suit. When this carte de visite is compared to the known photograph of Henry Wirz wearing his Confederate uniform, it is obvious that the carte de visite is a fake. Luckily for the modern historian, both the known photograph of Henry Wirz, taken in Paris in 1863, and the carte de visite show him standing next to a chair. The real photograph of Henry Wirz shows a much taller man with no indication of being humpbacked or dwarfish looking.

Old Capitol Prison

Another widely distributed image of Henry Wirz shows him with a full beard and a sinister countenance. This image appeared in the September 16, 1865 issue of *Harper's Weekly* and was attributed to the famous Civil War photographer Alexander Gardner.

During the Civil War, widely read periodicals hired experienced and talented artists who were able to take any photographic image and turn it into a line drawing that could be reproduced easily on newsprint. The *Harper's Weekly* illustration implies that the image of Henry Wirz came from an Alexander Gardner photograph. However, the photograph from which the image is supposedly taken has never been found and may never have existed, since it bears little resemblance to the well-known photograph of Henry Wirz.

General Lew Wallace, the Head of the Military Commission That Tried Henry Wirz

The Trial of Henry Wirz

Edwin Stanton was a tall man with a long graying beard that rested gently on his barrel-like chest. His hair was streaked with gray and usually disheveled; his clothes were always wrinkled and sometimes worn and ink stained. Stanton would peer at the visitors to his office from behind small oval glasses that gave him the appearance of a grumpy old owl. Stanton suffered from asthma and often had trouble controlling his breathing, especially when he was excited or angry. Those who conversed with him often complained that even when he carried on a normal conversation, Stanton wheezed when he spoke.[1]

During the Civil War, Edwin Stanton's power was nearly absolute. As secretary of war, he was the most powerful member of the executive branch of government, excluding the president himself. Stanton had under his control the thousands of men in the Union army as well as millions of dollars in government contracts. By the stroke of a pen, he could make a millionaire out of a government contractor or ruin the career of even the highest-ranking military officer. Only Abraham Lincoln had the power to restrain Edwin Stanton's power but seldom did so. Lincoln found Stanton to be a dedicated and hard-working cabinet member, who was, unlike his predecessor, above corruption and bribery. He was a man too dedicated and valuable to the war effort to antagonize.

Following the death of Abraham Lincoln, Stanton had become de-facto president of the United States. From his office in the War Department, he fired out orders that were never questioned and quickly obeyed. Not even the new president Andrew Johnson, whom Stanton disliked and distrusted, dared challenge the powerful secretary of war, for his foul temper and humorless personality were legendary.

104

In the hectic days following the death of Lincoln, Stanton virtually lived in his office at the War Department. He worked tirelessly, often eating and sleeping at his desk. The strain of the work load took a heavy toll on Stanton's mental and physical health. He often had trouble breathing, having to stop and gasp for air. His skin took on a pale and yellowish tint from never going outdoors.

Stanton also began showing signs of paranoia, no longer trusting even his closest associates and often speaking about devious conspiracies against him. He lost weight, developed a twitch in his eye, and flew into violent rages when his orders were not obeyed quickly enough.

Edwin Stanton worried that what had been won on the battlefield, would now be lost in the post-war peace. He feared that in the euphoria of peace, the former leaders of the defeated Confederacy would simply return to their positions of power, the former slaves would be politically disenfranchised, and life would continue in the South just as if the Civil War had never occurred.

Since Lee's surrender, many former Confederate leaders continued to hold their political offices, and many Southern states were passing so-called "Black Codes," special laws designed to discriminate against African Americans and prohibit them from taking their rightful place in a free society. Under these "Black Codes" former slaves could not carry weapons, travel at night, serve on juries, or vote. Edwin Stanton and his Radical Republican allies in Congress were determined that this disturbing trend in the former Confederacy would not continue.

Edwin Stanton's hatred of the leaders of the Old South was personified by one man, the former president of the Confederate States of America Jefferson Davis.

Edwin Stanton firmly believed that Jefferson Davis was in involved in the plot to assassinate Abraham Lincoln. In the wake of the tragic murder of the president, an unsubstantiated rumor had started in Washington that Jefferson Davis had mistakenly announced the death of Lincoln in Richmond, the day before he was actually shot in Ford's Theater. Edwin Stanton believed firmly in the truth of the rumor, even though no evidence could be found to prove Jefferson Davis had ever made such a statement.

At his desk in the War Department, Edwin Stanton labored day and night collecting evidence against not only Jefferson Davis but scores of other high-ranking members of the Confederate army and civilian government.

Northern abolitionists wanted Confederate General Nathan Bedford Forrest to be brought to trial for the slaughter of Black soldiers at Fort Pillow, Tennessee, in the spring of 1864.

Confederate Secretary of the Navy Stephen R. Mallory was considered by many to be a war criminal for his development of the submarine and underwater mine. Both of these weapons would come into common use in later wars, but in 1865 they were considered to be cruel and wanton instruments of destruction that no civilized person would ever consider using. Mallory was also being charged with piracy for his use of Confederate raiding ships, such as the CSS *Alabama* that attacked and burned unarmed civilian whaling vessels and merchant marine ships on the high seas.

Republican politicians from Kansas and Missouri wanted the Confederate Congress to be held responsible for the actions of Confederate Colonel William Clark Quantrill, who terrorized the region with bloody raids such as the one on Lawrence, Kansas, where over 150 men, women, and children were slaughtered. Quantrill had been killed late in the war, but people in Kansas and Missouri felt that the Confederate Congress should be held responsible, since it had passed the Partisan Ranger Act in 1862, which permitted the creation of guerrilla units such as Quantrill's band.

War crimes aside, there was the also the issue of treason, which is defined in the Constitution, Article 3, Section 3 as: "levying war against them (United States) or in adhering to their enemies, giving aid and comfort." Edwin Stanton, and some other Radical Republicans, firmly believed that key members of the Confederate army, navy, and civilian government were clearly guilty of treason.

Urged on by Radical Republicans in Congress, a Federal grand jury in Norfolk, Virginia had even gone so far as to return indictments for treason against Jefferson Davis and Robert E. Lee. Stanton supported the indictments and wanted a trial of Davis and Lee.

The indictment of Robert E. Lee cost Edwin Stanton one of his most powerful allies: General Ulysses S. Grant. When Lee learned of his indictment, he immediately contacted General Grant, who assured him that neither he nor any of his officers would be tried for treason, since they were all protected by the terms of surrender signed at Appomattox Court House. Privately, Grant was angered at the indictment of Lee, a man he admired and respected. Grant went to see President Andrew Johnson to urge him to issue a presidential pardon to put the matter to rest.[2]

This action by Grant embarrassed both Edwin Stanton and President Johnson. Both men disagreed that Lee should receive a pardon. However, neither Johnson nor Stanton wanted a public fight with the popular general. Neither did they want to publicly repudiate the surrender terms and paroles Grant had signed at Appomattox Court House. The net result was that Robert E. Lee and hundreds of other prominent ex-Confederates were left in a state of legal limbo, where the government was not taking any steps to bring them to trial, but could do so whenever it felt like it.

Even though there was a lot of support in the North for Edwin Stanton's plan to bring Confederate leaders to justice, there was also a strong and growing tide of public opinion to forgive and forget the sins of the nation's erring brothers of the South. Thousands of prominent Northern leaders agreed with Abraham Lincoln's words during his second inaugural address, when he called upon the people to "bind up the nation's wounds." Many openly questioned what good would come from high profile trials of Confederate leaders. Even within the Union Army, there was very little fervor for a long series of treason and war crimes' trials. Many were saying that enough blood had been shed and it was time to move on to other things.

Edwin Stanton was furiously angry at these attitudes. He felt that the security of the United States required that the architects of the Southern rebellion against the United States be punished. No nation in the history of the world allowed its traitors to escape retribution. Stanton firmly believed that if the leaders of the Confederacy were not punished that this would breed disrespect for Federal authority and simply cause another rebellion later on in the nation's history.

Stanton realized that Jefferson Davis was the key to his plan to punish the former leaders of the Confederacy. If Davis was allowed to escape trial, then certainly no other Confederate leader would be brought to account.

A large part of the resistance to further trials of Confederate leaders came about as a direct result of the trials and executions of the Lincoln conspirators. During their confinement, the Lincoln conspirators were kept chained hand and food aboard airless ironclad warships anchored in the Potomac River. They were not allowed to write letters, have visitors, or converse with their attorneys. They were not even allowed to talk to each other. They were forced to wear heavy padded hoods to prevent them from seeing or hearing anything. There treatment was so harsh that one attending physician feared that they would go mad from sitting for days in their own filth and sweat, not being allowed to see or hear anything.

To make matters worse one of the four accused conspirators had been a woman of advanced years named Mary Surratt. The charges against Mary Surratt were weak. She had operated a small boardinghouse in Washington where the conspirators sometimes held their meetings. There was no hard evidence that she ever knew what the men who used her house as a rendezvous spot were planning, even though her son John was one of the group.

Even after she had been convicted, no one really expected Mrs. Surratt to be hung. The commanding officer of the Washington Arsenal, where the executions were to take place, was so sure that President Andrew Johnson would commute her sentence at the last minute, he posted riders along the route from the White House to the Arsenal to quickly relay the message when it came. However, when the time for the executions arrived, only silence came from the White House when Mary Surratt became the first woman ever executed by the United States government.

This public hanging of a middle-aged widow caused a storm of protest to sweep over the nation. After her death, even strongly abolitionist Northern newspapers began to turn a skeptical eye towards the evidence against Mary Surratt and found it wanting. Other newspapers openly questioned why she was imprisoned under such unnecessarily harsh conditions. The cruelty of Mary Surrat's treatment and her execution also did a lot to quell the fervor in the North for more trials of Confederate leaders.

Edwin Stanton had personally supervised all aspects of the Lincoln conspirators' imprisonment, trial, and executions. It was by his order that the accused conspirators had been chained and hooded. Stanton was severely criticized in both foreign and domestic newspapers for the way in which the accused conspirators had been imprisoned and tried with no regard for their basic constitutional rights. Stanton also shared with Andrew Johnson the blame for the execution of Mary Surratt. Most critics felt that the notoriously vindictive Stanton had used his political power to persuade the new president to allow her execution to take place.

The political fervor against Stanton became even more ferocious when it was learned that he had ordered Jefferson Davis imprisoned under harsh conditions at Fortress Monroe, Virginia. Davis was being kept in a airless casemate that was so hot and humid that mildew grew on his shoes. The former Confederate president was kept under constant surveillance by two armed sentries who never let him out of their sight. Davis complained that to be constantly under observation without a second of privacy was torture more than a man could possibly endure.

When the news was leaked that Davis had been shackled, a political fire storm erupted against Stanton. Even those who had been bitter political enemies of Jefferson Davis before the war decried this humiliating treatment of a former U.S. senator and secretary of war. Finally, Stanton was forced to concede and ordered the chains removed from Davis' legs.[3]

The harshness of the criticism leveled against him for his treatment of the Lincoln conspirators and Jefferson Davis shocked and hurt Stanton. He realized the vital importance of public opinion in his plan to bring the leaders of the Confederacy to justice.

Edwin Stanton was determined not to make the same mistake again. He hoped that the upcoming trial of Henry Wirz would give him an opportunity to redeem himself in the public's eyes. He ordered that Wirz be spared the chains and padded hood forced on the Lincoln conspirators. While Wirz was kept under heavy guard, he was not forced to undergo any unnecessary cruelty or public indignities. Unlike the Lincoln conspirators, Wirz did not have to appear in court wearing dirty and sweat-stained prison attire. Each day he was provided with a clean suit of civilian clothes to wear in court. Edwin Stanton even allowed Henry Wirz certain special privileges. During his trial, when Henry Wirz complained of being ill and in pain, the court allowed him to recline on a couch that had been brought into the courtroom.

By the time Henry Wirz's trial was slated to begin, Stanton's case against Jefferson Davis for conspiracy to murder Abraham Lincoln was beginning to unravel. The trial of the four Lincoln conspirators had failed to produce any conclusive evidence that Jefferson Davis was involved in the plot to kill Abraham Lincoln. However, this did not deter Stanton who pushed ahead with a full scale investigation into Davis' possible role in the assassination.

Stanton's investigation crumbled when his key witness against Jefferson Davis, a small time hoodlum who called himself William Campbell (but was actually Joseph A. Hoare), confessed to the press that he and others had been paid large sums of money to lie under oath and say that Davis had been part of the Lincoln assassination plot. The War Department was unable to discredit Campbell, and his charges were widely believed in both the North and South.[4]

The death blow to Stanton's case against Davis for treason came when the Chief Justice of the Supreme Court, Salmon P. Chase, wrote Stanton a letter saying that in his legal opinion secession was not the same as treason, and that the charges against Davis should be dropped.[5]

By August of 1865, when the trial of Henry Wirz was scheduled to begin, even such hard line, anti-Southern abolitionists as Horace Greeley and Senator Thaddeus Stevens were calling for Davis to be released. Stevens, an ardent Radical Republican member of the House of Representatives, even offered to represent Davis as his attorney. Greeley, obviously attracted to the case of Jefferson Davis because of his passion for crusades and lost causes, wrote powerful editorials in his *Tribune*, calling for Jefferson Davis to be immediately freed from prison. Greeley also sent agents to Canada to examine Confederate records sent there for safe-keeping during the final year of the war. These documents showed that Jefferson Davis had urged humane treatment for Union prisoners of war and had resisted efforts to get him to retaliate against Union prisoners for reported harsh treatment of Confederate prisoners of war in Federal hands.

Edwin Stanton saw the Wirz trial as a tool to quash the growing clamor in the North to free Jefferson Davis. It was generally believed that Wirz's defense would be that he was only obeying orders, implying that he had been part of a plot to deliberately murder Union prisoners of war. Stanton hoped that this defensive strategy would give him evidence to use against Jefferson Davis.

However, unknown to Edwin Stanton, Henry Wirz's attorneys had decided that his defense would not be that he was only obeying orders, but rather that Wirz did the best he could with the resources he had to work with, and had not violated any of the rules of war. This defensive strategy may have cost Henry Wirz his life, but it also insured that Edwin Stanton would never be able to implicate anyone higher than the already dead General John H. Winder in the tragic events that occurred at Andersonville.

Edwin Stanton chose Colonel Norton P. Chipman, a twenty-six-year-old Iowa attorney with a deep dislike for the Confederacy, to head the prosecution team. Chipman had been born and raised in Iowa, where he

General Norton P. Chipman,
Who Headed the Prosecution of
Henry Wirz
U.S. Army Military History Institute

trained to be a lawyer. When the Civil War began, he was commissioned a major and given command of the 2nd Iowa Infantry. He was wounded at Fort Donelson in February 1862. Upon his recovery, he was promoted to lieutenant colonel and was made chief of staff to General S. R. Curtis. Later Chipman would be transferred to Washington where he caught the eye of Secretary of War Edwin Stanton who admired his hard work and legal knowledge.

Colonel Chipman considered his appointment to be a great honor and worked tirelessly for three months, interviewing former Andersonville prisoners and guards.

The head of the military commission was Major General Lew Wallace, the same officer who led the court during the trial of the Lincoln conspirators. General Wallace was a highly intelligent and deeply religious man, who had a flawed military record.

Wallace had risen to high military rank primarily because of political connections in his home state of Indiana, where he had raised the 11th Indiana Volunteer Infantry of which he was made commanding officer with the rank of brigadier general. He did well enough in the early fighting at Fort Donelson and was promoted to the rank of major general. However, General Wallace's military career took a serious setback at the Battle of Shiloh.

Wallace had been camped six miles from the battlefield when the Confederates launched their surprise attack. Ordered by General Grant to bring his division up as soon as possible, Wallace mistakenly took a route to the battle site that would have taken him to the Confederate rear where he would have surely been surrounded and easily defeated. By the time Wallace learned of his mistake, he had traveled such a distance he had to make a lengthy forced march back to his starting point and take a different route to the battlefield. Wallace's blunder at Shiloh would put his military career under a cloud from which he would never escape. Wallace would spend the rest of his life trying to explain why he had been late to the battle of Shiloh.

His lackluster performance in later battles in Kentucky and the Shenandoah Valley only aggravated the nagging questions about Wallace's courage and military judgment. Eventually he was relieved of combat command and assigned to administrative duties at which the bookish Wallace was very efficient.

Serving under Wallace on the commission would be six generals and three colonels. They were: Brevet Major General G. Mott, Brevet Major General John W. Geary, Brevet Major General Lorenzo Thomas, Brigadier General Franceis Fesseden, Brigadier General E. S. Bragg, Brevet Brigadier General John F. Ballier, Brevet Colonel T. Allcock, and Lieutenant Colonel John H. Stibbs. Seven of the nine officers on the military commission were from the volunteers; only two came from the ranks of the regular army. After the trial began, General Bragg became ill and was relieved from the commission. He was not present in final deliberations but was not replaced.[6]

Remembering the criticism leveled against him for not allowing the Lincoln conspirators to have adequate legal counsel, Edwin Stanton made sure that Henry Wirz was adequately represented. Defending Henry Wirz would be a team of attorneys that were part of the respected Washington law firm of Hughes, Denver, and Peck.

Wirz's attorneys did not challenge the makeup of the court, probably feeling that it would be as fair a commission as could be had under the circumstances. All the officers were distinguished gentlemen, highly respected for their intellect. They had all served in the Union army, but none had any type of deeply rooted prejudice towards Wirz's religion or of the South. No member of the court had ever written or said anything to indicate that he had any preconceived notions about Henry Wirz's guilt or innocence.

However, on closer examination, it would seem that the commission was top heavy with men too heavily involved in politics in their home states to risk jeopardizing their, hoped for, postwar political career by finding Henry Wirz not guilty. After the war, Major General Mott would become governor of New Jersey. General John W. Geary would become governor of Pennsylvania, and Lew Wallace would go on to become territorial governor of New Mexico. Other members of the commission would hold lesser political positions.

The trial of Henry Wirz began on August 21, 1865 with a colossal blunder on the part of the prosecution. Using the indictment in the Lincoln conspirator's trial as a guide, Colonel Chipman compiled a lengthy list of charges, accusing Henry Wirz along with Jefferson Davis, Robert E. Lee, and other high-ranking Confederate officials with "wanton cruelty" upon Union soldiers confined as prisoners of war at Andersonville, Georgia.

Edwin Stanton personally attended the opening day of the Wirz trial to read the charges against him without first having reviewed the document in private. After reading aloud the charges against Henry Wirz to a packed courtroom, a red-faced Edwin Stanton angrily ordered the court to adjourn until further notice. The indictment Edwin Stanton had read was filled with much of the same extravagant language that had so embarrassed him at the trial of the Lincoln conspirators. It would not do. The next day General Wallace tersely announced that President Andrew Johnson had ordered the commission "dissolved."[7] Wirz's defense team was elated with these unexpected developments. However, their joy was short lived, since the government quickly announced that the commission would soon reconvene.

The commission reconvened on August 23, 1865, with a second more carefully worded set of indictments that made no mention of Jefferson Davis, Robert E. Lee, or any member of the Confederate cabinet. Henry Wirz would be formally charged with two counts: "Maliciously, willfully, and traitorously, combining, confederating, and conspiring with John H. Winder, (the Commander in Chief of all Confederate prisons), R. R. Stevenson (Chief Surgeon at Andersonville), Joseph White (the head of the prison hospital), W. S. Winder (General Winder's son, who choose the prison site and laid out the stockade), and others unknown, (this designation would later allow Jefferson Davis or other high ranking Confederates to be charged if evidence was found to implicate them), to injure the health and destroy the lives of soldiers...then held as prisoners of war...so that the armies of the United States might be weakened and impaired; in violation of the laws and customs of war."

The second charge was "Murder in violation of the laws and customs of war." This second charge accused Wirz of deliberately murdering Union prisoners of war. He was specifically charged in the deaths of twelve Union prisoners of war. The indictment accused Wirz of personally causing the deaths of prisoners by such diverse means as: ordering a sentinel to shoot a prisoner (four counts); shooting a prisoner with his revolver (two counts); jumping upon and stamping a prisoner to death (one count); beating a prisoner upon the head with his revolver (one count); having a prisoner attacked by ferocious dogs (one count); binding the necks and feet of prisoners with chains and iron balls (one count); and by confinement in the stocks (two counts). All these counts of murder against Henry Wirz had one thing in common: in none of them could the prosecution produce the name of the murder victim.

The bringing of the second set of indictments was objected to as being double jeopardy by Wirz's attorneys. When the commission ruled against them, all of Wirz's legal team resigned except for Otis H. Baker and Louis Schade. Wirz protested strongly against the loss of his legal team, but the commission ruled that Baker and Schade were adequate counsel for the accused.

Colonel Chipman had a basic legal problem. After thoroughly researching the legal literature, he could not find any legal precedent for one nation trying a soldier of a foreign army for crimes committed during time of war. Chipman artfully sidestepped this tricky legal issue by refusing to admit that the Confederate States of America ever was a foreign nation, independent of the United States. Chipman found plenty of precedent for citizens being put on trial for acts committed during a time of rebellion. He referred to the Whiskey Rebellion, and the Aaron Burr affair, as prime examples.[8]

The next important issue to be resolved was the claim by Wirz that he had been promised safe-conduct back to his family at Andersonville by Captain Noyes, acting under orders from General Wilson. Both Captain Noyes and General Wilson testified strongly denying that Wirz was ever promised any type of safe-conduct implied or otherwise. Wirz's attorneys also argued that he had been covered by the parole agreement signed between Joseph Johnston and William T. Sherman. Colonel Chipman presented evidence that Wirz's command at Andersonville was not part of any Confederate army that had surrendered and was therefore not subject to any parole agreement. The court finally ruled that both arguments were irrelevant since only the president of the United States had the power to absolve crimes and offenses that were in violation of the rules of war.

With the loss of these two arguments before the court, the fate of Henry Wirz was sealed and his attorneys knew it. Their only hope left was to try and convince the court that it had no legal authority to put Wirz on trial. This effort also failed and from that point onward the trial followed a set formula with everything going the way of the prosecution.

By modern legal standards the trial of Henry Wirz was filled with all types of procedural errors and outright injustices. The commission allowed hearsay evidence to be admitted, ignored contradictory testimony, and probably knew that much of the testimony was outright lies on the part of former prisoners of war justly angered by their harsh treatment and caught up in the lynch mob fervor against Henry Wirz.

Colonel Chipman had wisely anticipated from statements that Wirz had made to General Wilson that the defense would probably claim that Henry Wirz was doing the best he could under the circumstances, rather than that he was just obeying orders as Edwin Stanton had guessed. Chipman put on a string of carefully selected witnesses to counter that argument. The most damning of which was Lieutenant Colonel Alexander W. Persons of the 55th Georgia Infantry, who commanded the prison at Andersonville from February when the prison received its first prisoners until late May of 1864.

Persons explained how the prison was divided into three separate and distinct departments: one was the commanding officer of the troops (Colonel Persons); the second was the commander of the prison stockade

(Wirz); and finally the officer commanding the post (General Winder). The quartermaster of the prison was Richard B. Winder who was in charge of the prison bakehouse and arranging rail transportation.

Persons testified that the railroad that serviced Andersonville was also being used to supply food and ammunition to the armies of Robert E. Lee and Joseph Johnston. He claimed that he had carried on a lengthy correspondence with the superintendent of the rail line and after much difficulty had arranged to have several train loads of lumber delivered to Andersonville to be used to build shelters for the prisoners. Persons testified that over fifty boxcar loads of cut lumber were delivered to the prison, but none of it was ever used to build badly needed shelters inside the stockade. Persons claimed that when he was relieved from duty at Andersonville he saw forty or fifty houses being erected in or near the town. Persons estimated there were between fifteen to twenty thousand prisoners inside the stockade when he left.

Colonel George Welling, of the 4th Kentucky Cavalry, assigned to General Wilson's command, testified to all the provisions he found in the region of Andersonville. Welling had accepted the surrender of the Confederate commissaries at Albany only thirty-five miles south of Andersonville. He testified that he found there more than 31,000 pounds of bacon and 700 pounds of salt. He did not remember how much corn was on hand, but he stated that the country through which he passed was full of corn and pork. There were three grain mills near Andersonville. One in Albany had two runs of grinding stones capable of grinding four to five hundred bushels of corn in twenty-four hours. There was also a bakery at Albany that had four ovens. Welling testified that he also found twenty wagons and thirty or forty mules.

Later, the prosecution argued that General Sherman fed an army of 65,000 men for a month during his famous "March to the Sea" from the rations his foragers found along the route of march through Georgia. Union soldiers reported finding larders and smokehouses filled with hams, corn, beans, and sweet potatoes. There was so much beef in Georgia that Sherman had managed to depart Atlanta with 5,000 head of cattle and had actually enlarged his herd to 10,000 head by the time his army reached Savannah, simply by collecting all cattle he found along the march route. All of this while Union prisoners of war were starving at Andersonville.[9]

Of course, what the prosecution did not say was that Henry Wirz was not an invading conqueror at the head of a 65,000-man army that empowered him to make up the rules as he marched along. Wirz was only a junior officer and had no legal authority to simply go out into the countryside and seize private citizens' crops and livestock. He also had no power to force his superiors in the Confederate army and civilian government to channel supplies away from Confederate armies in the field to feed the prisoners of war under his control at Andersonville.

Having established that Georgia had plenty of food to have fed the prisoners at Andersonville, if it had wanted to do so, Chipman proceeded to renew his attack against Jefferson Davis.

During his research for the trial of Henry Wirz, Chipman had found a detailed report written by Colonel D. T. Chandler, the Confederate assistant adjutant and inspector general. Chandler was a West Point graduate who had a reputation for being a conscientious officer with impeccable integrity. Chandler's report, dated July 5, 1865, informed Confederate authorities in Richmond about conditions at Andersonville based upon his inspection of the prison site. Chipman was sure that this document was the crucial piece of evidence he needed to prove that Jefferson Davis was responsible for the conditions at Andersonville. A fact that would no doubt give much pleasure to Edwin Stanton.

The document was introduced into evidence and read in court. It outlined in detail the horrible conditions inside the stockade and what caused these problems—no barracks or shelters for the prisoners, the poor position of the bakehouse, the inadequate medical care, water supply, and the prisoners' unhealthy diet. Chandler recommended that no further prisoners be sent to Andersonville and that new prisons be opened to relieve overcrowding. In his report Chandler made no recommendations as to who was to blame or level any criticisms against Captain Wirz.[10]

Chandler, obviously irritated that his report did not illicit a quick response from Richmond, submitted a supplemental report dated August 5, 1864. In this report Chandler does talk about personal changes needed at the prison. He commends Captain Wirz as an efficient officer, and closed with a recommendation that General Winder be replaced with someone "who unites both energy and good judgment, with some feeling of humanity, and consideration for the welfare and comfort, (so far as is consistent with their safekeeping), of the vast number of unfortunates placed under his control." Chandler went on to condemn General Winder for boasting that he had never been inside the stockade and having advocated leaving the prisoners in their present state until the death rate relieved the overcrowding. Chandler maintained that the exercise of a little energy and good judgment on the part of General Winder could have considerably improved conditions inside the prison.

Chandler's first report was presented to Inspector General Colonel R. W. Chilton, who forwarded it to the office of Confederate Secretary of War John C. Breckinridge. The prosecution called witnesses to verify that the document had indeed reached Richmond and had gotten as far as the Assistant Secretary of War J. A. Campbell, who wrote a memo to the secretary of War, urging that something should be done about conditions at the prison.

The prosecution then introduced a great amount of hearsay testimony, trying to prove that Jefferson Davis had seen Chandler's report.

They called witnesses who claimed to have heard aides to Jefferson Davis mention the report or claimed that they had heard Jefferson Davis speak about conditions at Andersonville and other Confederate prisons. All this testimony was given over the strong objection of the defense team, who maintained that Henry Wirz, not Jefferson Davis, was on trial and the evidence was therefore irrelevant. However, after deliberating among themselves, the court overruled the defense's objection.

Chandler himself was called as a witness and he told of several things that could have been done to improve living conditions inside the stockade. These included draining the water from the swampy area inside the stockade to a small stream on lower ground a few hundred yards beyond the stockade, and moving the bakehouse and Confederate guards' camp to a location where they did not pollute the prison's drinking water. Chandler felt that there was enough wood and labor readily available to enlarge the stockade, erect shelters, and provide the prisoners with enough firewood to cook their food.

What was not mentioned by the prosecution was that General Winder had already taken steps to implement all of Chandler's recommendations by the time the report was submitted to Richmond. By the first of September, the first barracks would be built, the cookhouse relocated, the stockade enlarged, and, most importantly, the logistics were completed to begin moving prisoners out of Andersonville.

Chandler's report was not quickly acted upon in Richmond for several reasons. The first was that General Winder took grievous exception to his report and had filed a counterreport disputing Chandler's claims. It was Winder's opposition to his initial report that caused Chandler to write his supplemental report critical of the old general. Winder's counterreport created some confusion in Richmond about who was correct. John Winder was a general, a respected Southern gentleman, and a close personal friend of Jefferson Davis. The general tendency was to believe that Chandler was a young colonel who may have become overzealous in his duties. Also, General Winder had made many enemies during his tenure as provost marshal of Richmond, and many wondered if Chandler's report might have been made in an attempt to discredit General Winder's career. It took some time before Confederate Secretary of War John C. Breckinridge, who had held the post only since February, could sort out matters and take some action to correct the problems at Andersonville.

Chandler wrote his initial report in early July, and by September, thousands of Union prisoners were being transported from Andersonville to new prisons at Millen, Thomasville, and Blackshear, Georgia. By early December the population had been reduced to only a few thousand unfortunate souls who had the bad luck to be left behind at Andersonville.

Still attempting to indict Jefferson Davis, Colonel Chipman called several low ranking enlisted men who worked in the Confederate War

Department. They repeated old Richmond gossip about the relationship between Jefferson Davis and General Winder, attempting to prove that Davis knew of Winder's incompetence and cruelty, but he refused to replace him because of their friendship. Others testified of signatures and initials trying to determine if Jefferson Davis had personally read the report of Colonel Chandler, or if those who did read it had spoken to Jefferson Davis about it.

Of course none of this had any bearing on the charges against Henry Wirz, and it was mostly hearsay evidence and gossip, that would never have been allowed in a regular civilian court. But, Colonel Chipman was not finished with his wild goose chase after Jefferson Davis. A detailed report on the medical conditions at Andersonville, written by Surgeon Joseph Jones, was introduced.[11] The Jones' report talked in detail about the gruesome conditions inside the prison hospital. The Jones' report was followed by redundant reports from other surgeons also describing in minute detail the problems within the prison hospital.

Again Chipman was trying to lay down a paper trail that would show that Jefferson Davis, the Confederate president, knew full well about the horrors at Andersonville and had done nothing to correct them. However, Chipman failed to provide proof that the spade of reports had ever reached the desk of Jefferson Davis, and if the Confederate president, who had no medical training, could have done anything to change conditions.

Even though Henry Wirz was a medical doctor, he was not a surgeon and was not placed in command of the hospital until it was really too late to do anything to correct the ghastly conditions there. Also, the conditions inside the hospital were in reality just a continuation of the suffering and misery of the stockade. It would have been impossible to change one and not change the other and Henry Wirz did not have the power or resources to do either.

When talking about the hospital, Colonel Chipman had to be careful not to give the defense an opportunity to introduce evidence about the Union naval blockade of the South. It had prevented much needed medical supplies from reaching the sick and wounded of the Confederacy, including civilian noncombatants. Abraham Lincoln had been urged by Northern humanitarian groups to allow medical supplies to pass through the blockade, but he had refused primarily because of strong opposition from Secretary of War Edwin Stanton and the Radical Republicans in Congress.

After having completed presenting an array of hearsay testimony in an effort to implicate Jefferson Davis, Colonel Chipman then launched into the heart of his case against Henry Wirz. Chipman would call a number of witnesses whose sympathies during the war had been to both the Union and Confederate causes. They would describe the terrible things they had seen at Andersonville with enough clarity to make military officers, hardened by battle, cringe at the tales.

During His Trial Henry Wirz Was Allowed to Recline on a Couch
Harper's Weekly, October 21, 1865

By this time it seemed that the court was taking the attitude that any evidence against General Winder was also evidence against his subordinate, Henry Wirz. It was an attitude also assumed by the journalists who were eagerly reporting the trial to the Northern reading public.

One such witness was Ambrose Spencer, a plantation owner from Sumter County, Georgia, who frequently visited the prison to sell vegetables to the prisoners and guards.[12] He reported that the militia of southwestern Georgia had been called out by order of Governor Brown and had been stationed at Andersonville. He said that their tents were floored with sawed lumber, and that a number of tents were protected from the sun by boards. Spencer also testified that a group of local women had collected several wagonloads of food, blankets, and clothing to deliver to the prison, but General Winder refused to allow the supplies to be delivered to the prison. Spencer claimed that when he spoke to General Winder, the old general swore and said that the whole country was becoming "Yankee" and that he would be damned if he would not put a stop to it. Spencer claimed that Wirz and Sidney Winder supported General Winder in his decision, and the Captain Wirz had even suggested building a house at the depot and use the women for "certain purposes."[13]

Colonel Chipman called former prisoners as witnesses who carefully presented an image of Henry Wirz as a man filled with venomous profanities. He was depicted to the court as some type of wild-eyed maniac, running around with a drawn pistol, screaming and cursing sick and dying Union prisoners of war. Other former prisoners of war such as James Madison Page of the 6th Michigan Cavalry, who were willing to attest that Henry Wirz had always treated him with courtesy and respect, was never allowed to testify. Page was so angered by this that he wrote a book titled *The True Story of Andersonville Prison, A Defense of Henry Wirz* that was published in 1908.

It appears from the testimony, which was allowed to be presented, that Henry Wirz was a man totally lacking any type of sense of humor, combined with a maniacal obsession with order and discipline.

Many of the charges of brutality towards Union prisoners of war brought against Henry Wirz centered upon two games played by prisoners. The first was something the prisoners called "playing roots."

For feeding and counting purposes, the prisoners at Andersonville were divided into detachments of 270 men with that group subdivided into smaller groups of 90 men each. Originally the prisoners had been grouped in units of 100 men each, but for some mysterious reason Wirz, or perhaps General Winder, had ordered that the men be grouped in units of 90 men each. This accomplished little except to make it harder to get an accurate count. Henry Wirz tried to use the daily ritual of issuing food to call the roll of prisoners and get a accurate count of the prison population.

Ideally, the way the system was supposed to work, each prisoner should have been standing patiently in a military formation of 90 men each morning to be counted. Later, at noon, wagons filled with the pork and cornbread rations entered the prison. The amount of food issued to the prisoners was based on the morning count.

Under this system, each morning the prisoners would file by in an orderly manner, while Wirz, or one of his subordinates, checked each prisoner's name, constantly referring to a faded green ledger book. This way the food was issued in a neat and orderly manner, and Wirz could get an accurate count of the number of men present in the stockade and would be able to show that all of his prisoners were accounted for and fed properly.

The only problem was that in order for this system to work the prisoners had to cooperate, and they simply didn't do so. The whole procedure was terribly slow and tedious, taking up to three hours to complete. It was unreasonable to expect the prisoners to stand out in the hot sun for that length of time without getting tired and restless. The bored prisoners would deliberately cause as much confusion as possible in order to obtain more food than was their due, thereby disrupting the procedure. Many of the men would slip into line two or three times in order to get extra rations, answering to the name of sick or dead prisoners. Others would start mock fights and other disturbances to allow other men to "play roots" by breaking into the line. While some of these prisoners were just being selfish, others were just having a little fun at the expense of their captors, while still others were attempting to get extra rations for men too sick or weak to stand in formation.

Henry Wirz had been given this aggravating daily duty by General Winder and it was simply too much responsibility for a man in his physical condition. He could not possibly watch all the thousands of men in the stockade adequately and his undisciplined Confederate guards provided him with little or no help. One former prisoner of Andersonville, Private John McElroy of the 16th Illinois Cavalry, writing in his book, *This Was Andersonville*, published in 1866, had this to say about the Southern people he met during captivity, including the Confederate guards and officers charged with counting the prisoners:

> Rebels as a rule are astonishingly ignorant of arithmetic and accounting. Generally they are good shots, fine horsemen, ready speakers, and ardent politicians. But, like all non-commercial people they flounder hopelessly in what people of this section would consider simple mathematical processes.[14]

While McElroy's remarks were undoubtedly a regional stereotype, deliberately written to belittle Southerners, it did have some measure of truth. Probably all the enlisted men assigned to guard prisoners at Andersonville were either illiterate or nearly so. Of those that could read most had never attempted to read any book other than the Bible. As for their mathematical skills, it was not uncommon to see Confederate soldiers having great difficulty counting their meager pay of less than ten dollars a month. It would have been totally impossible for them to have made an accurate count of hundreds of prisoners of war. This meant that the total burden of making an accurate count fell on Captain Wirz.

When Wirz did see a prisoner "playing roots" by jumping into line a second or third time, he would seemingly go insane with rage. Wirz would pull out his pistol and storm into the crowd of men shouting obscenities and yelling "I will learn a damn Yankee to play 'roots' upon me." Witnesses testified that Wirz would often hit or kick any man he suspected of "playing roots." Others claimed he would threaten to shoot the prisoner with his pistol.[15]

Instead of terrifying the prisoners, Wirz's escapades only seemed to provide them with some much needed amusement. Even the Confederate guards in their pigeon roost towers would laugh and yell taunts at Wirz while he was trying to get the prisoners to line up properly. Despite all of Wirz's bullying and threats, the counting system never worked properly.

To Henry Wirz the whole matter was deadly serious, not just a game played by mischievous and bored prisoners. When running a prison, it is vital for security reasons to know exactly how many prisoners you should have in custody, and how many you actually have.

In order to get the prisoners to cooperate and to stop the playing of "roots," Wirz resorted to the drastic step of withholding rations from the prisoners. This created a state of near rebellion in the stockade. Groups of prisoners openly talked about storming the gate rather than slowly starve to death. Some went so far as to form a secret society, called the "Plymouth Brigade," complete with secret oaths and elected officers. They planned to dig shallow tunnels under the log walls to allow more prisoners to exit the stockade and rush the gun positions outside the fence. Afterwards the survivors planned to march to Union held Apalachicola Bay or try to reach Sherman's army.

When Captain Wirz got word of these plots from informants, he posted notices on the North and South gates, threatening to open fire on the prison with artillery should the prisoners give him any reason to do so. He also banned any large gatherings of prisoners near the gates.[16]

This only gave more impetus to the agitators, who were marching around the stockade organizing men to rush the gates should the Confederates open fire. They vowed to die fighting like men rather than be shot like rats in a barrel.

To calm the situation, Wirz gave in and ceased withholding rations from the prison. He also ceased making threats to fire on the stockade with grape and canister shot. Wirz did all this even though the "playing of roots" continued unabated.

"Flanking" was another trick played by the prisoners. It usually oc- curred as a prelude to an escape attempt. "Flanking" was when men who were not assigned to work outside the stockade, would fall in with one of the work details made up of paroled prisoners. Once the work detail marched out through the gates of the stockade, the flankers would wait for an oppor- tunity to sneak away.

It was the duty of the sentries at the two gates to catch flankers, however, it was very difficult to do so since the prisoners carried no iden- tification, and their appearance usually changed radically after they entered the prison. Not all flankers were intent upon escape; some simply wanted to get outside in order to trade with the Confederate guards or local civilians.

Just as he did with the prisoners "playing roots," Henry Wirz seemed to take this disobedience as a personal affront, not the reasonable actions of men trapped in an intolerable situation, being forced to fight daily for their survival. Defenders of Henry Wirz would charge that it was normal for an officer subjected to public humiliation and massive disobedience to react violently. Would a Union general put up with this type of insubordina- tion? Didn't Union officers routinely inflict physical punishments upon their soldiers for violations of military regulations? During the Civil War Union soldiers were branded, flogged, and sometimes even executed for insub- ordination, desertion, and cowardice.

It was charged that Henry Wirz would often hit sick and wounded prisoners of war with his pistol. Some wonder if this was physically pos- sible. It was known that Henry Wirz carried a Le Mat revolver, one of the heaviest and most unusual Civil War handguns ever produced. It had been developed by Colonel Jean Alexandre Le Mat of New Orleans, who was first granted a patent for his revolver in 1856. Le Mat was a staunch sup- porter of the Southern cause and made every attempt to insure that his pistols would only find their way into Confederate hands. Le Mat revolvers were first produced in France, where Le Mat had relocated after getting a contract to produce pistols for the Confederate government. Later, Le Mat pistols were also made in Belgium and England. None were ever produced in the Confederacy.

The Le Mat pistols were produced with muzzles up to .42 caliber with an eight shot cylinder and a six and a half-inch barrel. Under the main barrel was a .18-gauge shotgun barrel so the shooter could spray an en- emy with buckshot if all else failed. The weapon was nicknamed the "grapeshot pistol" by Confederate enlisted men. The gun was very bulky and heavy although in combat it amply protected the officer carrying it, because of its tremendous amount of firepower. Such famous Confeder- ate officers as Pierre Beaureguard and J. E. B. Stuart proudly carried Le Mat revolvers.

Defenders of Henry Wirz maintained that a man with one arm, totally useless due to wounds, could hardly wield such a heavy pistol and strike prisoners with it. Wirz's accusers countered that if he could not have handled such a heavy pistol, he would not have carried one. Other defenders of Wirz doubted if an intelligent officer would risk damaging such a valuable firearm by using it like a club to beat prisoners. In the Confederacy the Le Mat revolver was a prized possession, usually carried only by high ranking officers. Wirz probably purchased his Le Mat pistol, using his own money, while he was in Paris.

During his trail, Henry Wirz was accused of brutality towards prisoners of war even though all the punishments he inflicted were in common use both in the Union army and in civilian jails and prisons to punish escapes, rebellion, insubordination, cowardice, and desertion.

One of the most common was called "bucking and gaging" which was a widely used punishment during the Civil War for unruly and drunken soldiers. When the order was given to "buck and gag" a soldier, the offender was sat on the ground and his knees were drawn up to his chest. The soldier's hands were then tied together in front of his knees and a stout stick was run over the arms and under the knees to prevent the slightest movement. Finally, a makeshift gag, usually made from a round stick held in place with leather straps, was placed in the soldier's mouth. Bucking and gaging may seem harsh to modern readers, but during the Civil War it was actually considered a minor punishment, especially useful with soldiers who had been brawling or who had too much to drink.

Another punishment used at Andersonville were the stocks, a punishment that dates back as far as pre-Christian Europe. During the colonial period of American history, the stocks were used in every English colony, but were most associated with puritan New England, where they were used for such minor crimes as profanity, drunkenness, and failure to attend church. At the time of the American Civil War, stocks were commonly found in civilian jails and prisons all across the United States. They were a widely accepted method of sobering up drunks and enforcing discipline among the prison population. The stocks were not commonly used by the Union Army only because of the difficulty of moving around the bulky apparatus. However, where Union commanders had stocks available, they used them to discipline soldiers.

The stocks used at Andersonville came in two varieties. The "foot stocks" were two wide boards positioned about a foot off the ground. The two boards had a metal hinge that allowed them to be opened like a giant jaw. The prisoner's feet were placed into circular holes cut between the two boards. The prisoner was then forced to sit on the ground or a small bench, exposed to the elements, unable to move his legs. Most prisoners found the foot stocks not all that uncomfortable. In many smaller European communities, that could not afford to maintain a jail, the foot stocks were used as a regular method of securing prisoners awaiting trial and were not even viewed as punishment.

Captain Wirz had ordered that the stocks be located under pine trees near the Confederate camp. Ironically, the men being punished sat under the shade of the pine trees enjoying cool breezes that could not be felt inside the stockade. Many prisoners were able to sleep comfortably in the foot stocks on makeshift beds of gathered pine straw, that protected them from the dampness of the ground. Some prisoners in the stocks were given extra rations or blankets by the Confederate guards who took pity upon them. Some even used it as an opportunity to barter and trade with the guards.

The other type of stocks called the "spread-eagle stocks" was much more cruel. The prisoner's head and shoulders were placed into holes cut between two heavy boards much like the foot stocks. Sometimes a man had to stand on his tiptoes to reach the stocks, other times he was horribly bent over. Even a short period of time in the spread eagle stocks would cause unbearable pain. To make matters worse it was impossible to eat while in the spread eagle stocks and only rarely was the prisoner given water. If the prisoner was not released in order to relieve himself, he had to suffer the indignity of being exposed to the jeers and taunts of Confederate guards while covered in their own body wastes.[17]

There was also much testimony about Andersonville's famous "chain gang." Twelve men had heavy iron collars placed upon either their ankles or necks. These iron collars did not have locks, but were secured by a piece of iron driven into place and bent double with a hammer. Most of the time the piece of iron would be only an old rivet or an iron nail that had been forged into position by the camp blacksmith. When it came time to release the prisoner the blacksmith would have cut the piece of iron using a heavy hammer and a metal chisel. The broken nails were saved and reused over and over again. Running through a ring on the collar was a heavy hand-forged chain that was attached to a 25-pound cast iron ball. According to witnesses, the worst thing about being on the chain gang was being chained to twelve other men. When one man wanted to move, all the others had to go along. If one of the men had diarrhea it created a terrible situation, since the slightest movement caused the round iron collars to rub against bare skin.

As with the foot stocks, the chain gang was a common sight in the United States during the Civil War period. Many small towns used them in lieu of a jail to hold prisoners awaiting trial. They were routinely used when slaves were being transported or were being prepared for sale. Civilian prisons often had chain gangs, that worked outside their walls maintaining roads or tending the fields that provided food for the prison population. Many Southern states still had "chain gangs" working on the roadways as late as the 1950s.

The Union army also used the ball and chain to confine soldiers accused of crimes. The Lincoln conspirators were bound with a ball and chain almost identical to the one used at Andersonville.

Evidence indicates that most Andersonville prisoners spent only a few hours in the stocks, and only a day or two on the chain gang. This wasn't because of any charity on the part of the Confederate prison staff, but rather the other prisoners were constantly getting into trouble and an angry Captain Wirz was ordering them into the stocks or chain gang. To make room for these troublemakers the men already confined to the stocks and chain gang had to be released.

General Winder had ordered that all Black prisoners of war were to be used for hard labor. They were put to work piling up dirt for earthwork fortifications, felling trees, uprooting stumps, and digging rifle pits. It was generally felt that Blacks were more "suited for" this type of hard labor than whites.

A common method of flanking, used by white prisoners to get out of the stockade, was to blacken their hands and faces with the heavy dark smoke that came from their pine wood fires. This procedure would make even the fairest skinned white man look enough like a Black to fool the Confederate guards at the gate. This practice infuriated Captain Wirz. For a white man to purposely attempt to look like a Black deeply violated his sense of racial pride.

When a white prisoner was found with his face blackened, Wirz ensured that he was harshly punished. One such prisoner was Vincenzo Bardo. When he was apprehended at the gate with a blackened face, Bardo was brought before Wirz for punishment. Wirz ordered him placed in the spread eagle stocks and given thirty-nine lashes. Frank Maddox, a member of the 35th United States Colored Regiment, captured at Olustee, Florida, testified that Wirz had once said to him (speaking of his flogging of Bardo), "the man blackened himself to be a nigger, and, god-damn him, he (Wirz) would give him a nigger's law."[18] Bardo himself would later be called as a defense witness to say it was not Captain Wirz who whipped him but another Confederate guard.[19]

The key issue at the trial of Henry Wirz was whether he had personally murdered Union prisoners of war. Wirz was charged with thirteen counts of murdering Union prisoners of war by such diverse methods as stomping and jumping on prisoners, confining them in stocks, shooting them with a pistol, beating them with a pistol, binding them with a ball and chains, having ferocious dogs attack and kill them, and ordering guards to shoot prisoners.

It was vital for the prosecution to prove these charges against Wirz, but it would be difficult to do so. Many of the witnesses could not recall the name of the alleged murder victim, or the date of the alleged murder. Others could remember only partial details. Others testifying as first hand witnesses had obviously received their information from other sources. Some were only repeating camp gossip. However, Colonel Chipman did produce some viable witnesses who were able to remember dates and names.

BALL & CHAIN.

SHOT ON THE DEAD LINE FOR A PIECE OF MOULDY CAKE.

An Artist's Conception of the Chain Gang and the Shooting of a Prisoner for Crossing the Deadline

Harper's Weekly, *September 16, 1865*

Private J. B. Walker, Company G, 141 Pennsylvania Infantry, testified of seeing a fellow prisoner he knew only by the name of Prendiville, shot by a sentry on the night of September 4, 1864. He claimed that Prendiville was a full three feet from the deadline when he was shot. Walker's testimony was supported by the hospital register which reads: "11,230, Prendivelle, M. Private, 7th Indiana, Company H, complaint unknown; died in quarters, admitted September 6th, died September 6th."

Charles E. Smith, Company K, 4th U.S. Cavalry, testified that he saw Wirz order a sentry to fire on a prisoner who was too near the deadline sometime near June 10. He did not know the man's name, but did recall the date.[20]

The fact that undisciplined Confederate guards did shoot prisoners unnecessarily was never in dispute. However, Wirz was forced to walk a fine line between preventing unnecessary killing, while at the same time trying to keep the equally rebellious Union prisoners of war behind the deadline. Wirz was within his legal right to shoot any prisoner attempting to escape, and under the rules of confinement laid down at Andersonville, crossing the deadline was considered attempted escape.

Wirz claimed that he never ordered a sentry to shoot, but it is doubtful if he could have performed his duty properly without doing so. His primary problem was that some of the young guards were too anxious to shoot, while others would not do so without direct orders. The whole problem was aggravated by the terrible overcrowding inside the stockade. Most of the shooting incidents occurred during the months of June, July, and August, when the stockade was most crowded. Some of the prisoners complained that they could simply roll over in their sleep, and be inside the deadline. Another problem was that prisoners had to force the deadline to get fresh drinking water, or to retrieve a root, or piece of bread, that had fallen across the line.

During the trial the accusation arose that Wirz (sometimes it was attributed to General Winder) promised the Confederate soldiers at Andersonville a 30-day furlough for killing a Yankee prisoner of war. If such an order was ever issued, it would have undoubtedly produced a blood bath of random shooting, and the number of men killed by sentries would have been much greater than it was. Wirz maintained that the charge was preposterous and that he could not possibly have spared a sentry for that long a period of time. He steadfastly insisted that no such order was ever issued.

The prosecution could not produce one shred of documentary evidence that either Wirz or General Winder ever issued any promise to the Confederate guards at Andersonville of a 30-day furlough for killing Union prisoners of war. What Colonel Chipman was able to produce was the testimony of a paroled prisoner named John H. Goldsmith, of the 14th Illinois Infantry, who was a clerk in Wirz's office. It was his duty to keep track of rations issued to the prisoners as well as keeping up the register of those prisoners who had died. Goldsmith claimed that he had personally written a 30-day furlough for a Confederate guard named Scott of the 4th Georgia Reserves, who had recently shot and killed a prisoner named Henry Lochmire, who belonged to a Pennsylvania regiment.[21]

According to Goldsmith's testimony, he wrote out the furlough in February of 1865, when the prison's population was very small and the random killing of prisoners had almost ceased. In all probability the prisoner killed was actually trying to escape, and the furlough was just a coincidence. Even if it was a deliberate, unjustified killing it does nothing to prove the charge that Wirz was giving furloughs for killing prisoners.

None of the charges of murder against Henry Wirz held much credibility except for one. It involved the killing of a one-legged, feebleminded cripple that witnesses identified only by his nickname "Chickamauga." Terms like "idiot" and "simpleminded" were used in testimony to describe him. While no one remembers his real name, all the witnesses were remarkably consistent in the details of his death. When all the testimony about the death of "Chickamauga" are taken together certain facts about him emerge. Jasper Culver, of the First Wisconsin Infantry, recalled that "Chickamauga" was from the 96th Illinois Infantry.[22] Private Thomas Walsh, of the 74th New York Infantry, recalled that the shooting of "Chickamauga" occurred on May 15, 1864, because it was Whit-Sunday. He also recalled that "Chickamauga" was in the same building with him when he was a prisoner in Richmond.[23]

It seems that "Chickamauga" was well known in the prison as a buffoon, a moocher, a possible informant, and a general nuisance. The bored prisoners seemed to take a sadistic delight in teasing and mocking him. He was a favorite victim of the Raiders who frequently beat him up to steal his food ration or sometimes just for the entertainment of it. Besides being psychologically off balance, probably mentally retarded, and the victim of almost constant harassment, "Chickamauga" was also tormented by his amputated leg. The leg had not healed properly after it had been removed and the unsanitary conditions inside the stockade caused it to continually become infected. When this happened the raw and bloody stump of his leg would swell, drain pus, and throb with pain.

With his body emaciated by malnutrition and with his leg in constant and unbearable pain, the poor tormented and crippled man decided that even death was better than the life he was leading.

One day "Chickamauga," who was constantly begging the Confederate guards at the gate to admit him to the hospital, only to be made fun of and dismissed, deliberately crossed the deadline and invited the guards to shoot him. Instead of shooting him, the guards sent a messenger to summon Captain Wirz to the stockade. According to witnesses, Wirz entered the stockade with his pistol drawn, cursing violently. He confronted

"Chickamauga" near the North Gate and ordered him back across the deadline. "Chickamauga" pitifully begged with tears in his eyes for Wirz to allow him to go to the hospital. Wirz refused, probably fearing that if he gave into "Chickamauga's" demands, other prisoners would pull the same stunt. Union prisoners, who had gathered to watch, urged "Chickamauga" to return across the deadline, but he refused. Wirz was set on the course of action he had chosen. According to witnesses, at this point Wirz, probably fearing a riot, flew into a violent rage and ordered the guard in the tower to shoot "Chickamauga." Instead, the teenage sentry yelled at "Chickamauga" to return back across the deadline. According to witness Joseph Adler, Wirz castigated the sentry for talking too much and asked him, "Why didn't he use his musket at once and shoot the man down."[24] The guard then fired hitting "Chickamauga" in the jaw. "Chickamauga" was knocked down by the gunshot but was soon on his feet again with his jaw shattered, bleeding profusely, and unable to speak. At this point, a second shot struck him in the chest, giving the poor crippled veteran the death he desired. In Wirz's statement to the court, he gives his version of the Chickamauga incident:

> On the evening in question the sergeant or the officer of the guard came to my quarters and stated that there was a man within the deadline, jawing with the sentry and refusing to go inside, and there was a crowd of prisoners around him and a good deal of disturbance. I rode my horse down to the stockade, dismounted outside and went in. There I found things as they had been described to me. I went up to Chickamauga and asked him in a rough tone of voice what the hell he was doing there. He said he wanted to be killed. I took my revolver in my hand and said in a menacing manner, that if that was all he wanted I would accommodate him. I scared him somewhat and he was taken outside by some of the prisoners. I then in his presence, and solely as a menace, told the sentry to shoot him if he came in again. I little thought that he would come back or that his comrades would permit him, after hearing the order, to go once more across the forbidden line. I left the stockade remounted my horse and was on my way back to my quarters when I heard the report of a musket. I hastened back and ran up to the sentry-box from which the shot had been fired.[25]

While Henry Wirz denies directly having "Chickamauga" shot, he does make one important point: In almost any prison, crossing the deadline was seen as an escape attempt and lethal force to prevent the escape of a prisoner is accepted practice.

> There can be no doubt that the unfortunate man, whose name appears to be unknown, and whose only appellation in this court is derived from the name of the famous field of battle where he lost his leg, was shot in consequence of a violation of a rule of prison discipline; not an unnecessarily harsh rule nor an unusual one; because at Andersonville it was absolutely

indispensable to the security of the prison and because the same rule was enforced at Macon, Florence, Salisbury, Belle Isle, and the other principal prisons of the Southern Confederacy.

I have certainly heard of cases occurring in the very prison where I am now confined, of prisoners being shot for similar violations of prison discipline. ...The court will take cognizance of the fact that the rules of the prison at Andersonville were printed and posted on conspicuous places all through the stockade, that the internal police of the stockade was exclusively in the hands of federal prisoners, and the squads of ninety men into which the occupants of the stockade were divided were officered by federal soldiers.[26]

Another incident at Andersonville involved a prisoner referred to in testimony as "Frenchy." Henry Wirz was charged with causing his death by allowing "Frenchy" to be torn to bits by a pack of ferocious dogs after he had been captured following an escape. In his written statement, Wirz describes "Frenchy" as a "little, wiry, fellow, whom bolts, stocks, and guards were alike powerless to prevent from escaping."

"Frenchy" was Andersonville's resident escape artist. He had managed to flee the prison a half dozen times but seldom got far. The countryside around Andersonville was alive with local militia patrols, looking for runaway slaves and provost seeking out Confederate deserters. Every farmer in the region was well armed and alert for any strangers in the area. Union prisoners who escaped reported that they could expect help from Black field hands, but house servants often turned them in. Each time "Frenchy" escaped from Andersonville, he was returned by local planters to the embarrassment of Henry Wirz, who usually didn't even know he was gone. According to Wirz's statement, he became so tired of chasing "Frenchy," he decided to grant him a parole, hoping that by releasing him from the stockade and granting him extra rations and soft duty, he could keep "Frenchy" from running off. The first day after "Frenchy" was granted parole, he was again gone. Wirz didn't even bother to launch a search party and "Frenchy" returned voluntarily the next afternoon. He told Wirz he had been out picking blackberries. Wirz decided that picking blackberries would be a good job for "Frenchy" and assigned him that duty permanently. However, the obstinate little man declared that he would do no work, thus rejecting the parole agreement.

Still Wirz did not put him back in the stockade. The next day "Frenchy" was gone again. Wirz claimed that he did not launch a search for "Frenchy" because he was "glad to get rid of him." Three or four days later, a group of local planters returned "Frenchy" to the prison. This time Wirz felt that he had to take some kind of disciplinary action and ordered "Frenchy" put on the chain gang. While he was being led to the blacksmith to have the shackles put on, "Frenchy" broke free and leaped into a thicket disappearing within seconds. Wirz ordered the dogs out and launched a manhunt for the elusive "Frenchy," probably wanting to get him back into custody before he again encountered local planters, who were complaining to Georgia state officials about the number of runaway prisoners. Within a short period of time, the dogs had chased "Frenchy" down. The little man had climbed a tree in an effort to elude the dogs. When the search party caught up with the dogs, "Frenchy" refused to come down from the tree, and the head of the search party (not Wirz) fired a shot to force "Frenchy" out of the tree. "Frenchy" was not hit by the bullet, but it did come close enough to cause him to fall out of the tree into a mud hole. While he was laying in the mud, the dogs descended on "Frenchy," but according to Wirz's statement, they were quickly driven off by members of the search detail. Wirz claimed that "Frenchy" had some scratches, was covered with mud, and his clothes were badly torn, but otherwise unhurt.

"Frenchy" was marched back to prison and placed under heavy guard in one of the tents in the guard's camp until Henry Wirz arranged a special prisoner exchange just for him. A few days after his last escape from Andersonville, "Frenchy", whose real name was Trado, was put on a train headed to an exchange point. Wirz claims that he did not know what became of "Frenchy" after that and any military records pertaining to him were not given to the defense team by the prosecution.[27]

The most ridiculous and unfair charge leveled against Wirz by the court was conspiracy to murder Union prisoners of war, by allowing the conditions at Andersonville to exist. Wirz answered it eloquently in his written statement to the court, pointing out the simple fact that he did not report for duty until March 27, 1864, long after the prison had been laid out in the winter months of 1863 by Captain W. Sidney Winder, more than a month after the first prisoners had arrived. Simply put, by the time Henry Wirz arrived at Andersonville, the conditions that caused so much death and suffering were already in place, and Wirz, who had no hand in creating them, did not have the power to change them once they were in place.

There were thirty-two witnesses who testified for the defense. Of these, twelve were former Union prisoners of war who testified to acts of kindness or fair play by Captain Wirz; four were Confederate surgeons who testified as to the near impossibility of changing anything at the hospital under the circumstances that existed at Andersonville; five were former Confederate officers who were on duty at Andersonville, Richmond, or Macon, one of which had also been a witness for the prosecution.

The defense also called three clergymen who had visited the prison while it was open. The most impressive by far was Father Peter Whelan who had been sent to Andersonville by the Catholic bishop of Savannah.

Father Whelan was one of the true heroes of Andersonville. Although he was over sixty years of age, he lived under primitive conditions near the prison stockade for over three months. While at Andersonville, the elderly priest slept in a small cabin and ate mostly the same food as the prisoners and Confederate guards. Father Whelan daily entered the filthy prison stockade braving all manner of disease to minister to the men's spiritual needs. He was present at the prison from June 16 to sometime near the first of October. It was Father Whelan who had ministered the last rites to the four Raiders, who were hung at the prison in July of 1864.

He stated, without hesitation, that he never saw Captain Wirz inflict any personal violence on any prisoner, neither did he hear of it during his stay. Whelan went on to stay that it would have been nearly impossible for him to have not heard about any brutality inflicted at Andersonville due to the fact that he was personal minister both to the Union prisoners and Confederate guards of the Catholic faith. He admitted that prisoners had complained about Wirz's use of profane language, but none relayed to him any accounts of personal violence. He reported that Captain Wirz afforded him every facility to visit the prisoners and allowed him to provide any relief from their suffering in his power. During his stay Father Whelan had managed to borrow $16,000 in Confederate currency (about $500 in Federal money) and Captain Wirz freely allowed him to use the money to buy vermin—free flour for the prisoners.

The elderly Father Whelan was assisted by Father Henry Clavreul, who worked at Andersonville from July 15 to August 20, 1864. He, like Father Whelan, had been sent to Andersonville by Bishop Augustin Verot of Savannah, who also visited the prison for two days at the end of July.

The French-born Bishop Augustin Verot had lived for years in the South and had become somewhat of a Confederate hero for his defense of slavery based on cannon and civil law. However, the things he saw at Andersonville filled him with horror. With no regard for his own health, he joined Father Whelan and Father Clavreul in the stockade listening to confessions and administering last rites until he was too exhausted to continue.

After the war was over, several former Andersonville prisoners complained bitterly that in a mostly Protestant region of the country, only Catholic priests bothered to visit the stockade.[28]

The trial of Henry Wirz abruptly came to an abrupt close on October 24, 1865. The trial of Henry Wirz did not come to a climatic end with emotion filled final arguments as any modern trial would have ended. Instead, General Wallace just suddenly declared that the court had heard enough testimony and ordered the proceedings closed, leaving twenty-nine defense witnesses still waiting to be heard. It was as if the trial had ended by reason of exhaustion. The officers of the court felt that further testimony by either side would be redundant, and that both sides had made their point as well as it could.

This high-handed action by General Wallace would have totally flabbergasted any civilian court and would have certainly won Henry Wirz a new trial on appeal. However, Wirz was being tried by a military tribunal under the emergency conditions of martial law. Therefore, the only person who would review the finding of this court would be Secretary of War Edwin Stanton. President Johnston could have commuted Wirz's sentence, but no one really expected the hard-drinking president to use his authority as commander in chief of the armed forces to do so, since he had refused to interfere in the verdicts of the Lincoln conspirators. The highly conservative Supreme Court had also taken a hands-off approach to the military trials conducted after the Civil War.

The trial had lasted sixty-three days and had generated over 5,000 pages of recorded testimony. The prosecution had called 160 witnesses. The defense had subpoenaed 106 witnesses, but only sixty-eight had reported to testify.

There was never any doubt in anyone's mind as to what the verdict would be. Public opinion and political pressure demanded that Henry Wirz be convicted and hung. It was General Lew Wallace, as head of the court, who read the verdict on November 3, 1865, only nine days after the trial ended. Henry Wirz was convicted of one count of conspiracy to commit murder, by allowing the conditions at Andersonville to exist, and eleven of thirteen specifications of actual murder. Wirz was convicted of the murders of both "Frenchy" and the one-legged "Chickamauga." Wirz was found not guilty of one charge of beating a prisoner with his pistol, and one charge of shooting a prisoner with his pistol.

The sentence was imposed the same day the verdict was read: death by hanging. The date of the execution was set for November 10, 1865, pending a review by the secretary of war and the president of the United States.

According to the Catholic priest who attended Wirz as he awaited execution, the condemned former Confederate captain was approached by unnamed government officials in the final days of his life and offered a deal that would save him from the gallows. Wirz was told that he would receive a presidential pardon if he would testify that Jefferson Davis ordered the atrocities at Andersonville. Wirz refused.

After the end of the trial of Henry Wirz, the scholarly Lew Wallace would go on to become territorial governor of New Mexico from 1878 until 1881. This was the same time as the famous Lincoln County cattle wars in which the teenage outlaw William H. Bonney, better known by his alias "Billy the Kid," would become famous for his cattle rustling and killing. Wallace was a lot more charitable with this young cattle rustler, horse thief, and cold-blooded murder than he had been with Henry Wirz. After a secret meeting with the outlaw, Wallace issued him an amnesty, only to see it ignored by New Mexico lawmen who arrested Bonney anyway. The elusive "Billy the Kid" managed to escape from jail but was later shot to death at age 21 by Lincoln County Sheriff Pat Garrett.

After his tenure as governor of the New Mexico territory, Wallace would also serve as minister to Turkey, traveling extensively in Europe and the Middle East.

Wallace's greatest achievement would be a novel he wrote, that was set in the Roman Empire at the time of Christ. The deeply religious Wallace would name his novel after the main character, a wrongfully imprisoned man named *Ben Hur*. The book would become one of the most successful best sellers in American literary history, making Lew Wallace much more famous as an author than he would ever be for his badly flawed and controversial military career. *Ben Hur* would be made into a movie twice in the twentieth century—once as a black and white silent classic famous for its dramatic chariot race scene and later in color starring Charlton Heston.

Wallace also wrote several other works of fiction including *The Fair God* (1873) about the conquest of Mexico and *The Prince of India* (1893). Lew Wallace's autobiography would be published a year after his death in 1905. He was 78 years old.

The Death Warrant Is Read to Henry Wirz

The Execution of Henry Wirz

The United States government issued 250 spectator tickets for the execution of Henry Wirz.[1] They were eagerly sought after by reporters and influential government officials. Secretary of War Edwin Stanton, who wielded absolute control over this well-staged media event, carefully screened the reporters who would view the execution to insure that they were all sympathetic to the Radical Republican cause.

To record the event for posterity, Edwin Stanton summoned his favorite photographer Alexander Gardner. The Scottish-born Gardner had lived in Great Britain, working as a jeweler, journalist, and businessman until he migrated to the United States in 1856. Gardner, a bright and creative man, was attracted to the new technology of photography because of his interest in chemistry. He decided to use this new medium to seek his fortune in America. Gardner made contact with Matthew B. Brady and obtained employment in his photography studio in New York City.

Matthew B. Brady was the premier photographer in the United States. Stating with very little, he had worked long and hard to perfect new techniques for improving the photographic process. Not content to stay in his studio taking formal portraits, Brady was anxious to find ways to improve his camera equipment so that he could photograph things outside of his studio under less than perfect conditions. During the 1850s the wet-plate process had been perfected, that allowed photographs to be reproduced in unlimited numbers. Brady found that he could photograph important people and famous places and sell these images in what were known at the time as a *carte de visite*. The selling of carte de visite and the taking of formal studio portraits of New York City's wealthy elite allowed Brady to develop a lucrative business, and hire several apprentice photographers. One of them was Alexander Gardner.

When the Civil War began, Matthew Brady was determined to capture as much of this great conflict as possible on his glass photographic plates. He loaded his bulky photographic equipment aboard wagons and sent out teams of camera men to document the Civil War in photographs. Brady spent most of his time capturing the aftermath of battles and the soldiers who fought them.

Action photos were out of the question due to the slow shutter speed of the primitive cameras. Also, the glass plate negatives had to be developed immediately after exposure, so each photography wagon had to be a darkroom, as well as a storage area for the bulky cameras, and the photographer's living quarters when he was in the field. It was no wonder that Civil War soldiers referred to the strange looking conveyances as the "what's it wagon."[2]

During the Civil War, Matthew Brady, and others who followed him, would take over one million collodion glass negative prints of everything from high-ranking generals to wide-eyed teenage privates. Beginning at the first battle of Bull Run, and continuing to the end of the war, the men in the "what's it wagons" would make the Civil War the first American war to be recorded extensively in photographs.

In 1862, Matthew Brady opened an exhibit of his photographs in New York City called "The Dead of Antietam". It was a collection of the best photographs Brady had taken immediately after the bloody one-day battle in western Maryland. For the first time in the history of the United States, ordinary American citizens could see what war looked like through the brutally honest lens of a camera. Brady's images were a far cry from the stylized images of bloodless heroism that the public was used seeing in newspapers, books, portrait galleries, and public statuary. Brady's photographs showed war as it really was. His black and white images of bloated dead horses and decaying corpses shocked and upset all who saw them. His exhibit generated an infant anti-draft and anti-war movement in Northern states that grew stronger and more vocal as the number of casualties in the Civil War continued to rise. Brady's exhibit angered Secretary of War Edwin Stanton who considered him a defeatist, a man attempting to destroy the Northern public's support for the war effort.

Early in 1863, Alexander Gardner broke away from his mentor Matthew Brady and started his own studio in Washington, D.C., making portraits of the important personages of the city. Gardner exploited the rift that had developed between the Union War Department and Matthew Brady for his own financial gain. By accommodating Secretary of War Stanton's wishes, Gardner could obtain access to critical events and people closed to other photographers.

Gardner freely lent his facilities to the Union Secret Service for intelligence work. He allowed the Secret Service to examine his photographs of Union soldiers for known Confederate spies. He photographed strategic bridges, railroad yards, river landings, and possible battlefields at the request of the Union commanders. Gardner even assigned his associates to copy maps and charts for the Corps of Engineers.

Alexander Gardner was rewarded for his cooperation by being given an honorary captain's commission in the Union Army and being allowed unlimited access to battlefields, Union Army encampments, and important events. By 1865, he was the photographer of choice for the Union War Department and a close ally of Edwin Stanton.

Alexander Gardner was given exclusive permission to photograph the Lincoln conspirators and was also given sole permission to photograph the execution of the four conspirators on the grounds of the Washington Arsenal.

When it came time for the execution of Henry Wirz, Alexander Gardner was again summoned to the office of the secretary of war to receive a photographic commission to record the execution.[3] Unlike the Lincoln conspirators, Henry Wirz would not be executed at the Washington Arsenal, but rather in the courtyard of the Old Capitol Prison. Gardner would photograph the execution from a special perch atop wooden bleachers especially built for the spectators. Gardner framed his image carefully. In the foreground would be the gallows surrounded by four companies of Union soldiers in tight military formations. In the background would be the newly completed capitol dome, shining white and glorious against the clear fall sky, clearly visible behind trees that had already lost their leaves for winter.

While Wirz awaited execution, rumors about his final hours circulated around Washington. One story related how his wife had tried to slip Wirz poison in a kiss. In reality, Henry Wirz's wife and children had returned to Cadiz, Kentucky after his arrest, and no record exists that the family ever visited him during his imprisonment in Washington.

Wirz's wife and children were left totally impoverished and alone after he was arrested and taken to Washington for trial. Exactly how she managed to get back to Kentucky is unknown, but it was probably either through help from her family in Kentucky or friends she had met while at Andersonville. Another possibility is Wirz's lawyers, who were extremely supportive of their unpopular client.

Elizabeth Wirz would live the rest of her life in extreme poverty, doing menial jobs to support herself and her two children. The last record of her comes from the 1870 census report that lists her as a widow with two children living in Trigg County, Kentucky. Today, the widow of Henry Wirz lies in a pauper's grave in rural western Kentucky, where she was buried following her death sometime after 1870.

Wirz's daughter Cora eventually married James Sessions Perrin, a businessman from Mobile. The Perrins settled in Natchez and Cora became a member of the United Daughters of the Confederacy and a strong defender of her father's name.

Other stories claimed that Wirz remained in a constant drunken state due to all the spirits he had consumed with the two Catholic priests who tended him. One witness to the execution claimed that Wirz's face was flushed with drink when he walked to the gallows.

The fact that the Catholic Church used wine during Mass was antagonistic to certain Protestant denominations that denounced the use of alcoholic beverages in any form, including religious ceremonies. One of the most common anti-Catholic slanders was that all Catholics were secret alcoholics, who used their faith to consume large quantities of alcoholic beverages.

The morbidly curious, who could not get tickets for the hanging of Henry Wirz, climbed trees outside the walls of the prison courtyard, while others paid for the privilege of sitting on the roofs of buildings that overlooked the prison. On the day of the execution, the area around the Old Capitol Prison was jammed with soldiers in spit and polish uniforms, government officials, stoic-looking reporters, and intoxicated revelers, offering large sums of money for one of the coveted tickets to the execution. Taverns in the area did a brisk business the morning of the execution and very few spectators to the execution of Henry Wirz did not have a bottle of whiskey somewhere on their person.

Alexander Gardner was one of the few people at the Old Capitol Prison that morning who was sober and business-like. He arrived early for the execution to make sure all his equipment was properly positioned and ready to record the historic event.

Probably to test his camera equipment, Gardner decided to photograph a group of reporters who had arrived to witness the execution. They were carefully positioned by the photographer on the wooden steps leading into the courtyard of the Old Capitol Prison. The men characteristically held note pads and pencils and struck exaggerated poses. One Washington policeman and a Union Army sentry also stood with the slightly inebriated group of reporters. After taking the photograph, Gardner rushed the wet plate to his darkroom and quickly developed it. The print turned out fine, so he returned to the prison to finish setting up for the execution.

Shortly after 9:00 A.M., the Union soldiers, assigned to the execution detail, marched sharply into the courtyard and assumed their positions before the gallows. The soldiers looked splendid in their freshly laundered uniforms and starched collars. Their fixed bayonets and brass buttons glistened in the bright morning sunlight as they waited for the condemned Henry Wirz to arrive.

The Noose Is Adjusted Around Wirz's Neck

Library of Congress

    After all the soldiers were in place, the crowd of ticket holding spectators were admitted to the courtyard of the Old Capitol Prison. As they waited for the execution to begin, the drunken crowd of spectators started to become restless and rowdy, yelling curses and chanting Wirz's name.

    At 10:15 A.M., Wirz appeared at the door of the prison flanked by two Catholic priests, Fathers Francis E. Boyle and Bernardin F. Wiget. When the crowd saw Wirz, they erupted in a thunderous roar of jeers, catcalls, hoots and whistles. The four companies of Union soldiers standing around the gallows came to attention, and as Wirz was led to the gallows, they began to chant in unison "Wirz remember Andersonville", "Wirz remember Andersonville". When the spectators in the bleachers joined in the chanting, the noise level in the prison courtyard rose to a point where it was almost deafening.

    Dressed in a black robe and hood with his wounded arm in a sling, Henry Wirz walked to the gallows with his head up and shoulders back, flanked by the two priests and an armed escort of soldiers. Wirz climbed the steps of the gallows unaided, coming to rigid attention in front of Major Russell, the officer in charge of the execution.

Exactly what was said on the gallows platform that day is unclear because of the noise of the crowd, but according to some witnesses, Major Russell apologized to Wirz for the undignified way the execution was being carried out saying he was only obeying his orders. Wirz supposedly replied, "I know what orders are Major, and I am being hanged for obeying them."

At this point, one of the two priests asked Wirz if he had anything he wanted to confess. Wirz replied that he had done nothing wrong to confess. In this obviously well-rehearsed scenario, Henry Wirz put his very soul in jeopardy by publicly proclaiming his innocence of the charges for which he was about to be hung. If Wirz was guilty, he would die with a lie on his lips.

Wirz continued to stand alone and unaided, head slightly bowed, while the order of the court was read by Major Russell. The chanting of the

With the Crowd Chanting "Wirz remember Andersonville," the Trap Is Sprung

Library of Congress

soldiers and jeering of the crowd continued during the reading. The offi-cials on the gallows had to huddle close together so they could hear what was being read. No Union Army officer or government official stepped forward to order the soldiers to cease the chanting, or to make any effort to silence the rowdy spectators.

After the reading of the court order, Wirz proclaimed in a loud voice: "I go before my God and Almighty God who will judge between us. I am innocent and I will die like a man." At this point the black cloth hood was placed over Wirz's head, and the noose was positioned around his neck. Wirz's military escort, the two priests, and the other officials on the gallows descended the steps of the scaffold, leaving Wirz standing alone on a small raised platform, waiting for soldiers under the gallows to release the wooden beams holding up the trapdoor.

At exactly 10:32 A.M. the trap was sprung and Wirz fell through the open-ing. The rowdy, drunken spectators were hoping for a gory spectacle and they got it. The fall had not broken Wirz's neck, and he could be seen violently twisting and straining against his bonds. Wirz continued to squirm and fight for air for several minutes until his body went limp and lifeless. While Wirz was slowly and painfully strangling to death, the crowd was wild with excitement, cheering and yelling at the top of their voices. The soldiers maintained their discipline, standing at attention and repeatedly chanting over and over: "Wirz remember Andersonville, Wirz remember Andersonville."

The fact that Henry Wirz died slowly and painfully by strangulation was probably not an accident, but a deliberate act of cruelty.

Hanging was the most common form of capital punishment in the nineteenth century, being almost routinely applied for everything from murder and rape to horse stealing.

Whether the hanging resulted in a quick death or a prolonged gory mess, depended on the skill and knowledge of the hangman. For an ex-ecution to go smoothly, certain things had to be taken into consideration. First was the length of the drop. Too short of a drop and the neck would not break. Too long a drop and the downward force could literally tear the person's head from his shoulders. The general rule was that the length of the drop should be half the length of the condemned man's body height. However, this depended largely on the weight of the person being executed. The heavier the weight of the person being hung, the shorter the drop. This was far from being an exact science and each hangman had his own theory of how long a drop to use. In an effort to end the confusion, the U.S. Army published a "drop chart" in its Procedure for Military Executions. This "drop chart", which was based on the height and weight of the condemned, was to be used at all official executions.[4]

The second factor in a hanging was a well-stretched rope. Hemp, the plant fiber from which ropes were made in the nineteenth century, was naturally elastic. When a weighted hemp rope was dropped, the weight at the end of the rope would often bounce up and down several times before finally coming to rest.

This bouncing motion during a hanging could easily rip the condemned person's head off. This bouncing was easily corrected by stretching the rope until it had no more bounce. Hemp fibers quickly lose much of there elasticity when stretched. The normal way in which a rope was stretched was by attaching a heavy weight to the end of it, usually a bag filled with sand and rocks, then dropping it repeatedly from a height. A prisoner scheduled for execution would often be tortured for days before his death by being forced to listen to the trapdoor of his gallows repeatedly being sprung, followed by the low groaning noise produced by a rope under pressure.[5]

The final and most crucial element was positioning of the rope around the condemned person's neck. To cause the neck to break quickly, the knot of the noose should be positioned under the right or left ear. When the trap is sprung, the condemned falls straight down and at the end of the drop the rope jerks sideways with great force breaking the condemned man's neck. A hangman, who wants to be deliberately cruel, can greatly increase the suffering of the man being hung by deliberately misplacing the noose. Putting it behind the neck or under the chin would cause the condemned to slowly strangle to death.

The photographs of the execution of Henry Wirz taken by Alexander Gardner are not clear enough to show if Wirz's rope knot was positioned under the ear. It does appear that the amount of the drop was adequate. If Wirz's execution was a deliberate act of cruelty, or simply a bungled execution by an inexperienced hangman, is an issue that probably will never be fully resolved. However, the other circumstances surrounding the execution, the cheering, the taunts, and the obviously organized chanting, indicate that the slow, painful death was part of a much larger scheme to cause Wirz as much pain and humiliation as possible.

Following the execution, Wirz's body was cut down and taken into one of the rooms of the Old Capitol Prison for an autopsy. An autopsy of a man who had just been publicly hung was totally unnecessary. Pathological techniques that existed in the mid-nineteenth century couldn't possibly reveal any useful information about the life or death of Henry Wirz. Defenders of Henry Wirz claimed that the autopsy was only an excuse to mutilate the body and photograph the corpse.

Alexander Gardner had taken four remarkably clear photographs of the hanging. The first showed the order of the court being read; the second showing the noose being placed around Wirz's neck; the third showing the trap being sprung; and the fourth showing Wirz hanging, his hooded head clearly visible between two horizontal planks of the side rail of the scaffold. After the execution, Gardner had to quickly develop the glass negatives in his portable darkroom before moving his bulky equipment into the prison to photograph the autopsy.

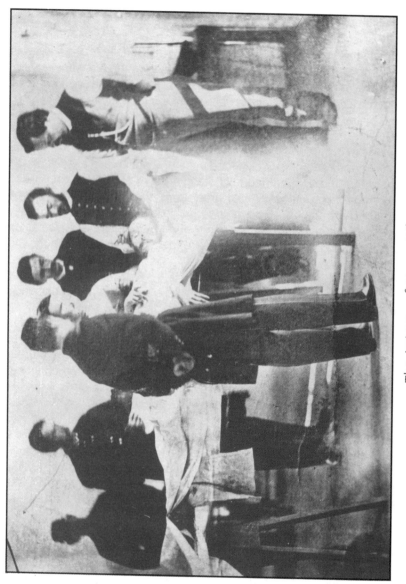

The Autopsy of Henry Wirz

The autopsy photograph is of a much poorer quality than the images made of the outdoor hanging in bright sunlight. Gardner had to use a flash to get the indoor picture, and the image is badly overexposed. Only one image of the autopsy has ever been found.

The autopsy photo shows a group of Union Army doctors in shirt sleeves standing around the body of Wirz. One of the doctors holds a scalpel to his head. Wirz's body appears to be laying on an ordinary wooden table. Another table had been quickly put together with boards and a carpenter's sawhorse to hold the autopsy instruments. Wirz's feet are protruding from under the sheet that covers most of his naked body. The feet are black from the postmortem settling of blood while the body was hanging from the gallows. Wirz's face is unmarred and looks remarkably calm and peaceful.[6]

On November 25, 1865, only ten days after the execution of Henry Wirz, Congress declared the prisoners' burial grounds at Andersonville a national cemetery. This act insured that the prisoners' cemetery would be forever protected and preserved by the Federal government. The dead prisoners of Andersonville would rest in the honored glory of their fellow countrymen. The same would not be true for the mortal remains of Henry Wirz.

In a letter dated November 11, 1865, Major General C. C. Augur, commanding general of the department of Washington, wrote a letter to Assistant Adjutant General E. D. Townsend, officially reporting that the sentence and orders of the president in the case of Henry Wirz, as promulgated in General Court Martial Orders No. 607, had been duly executed the day before between the hours of 10:00 and 11:00 A. M., and that Henry Wirz had been interred by the side of Atzerodt on the grounds of the Washington Arsenal.

However, Henry Wirz's attorney Louis Schade claimed that the body of Henry Wirz remained unburied for three years. During that time his embalmed body was stored in wooden rifle boxes somewhere in the War Department building. According to Schade, parts of Wirz's body were removed by army officers as souvenirs, and the head was put on display with people being charged a fee to view it.

Schade's accusations echoed a rumor that was circulating around Washington concerning the corpse of executed Lincoln conspirator Mary Surratt. According to the back fence and bar rail gossip of the day, Mary Surratt's body had not been buried in the Washington Arsenal grounds with the other three Lincoln conspirators, but instead her body had been secretly embalmed and transported to the basement of the War Department building, where Edwin Stanton would visit it from time to time.[7]

While none of the charges made by Louis Schade, or the rumors about Mary Surratt's body can be proven, certain events in the life of Edwin Stanton give them a great deal of credence.

Edwin Stanton had a morbid fascination with death that bordered on insanity. When his young daughter Lucy died, Stanton was so overwhelmed with grief, it almost drove him to suicide. He had her already buried body exhumed and kept the embalmed body in his bedroom for two years until family members convinced him to allow the young girl to be reburied. When his wife died in 1844, he had her body placed on a bed in his home where he compulsively dressed and undressed his wife's corpse in her wedding dress. Stanton would also decorate the corpse with his wife's personal items. Friends became understandably upset with this arrangement and urged Stanton to allow the body to be buried. After he reluctantly complied, Stanton went temporarily insane walking about the house late at night babbling "Where is Mary?" Where is Mary?"

When Stanton's elder brother Darwin committed suicide by cutting his own throat, Stanton again went insane with grief, running wildly through the woods sobbing hysterically. Relatives had to chase him down and restrain him by force. After Abraham Lincoln was assassinated, Stanton had the blood-stained chair in which the late president was sitting in Ford's Theater brought to his office in the War Department building. He kept the gory souvenir in his office for over a year, placing it so that his eyes would fall on it daily.[8]

Louis Schade worked just as hard to get Henry Wirz's body properly buried, as he had to prove his client's innocence. Schade wrote numerous letters to members of Congress and sympathetic newspapers. Schade's campaign received much public support in Democratic newspapers throughout the South.

During the nearly four years Louis Schade was crusading to have Henry Wirz properly buried, two important events occurred that greatly aided his cause. First, Edwin Stanton was removed from his post as secretary of war by President Andrew Johnson. This removal was so bitterly opposed by the Radical Republicans in Congress, they launched a failed attempt to impeach Johnson. Secondly, in 1868, Ulysses S. Grant was elected president. Grant wanted to appoint Stanton to the U.S. Supreme Court but was concerned about all the rumors and accusations concerning the ghoulish treatment of the corpses of Mary Surratt and Henry Wirz. Grant felt that the best way to silence all the rumors about Edwin Stanton's abnormal fascination with death was to have the bodies removed from the Washington Arsenal grounds and buried in civilian cemeteries.

In the summer of 1869, military officials of the U.S. Army, District of Washington, ordered all the bodies removed from the Washington Arsenal grounds, including the remains of John Wilkes Booth, which had been secretly buried under the flagstone floor of one of the Arsenal's warehouses. All remains were to be turned over to the next of kin and reinterred in civilian cemeteries.

The Execution of the Lincoln Conspirators, Showing Their Open Graves. Henry Wirz Was First Buried Next to the Body of Conspirator George Atzerodt on the Grounds of the Washington Arsenal.

Mount Olivet Cemetery. The Grave of Henry Wirz Is in the Foreground.
Peggy Sheppard

The remains of Henry Wirz were saved from a pauper's grave by Louis Schade, who took on the financial responsibility of buying a cemetery plot. Louis Schade claimed Wirz's body at the Washington Arsenal. At this time, Slade may possibly have examined the corpse, prompting his claim that the head had been removed and certain body parts were sold as souvenirs.

Mount Olivet was the only Catholic cemetery in the Washington D.C. area. It had only been opened in 1858 by the Archdiocese of Baltimore for the city of Washington's small, but growing, Catholic population. Louis Schade arranged to have Wirz's body taken to Mount Olivet Cemetery for burial.

Louis Schade and a Catholic priest were present when Wirz's remains were reburied, to pay their respects and make sure that the body was handled with dignity by the cemetery workers and soldiers who had escorted it from the Arsenal grounds.

Mary Surratt, who was also Catholic, was also buried in Mount Olivet. John Wilkes Booth's body was reburied in Greenmount Cemetery in Baltimore, Maryland. The bodies of the other three executed Lincoln conspirators, David E. Herold, Lewis Payne and David Atzerodt, were all claimed by family members or friends and reburied in civilian cemeteries.

Henry Wirz's body rested in an unmarked grave in Mount Olivet Cemetery until 1959 when Thomas Spencer, an Atlanta writer and strong defender of Henry Wirz, purchased at his own expense a simple marble headstone for the grave. It was installed in a formal ceremony by the United Daughters of the Confederacy. The inscription read: "Captain Henry Wirz C.S.A.— Confederate Hero Martyr— Died November 10, 1865."[9]

Except for a brief Catholic service when his body was moved to Mount Olivet Cemetery and the dedication ceremony of his headstone, Henry Wirz never had a formal funeral service. This was corrected on the 125th anniversary of his execution.

On November 10, 1990, a group of people assembled in Mount Olivet Cemetery at the grave of Henry Wirz. About two dozen Civil War reenactors, in full period costume, stood at attention in a cold rain outside a green funeral tent erected over the grave. Inside the tent were two dozen members

The Marble Headstone of Henry Wirz

Peggy Sheppard

of the Jefferson Davis Camp No. 305 of the Sons of Confederate Veterans. They were led by their commander Charles Goolsby who had organized the ceremony. With this group was Swiss Army Colonel Heinrich Wirz, the great grandnephew of his famous Civil War namesake.

Colonel Wirz laid on the grave a wreath bearing the colors of Switzerland, the city of Zurich, and the Wirz family crest. Two other wreaths, one made from tobacco leaves, an old western Maryland funeral tradition, the other of red and white carnations, were also formally placed on the grave as wisps of incense smoke filled the inside of the green funeral tent. The grave was flanked by the stars and stripes of the flag of the United States of America and the stars and bars of the flag of the Confederate States of America.

Reverend Ed Raffetto, an Episcopal priest and chaplain of the Sons of Confederate Veterans, stepped forward to conduct the funeral service. He prayed "Grant that our brother may sleep in peace, until you awaken in glory." About fifty yards away Confederate reenactors loaded powder charges into a 3-inch mountain howitzer and fired a 21-gun salute.[10]

PART THREE

'The word soldier makes me mad, while the sight of a uniform makes me froth at the mouth."

Dorence Atwater at Age 21

Andersonville National Historic Site

– 10 –

Dorence Atwater

If there was a true hero in the awful mess that was Andersonville, it was a young cavalry trooper from Terryville, Connecticut by the name of Dorence Atwater. Born on February 3, 1845, he came from a hard-working Yankee family, the third in a family of eight children. His father was a mason by profession, but he also served as a justice of the peace and was a successful school teacher. Atwater's mother was described as a strong woman with an "active temperament" that her son inherited. She had instilled within her son the typical Yankee virtues of hard work, duty, and honesty.[1]

Dorence Atwater was a large youth with broad shoulders, thick black hair, and full of spirit. He was also very bright. When he was only fourteen years of age, he got a job as a clerk in a store and later in a post office. His duties as a storekeeper and clerk required him to keep close records of all purchases and inventory. His employer must have been well pleased with Atwater's work, since he kept his job until the outbreak of the Civil War, when he decided to quit in order to enlist in the Union Army.

Although he was only sixteen years old, Dorence Atwater adapted well to the discipline of military life. His officers found the young man to be a hard worker, who seldom complained about the discomforts and rigors of campaigning. Atwater also had a reputation for dependability, integrity, and conscientious behavior.

He earned the respect of the older cavalry troopers by his skill at horsemanship and courage in battle. He participated in hard campaigning with the First Connecticut Cavalry and the Harris Light Cavalry of the 2nd New York Regiment. Atwater was under the command of Lieutenant Colonel (later General) Judson Kilpatrick and was part of the dashing band of Union cavalrymen who boldly raided into southern Virginia during the summer of 1862.

Atwater had only a minimum public school education, but he was highly intelligent, a fast learner, with good common sense. He was also a good reader and had a flair for penmanship, learned during his years as a store clerk. These attributes plus his skill at horsemanship and a reputation for dependability landed him a job as a courier, relaying dispatches by horseback between Union commanders in the field.

Dorence Atwater was on a routine mission near Hagerstown, Maryland, only four days after Pickett's famous charge at Gettysburg, when he was surprised by a superior Confederate cavalry force and was taken prisoner. On the day of his capture, Dorence Atwater had a letter in his pocket from his father informing him of the recent death of his mother.[2]

Dorence Atwater was taken to Belle Isle, Virginia where he would languish for five months until his captors discovered his clerical abilities. Atwater was granted a parole to work as a clerk at the Confederate prison in Richmond that had been Smith's Tobacco Warehouse before the war. He was charged with keeping track of supplies sent by the U.S. government and packages forwarded by the families of Union prisoners of war. As a paroled prisoner he was issued double rations, and his living conditions, although primitive, were a great improvement over sleeping in the mud of Belle Isle.[3]

Shortly after assuming his new post, Atwater discovered that a Confederate officer was pilfering packages sent to Union prisoners of war. With items such as coffee and canned meats in such short supply in the South, it was common practice for the guards to steal hard to find items from prisoners' packages. Seldom was anyone caught at it and even more seldom was anyone punished. It was almost unheard of for a prisoner on parole to be so brave as to accuse one of his captors, especially an officer, of theft.

With the full knowledge of the possible consequences of his actions, and disregarding the advice of his fellow prisoners to keep quiet, Dorence Atwater went to the commanding officer of the prison and reported the theft. The commander ordered an investigation, which eventually proved Atwater's accusations to be truthful. The Confederate officer was punished, but at the same time, Dorence Atwater was ordered to be transferred to another prison outside of Richmond. Atwater probably assumed that he would be sent to Danville, Virginia, but soon he realized that his new home would be the newly opened prison at Andersonville, Georgia.

Like thousands of other prisoners, Dorence Atwater endured the long, stop and go, train ride to Andersonville crammed into an overloaded boxcar. He arrived in February of 1864, only a few days after the prison was opened. He remained inside the rapidly filling pine log stockade with the other Union prisoners until the middle of May, when he was admitted to the hospital, which at that time was on high ground in the far northeast corner of the stockade. In June, he accepted a parole to work in the office of surgeon J. H. White.[4]

Dorence Atwater's duties were mostly clerical in nature. He was assigned to keep a record of all Federal prisoners admitted to the hospital and to maintain a separate record of those who died, recording their names, units, date and cause of death, as well as their grave number.

Atwater had been told by Surgeon White that the list of dead prisoners would be turned over to Union officials at war's end. However, Atwater had serious doubts if the Confederates really intended to do so. Like many of the prisoners at Andersonville, Dorence Atwater believed that the Confederates were deliberately attempting to kill and maim as many prisoners of war as possible so they would be unfit for battle. He also believed that when the war ended, the Confederates would try to hide the evidence of their crime. Atwater believed that the rolls on which he was working every day would be quickly destroyed as soon as the prison was in danger of liberation by Union troops or closed at the war's end.

At some time after assuming his duties as a hospital clerk, Dorence Atwater secretly began to compile a second list of the dead prisoners of war. Atwater would copy his second list on rough buff paper, which could be quickly hidden inside his shirt or pants pocket whenever a Confederate officer entered the office.

Hidden somewhere in his she-bang inside the stockade, Atwater had a ledger book that he had somehow secretly acquired at some point during his captivity. Upon returning from work each night, Atwater would carefully transfer the names from the rough pieces of buff paper into his ledger book, carefully checking to make sure each name was correct. Once the names were recorded, Atwater would carefully wrap his ledger in waterproof oil cloth and hide it in a dry spot.

The prison hospital was moved outside the stockade the first week in June. The new hospital was situated south of the main stockade on high ground behind the star fort. The hospital was about four acres in size, surrounded by a pine board fence six feet high. Chief Surgeon Isaiah White had laid out the hospital wards between neat pathways the prisoners called streets. Since there were no beds, the sick men had to lay on a thick bed of layered pine straw. Their only shelter was a square piece of canvas, large enough to cover eight to ten men which was pitched like a tent over each ward. Each surgeon was assigned a certain number of wards, and as the prison population climbed, the surgeons were assigned more and more prisoners to care for.

Chief Surgeon White believed that a simple thing like clean drinking water would do a lot to improve the men's health. He had a deep well dug at one corner of the hospital, far removed from the outhouse latrine that was built over a small stream, that flowed through the opposite end of the hospital compound. This way he hoped to keep the patients' drinking water from becoming contaminated by human sewage like the water in the stockade.

The patients' diet was basically the same as the men in the main prison stockade with the addition of a small measure of white flour, just enough for one biscuit.[5]

As the prison population grew, so did the hospital. In order to make additional room for patients, Surgeon White ordered the headquarter's tent, drug dispensary, and dissecting house (operating room) moved outside.

Dorence Atwater worked at a small desk in the headquarter's tent, maintaining his ledgers and preparing quarterly and monthly abstracts of the hospital's patients and the number of dead. When some of the ledgers were water damaged in a thunderstorm, Captain Wirz ordered Atwater to move his operations from the leaky tent into his small clapboard shack of an office near the star fort. This move gave Atwater much more privacy, allowing him more time to copy his second list of the dead. It also made him very familiar with Captain Wirz and General Winder, since he worked only a few feet from the two men, watching them make life and death decisions that affected the lives of thousands of Union prisoners of war.

Dorence Atwater returned each night to the stockade, sharing a she-bang with men from the First Connecticut Cavalry. As a paroled prisoner, he could have lived outside the stockade, but he needed his friends inside the stockade to guard his precious rolls while he was at work in the hospital and Wirz's office. Atwater was also probably smuggling food and medicines into the stockade in return.

Atwater hated the filthy stockade and couldn't wait to get outside each morning. He always arose before dawn and waited patiently by the North Gate as the night's dead were collected to be taken to the outside at first light.

As the first rays of sunlight filtered through the dark pine forest, Atwater would check out at the North Gate not to return until late that evening. Atwater's first stop would be Captain Wirz's office where he would pick up a canvas haversack in which he would put his ledger books along with his pen and ink supply. Atwater was always careful to keep his writing materials tightly wrapped in watertight oil cloth to guard against sudden rain showers and the heavy humidity of the Georgia summer.

With his haversack flung over his shoulder, Dorence Atwater would walk the two miles to the prison cemetery and then wait until he saw the first load of dead bodies slowly coming up the narrow dirt road from the main stockade. The bodies were loaded onto heavy wooden wagons, pulled by a pair of tired and underfed mules. The mules strained against their heavy loads, and the wagons made mournful creaking and groaning sounds as it moved along.

Many of the bodies had been stored in the "dead house" most of the night and were already stiff with rigor mortis by morning. They were often frozen into grotesque positions with arms and legs protruding from the wagons. As the wagons would hit a bump or depression in the dirt road, the cold dead arms would sway back and forth. It appeared to some of the men who witnessed this morbid scene, almost like the dead were waving good-bye to the filthy, disease ridden, prison pen they were leaving behind.

The wagons were followed by a detail of Union prisoners of war, carrying picks and shovels over their shoulders. Their pockets were stuffed with hundreds of dollars of Yankee "greenback" currency, ready to buy badly needed items for themselves and their mess mates back inside the stockade. The grave diggers were followed by a small detachment of Confederate guards, almost all of whom had their pockets and haversacks bulging with things they wished to trade for the coveted Yankee money. The wagons would be met at the cemetery by groups of local civilians, also carrying bundles of trade goods.

The prisoners on the grave-digging details had actually paid a bribe to perform this grisly duty, since the grave-digging detail offered the best, and sometimes the only, opportunity to trade with the Confederate guards and local civilians.

At the cemetery each morning, avarice triumphed over respect and grief. The dead men were only background scenery to all the bartering and deal making going on. As one group of prisoners would dig the graves and unload the corpses, the rest would be busy making deals with the motley bunch of civilians and gawking Confederate guards. When one group of prisoners were finished trading, they would switch places with the men so callously unloading and burying their dead comrades, and a new round of bargaining would begin.

Within an hour the work was done and the wagons would return to the stockade for another load of dead prisoners. On the return trip, the wagon that had previously carried the corpses was now loaded with cheap burlap sacks filled with tomatoes, turnips, sweet potatoes (which the prisoners usually called by the Yankee name of "yams"), sweet corn, beans, peas, and each man's pockets would be bulging with onions and boiled eggs.

Dorence Atwater probably took part in this grisly trade as much as the rest of the men. His survival and the survival of his comrades in the First Connecticut Cavalry depended upon him bringing fresh vegetables into the stockade to ward off scurvy. While he certainly had respect for the dead, he also had to think about the living.

Atwater's duty at the cemetery was to record the name and grave number of each dead prisoner. Prison regulations stipulated that each body be identified with a small slip of paper attached to one of the man's limbs before he was carried to the "dead house." However, many times these tags were water damaged or were poorly written in pencil by the light of a pine tar lamp inside the guard shack by the gate. Sometimes there simply wasn't any tag. When this happened Atwater would do everything in his power to identify the unmarked body. Usually, the men in the burial detail

The Burial of the Dead in Shallow Trenches

were friends of the deceased and could give him the information he needed. However, there were some times when they couldn't. There were a lot of men inside the stockade who had been driven to insanity by their confinement and died friendless and anonymous on the edge of the muddy swamp where such deranged men were exiled. They were carried to the "dead house" by strangers, who only wanted to get them out of the stockade before they began to decay. When Dorence Atwater encountered such a body, all he could do was write the very sad word "Unknown."[6]

To Dorence Atwater every "Unknown" in his journal was a bitter personal defeat. Atwater's list of the dead was his reason for living each day. It was how he psychologically fought off death and existed for the day he would be free. To Dorence Atwater to have to lie forever in an unmarked grave was a terrible tragedy, made worse by the knowledge that he might have been able to do something to prevent it.

The greater the number of dead, the longer it took each day to bury them. At midday the burying had to cease, since the wagons were needed to haul the prisoners' rations inside the stockade. When the issuing of rations was completed, the burying of the dead would resume and continue until late afternoon when it was finally finished. When the last of the day's dead were covered by the soft Georgia clay, the tired and hungry burial details would limp back to the stockade, wearily carrying their tools over their shoulders. There was no trading this late in the day; most of the financial transactions were completed by the noon meal break. The afternoon burials were simply a long and tiring chore.

After Dorence Atwater left the cemetery, there was still much left for him to do. His first job was to report to Chief Surgeon Isaiah White the correct number of the days dead. The chief surgeon would compare the names of the dead with the hospital rolls. This would tell him how many patients had died and also how many new patients he could admit to the hospital during the next day's sick call.

Atwater would then retire to his small desk in Captain Wirz's office where he would compare the names of the dead men with hospital records to find a cause of death for each buried prisoners of war. He would then update his rolls and compile the quarterly abstracts. At some point during this process, Dorence Atwater would find the time to secretly make a second list of the day's dead, which he carefully kept hidden.

Periodically, Atwater would help out at the hospital. He would accompany the doctors on their rounds, making a record of the treatments ordered and medicine given each patient. The doctors never approached the patients too closely due to the filth and lice that surrounded each man. Usually, the doctor would stand back a few feet and question the man about his condition. After listening to the man's complaints, he would prescribe medications or order the surgical removal of infected body parts.

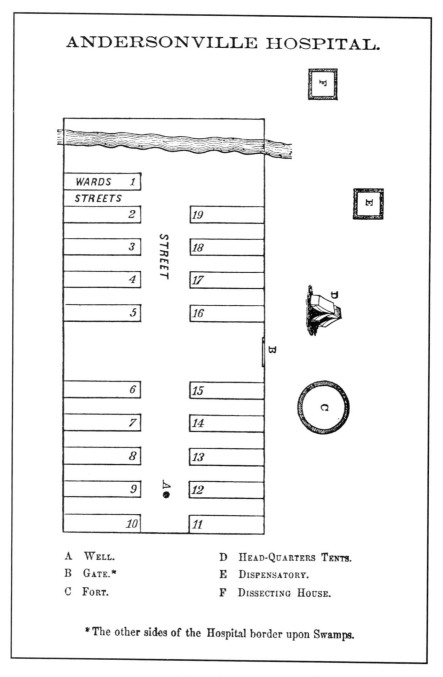

ANDERSONVILLE HOSPITAL.

WARDS 1	
STREETS	
2	19
3	18
4	17
5	16
6	15
7	14
8	13
9	12
10	11

STREET

A WELL.
B GATE.*
C FORT.
D HEAD-QUARTERS TENTS.
E DISPENSATORY.
F DISSECTING HOUSE.

*The other sides of the Hospital border upon Swamps.

Map of the Prison Hospital

Surgery at Andersonville was horrendous; but, with no antibiotics available, it was the only possible treatment for most afflictions. Skin infections would be lanced so that the infected blood and pus could drain. Limbs that were infected with gangrene were amputated at the nearest joint above the infection. Most patients had to have toes, feet, or legs removed because they were the body parts that most often came in contact with the filthy, disease-ridden floor of the stockade.

The removal of hands and arms was less common, but such surgery was performed with regularity. The most difficult surgery was the removal of an infected eye. With no knowledge of germ theory, and with no sterile place to operate, it was nearly impossible to stop infections from spreading from the eye socket to the brain and eventually causing a painfully slow death.

Each morning the surgeons would gather in the dissecting room to don their leather aprons and scrub their instruments. The patient was tied or strapped to a rough wooden table and the primitive surgery would begin. The cutting and sawing went on continuously from eight in the morning until one or two in the afternoon. Thousands of hands, arms, feet, and legs were amputated without benefit of proper sanitation, antibiotics, or anesthesia. Many men who did not have the strength to withstand the terrible pain and shock to their system died on the operating table. Others only developed worse infections from the surgery, once they were returned to the squalor of the hospital wards.[7]

Despite all the pain and suffering that went on in the hospital, many former patients praised the surgeons for their kindness. After the war it was revealed that many of the surgeons were secret Union men who used their knowledge of medicine to avoid combat in the Confederate Army. When no one was listening, they would cheer the sick prisoners with stories about Union victories, rumors of prisoner exchanges, and sometimes even information that would help prisoners escape.[8]

Dorence Atwater had to be back in the stockade before darkness fell. During the long days of summer, he could work in his small office until after eight o'clock. However, if he was late, his life could be in danger. The hot-headed teenage guards would eagerly fire at any prisoner seen outside the stockade after dark.

Once darkness fell, the surgeons abandoned the hospital to a squad of armed Confederate guards who would wander about inside the board fence. The patrolling sentries built small campfires to illuminate the fence, even though the patients in the hospital were much too ill to even try to escape. One chilly night, a hospital patient was shot by one of the guards while he was trying to warm himself by one of the watch fires. The surgeons in the hospital had heard rumors of unnecessary killings in the main stockade and were not about to allow such a thing to happen in the hospital. Chief Surgeon Isaiah White led a delegation to see General Winder to strongly protest the shooting.

During the period of time that Andersonville was in operation, the entire state of Georgia became one huge military hospital. Wounded soldiers from the battles of Chattanooga and Chickamauga had been shipped south on the Western and Atlantic Railroad to fill the hospitals of Atlanta. When Sherman's army began moving south towards Atlanta, every major city in the state began receiving train loads of wounded soldiers. Churches and saloons were turned into dressing stations. Fairgrounds, livery stables, and rail yards were turned into huge hospital wards. When the military hospital in Americus burned down, local citizens managed to find room for over 2,000 wounded soldiers in private homes. The city of Macon had some six thousand wounded and sick Confederate soldiers to care for, a number that was equal to the population of the city. Therefore, everything even remotely related to medical care—bandages, ointments, medicines, even surgical tools—were in short supply all over Georgia.[9]

The medicines for the hospital at Andersonville arrived by train from a laboratory in Macon. A month's supply of drugs might last ten days, if it was used very sparingly. After the medicine was gone, no more would be available until the next shipment. Chief Surgeon White, like most Southern physicians, had built up a lifetime knowledge of regional home remedies and folk medicines. The woods around the prison were filled with all types of plants, berries, and tree barks that could be used to treat various illnesses. White oak bark could be used to give relief from diarrhea. Sweet fern and sumach berries were used to ward off scurvy.[10] Exactly how well these folk medicines worked is unknown. However, it was certainly better than doing nothing. But more importantly, it showed that the surgeons in the prison hospital were sincerely trying to do something to help the sick Union prisoners of war.

By the first day of September over 10,000 prisoners had already died at Andersonville. That same month, the Confederate authorities began the wholesale movement of prisoners out of Andersonville. Most would go to the new prison at Millen, only to be moved again, only a few weeks later, as Sherman's army began to close in on Millen during his famous "March to the Sea." Black and healthy white prisoners were sent to Savannah to help dig earthwork defenses. Other prisoners were sent to the newly opened, makeshift prison near the south Georgia swamp town of Blackshear. Other prisoners were funneled to Salisbury, North Carolina and Columbia, South Carolina.

Dorence Atwater stayed behind to continue his work at the hospital and secretly record his register of dead prisoners. Every day, he continued his daily routine at the cemetery. However, with the rapid decline in the prison's population, Atwater didn't have to spend as much time recording graves each morning as he had during the summer. This gave Dorence Atwater an opportunity to make a detailed map of the cemetery, that would be most valuable later on. Atwater was able to visually pinpoint the beginning of each row of graves, using fixed points as a survey reference. These fixed points were usually large oak trees or the center of the road leading from the stockade. Using this system Atwater found a foolproof method of locating the beginning of each row of graves and from these points any single grave could be easily found.

Atwater endured the bitter winter of 1864–1865 when the Andersonville prisoners suffered terribly in the cold and damp of the muddy stockade. The rigors of prison life had taken a heavy toll on Atwater's health. Even with double rations and access to the prison hospital, Atwater was ill much of the time fighting off diarrhea, fevers, and pneumonia. Through it all, he carefully hoarded his rolls, keeping them securely wrapped and carefully hidden.

By February 1, 1865, Dorence Atwater had 12,636 names recorded in his register. During the next three weeks, he would continue to add names as the men died and were buried in the cemetery. The last burial at Andersonville would take place on April 28, 1865, but Dorence Atwater would not be there to record it. On February 20, he was told to pack his belongings and board an awaiting train. His destination was to be the Confederate prison at Columbia, South Carolina.[11]

Atwater was certainly glad to be leaving Andersonville, but he worried that some meddlesome Confederate officer would find his rolls and confiscate them. So, he carefully hid his rolls inside his tiny bundle of personal possessions. He hoped that with the Confederacy collapsing all around him, no Confederate guard would bother to search his bundle. If one did, Atwater hoped he would be illiterate, or too dumb, to know what he was looking at.

Dorence Atwater never reached Columbia. In Macon, they discovered that the South Carolina capital had been captured by Sherman's army, and it had been mostly destroyed by a great fire, that the Confederates claimed was set by rioting bands of newly freed slaves, released prisoners of war, and Union soldiers. With this news, the train was detoured to the Confederate prison at Salisbury, North Carolina.

The prison at Salisbury was an old, four-story, brick, factory building, surrounded by a high board fence with a catwalk for patrolling Confederate guards. Inside the fence were a collection of smaller buildings and tents.

Salisbury was a much smaller prison than Andersonville and its cemetery was only about one-third as large. At Salisbury, the graves were marked with a single wooden shingle, but summer rains had made the crude pencil grave markings mostly illegible. It was nearly impossible to tell who was buried in each grave, since the graves had not been numbered and mapped as they had been at Andersonville.

However, the poor condition of the cemetery did not mean that records of the dead prisoners were not maintained. Two civilian prisoners, A. D. Richardson and J. H. Browne, who were captured reporters for Horace Greeley's *New York Tribune*, had recorded the names of 1,400 men who had died at Salisbury. They took their lists with them when the two reporters escaped in December of 1864. A list of 1,200 more names were smuggled out later by released prisoners of war. After the war, captured Confederate records turned up even more names.

Horace Greeley, the eccentric publisher of the *New York Tribune*, published both lists of the Salisbury dead in his widely read newspaper. The publication of the names made Greeley a hero to the families of the missing men. It was not until the lists were published in the *Tribune* did the families of the dead men finally learn of their fate.

The publication of these lists did not set well with the politically sensitive Secretary of War Edwin Stanton. After the lists appeared in his newspaper, Greeley was visited by stern-faced representatives of the War Department, who demanded that he turn over the original lists, allegedly so the families of the dead prisoners could collect the back pay due them. Greeley reluctantly complied.[12]

After only two days at Salisbury, Dorence Atwater was paroled to the Union lines near Wilmington, North Carolina. He was to be one of the first of a group of ten thousand prisoners of war to be released to Union officials. Dorence Atwater's release early in the month of February ended twenty months of brutal captivity behind enemy lines. Atwater remained in the Wilmington area until mid-March, when he was sent by ocean steamer to Camp Parole, Maryland.[13]

What became known in Civil War history as Camp Parole, was in reality part of the United States Naval Academy at Annapolis, Maryland. When the Union prisoners of war were finally released, the cadet barracks had been hastily converted into a hospital to receive the pitiful wrecks of humanity that were arriving daily on the Annapolis wharfs from the rapidly closing Confederate prison pens. When all the barracks were filled with hollow-eyed and emaciated prisoners of war, large field tents were put up on the parade ground to provide extra quarters for the overflow.

Teams of women from the U.S. Sanitary Commission, a privately funded, civilian, organization that cared for sick and wounded soldiers and their families, would feed the starved prisoners fresh boiled vegetables, ground to a soft mush; and nurses (both male and female) would wash the filthy prisoners and apply fresh bandages.[14]

Dorence Atwater, the once strong and healthy young man who had enlisted in the Union Army, was now little more than a living skeleton. Weakened by twenty months of malnutrition, his body was now ravaged by fevers and diarrhea. Despite his feeble condition, Dorence Atwater wrote two letters from his hospital sick bed. The first was to the commander of the hospital requesting an immediate furlough to return home. Atwater desperately wanted to get home to his ailing father in Terryville. The second letter went to Secretary of War Edwin Stanton, telling him about the list of dead prisoners that Atwater had so carefully guarded and brought out of his confinement.

Due to the overcrowding at Camp Parole, Atwater's request for furlough was almost immediately granted. With little advance notice, he was ordered to be sent home. Although he had developed diphtheria, Atwater immediately departed Camp Parole. By the time he arrived at his home in Terryville, Atwater was near death.

For a few terrifying days, Dorence Atwater hung perilously between life and death in the bed in which he slept as a child. After a week of intense care by his loving family, the fever broke and he slowly began his recovery. Soon he was sitting up in bed and receiving family and friends, who were shocked at his emaciated appearance. Dorence Atwater spent as much time as possible visiting with his father, who was also seriously ill.

The young cavalryman was much improved, but was far from recovered, when he received a telegram on April 12, ordering him to report to the War Department building in Washington and to bring his rolls of the Andersonville dead with him. Against the wishes of his family, Dorence Atwater heeded the call and departed for Washington.

Clara Barton

Clara Barton

Dorence Atwater arrived in Washington on the afternoon of Friday, April 14, 1865. He was familiar with the city, having spent much time in Washington while he was part of the Army of the Potomac. Atwater went directly to the War Department and reported to the chief clerk. He was told that the person he needed to contact was Major Samuel Beck, but Major Beck was out of town, attending the ceremony in Charleston, where the Stars and Stripes were being raised over the pile of rubble that had been Fort Sumter. Atwater was advised to find a room and wait for the Major's return.

To Atwater's surprise, the chief clerk then ordered him to hand over the rolls he had mentioned to the secretary of war in his letter. Atwater had carefully hidden and guarded his rolls all during his long captivity and was now reluctant to give them over to a total stranger. However, the stranger wore the uniform of the United States Army, and not suspecting treachery by his own government, the young clerk carefully retrieved the small ledger book from his suitcase and handed it over to the chief clerk.

That night, as the still very ill Dorence Atwater tried to sleep in his cheap Washington hotel room, a single gunshot rang out in Ford's Theater and Abraham Lincoln slumped over mortally wounded. Atwater awoke the next morning to find the city in a state of panic and profound grief. Atwater spent much of Saturday and Sunday in bed fighting off his illness. When he ventured from his small room, Atwater would buy newspapers and tearfully read about the death of President Lincoln.

On Monday, a messenger from the War Department arrived at Atwater's hotel and told him that Beck had returned from Charleston and wanted to see him. Dorence Atwater hurriedly made his way to the War Department and was quickly ushered into the office of Major Samuel Beck.

This was not a good day for Dorence Atwater to talk with Major Beck. The Major was tired and testy from his journey to Charleston and he had gotten very little sleep since his return to Washington. Secretary of War Edwin Stanton was tirelessly obsessed with the search for the person or persons who had committed the heinous crimes against President Lincoln and Secretary of State Steward. Everyone at the War Department was putting in long hours.

Major Beck seemed irritated to be diverted from the important work of hunting for the assassins to deal with Atwater. He intended to spend no more time than necessary with the youthful former prisoner of war. He was cold and aloof towards Atwater. It was the posture the Major felt was appropriate when a field grade officer deals with an enlisted man. He kept Atwater waiting at attention while he finished some last minute paperwork.

After a suitable period of time had elapsed, Major Beck glanced up at the thin and pale young man who was standing before him. He curtly informed Atwater that the secretary of war thanked him for the gift of his lists of dead Union prisoners of war and that the secretary had authorized the payment of $300 to Atwater for his troubles.

Atwater was shocked at what he heard! He feebly tried to explain that he had not copied the rolls for money, but instead he wanted the War Department to help him get his rolls published so the next of kin of the dead prisoners would know of their deaths in Confederate prisons.

Major Beck did not say so at the time, but he knew that certain high-ranking officials in the War Department had already decided that the publication of the lists of nearly 13,000 dead prisoners of war would not be good for the nation's moral.

Secretary of War Stanton was still irritated that the lists of dead from Salisbury Prison had been published by Horace Greeley's *New York Tribune*. Stanton considered Greeley to be a political enemy of the Republican Party and the Lincoln administration.

Major Beck had been given the job of making sure Atwater was silenced and that the bothersome rolls remained secured in a safe in the War Department building. However, both the secretary of war and Major Beck had seriously underestimated the tenacity of Dorence Atwater.

Major Beck responded to Atwater's protests by attempting to browbeat the young cavalryman. The Major stood up and became very stern. He told Atwater that the $300 offer was more than generous and that he should accept it with gratitude. Beck then threatened to treat the rolls as captured enemy documents and pay Atwater nothing.

For the first time Dorence Atwater became aware that the War Department was going to actively attempt to suppress the rolls, rather than help him get them printed. He also became acutely aware of the fact that he had made a serious mistake by surrendering his rolls to the chief clerk when he first reported to the War Department.

Atwater knew he was operating from a position of weakness, but he had a strong resolve. He had seen his share of combat and had survived the horrors of the Confederate prison system; he was not about to be intimidated by a rear echelon desk soldier.

Atwater stood his ground. He maintained that his rolls were not captured documents since no enemy soldier had ever touched them. They were his personal property, and he wanted them back, or he would charge Beck with theft, just as he had the Confederate officer in Richmond. Atwater also reminded Major Beck that his enlistment in the Union Army had expired while he was a prisoner, and although he still wore the uniform and had not been officially discharged, he was no longer legally in the army.

What resulted was a heated argument where Atwater's tone of voice crossed over the line into insubordination. However, it was Beck who decided to give in. After much give and take, the two men decided on a mutually agreeable course of action: The War Department would return Atwater's list of dead prisoners as soon as they could be copied, and Dorence Atwater would be further rewarded with a position of clerk in the War Department, with the rank of sergeant in the regular army of the United States. Dorence Atwater may have suspected, but had no way of knowing for sure, that Major Beck was lying and had no intention of ever returning his rolls.

Atwater was desperately in need of a job and the $300 would pay off his father's medical bills and debts. It was a hard offer for the young soldier to resist. However, there was one severe danger. To assume the position as clerk, Dorence Atwater would have to reenlist in the United States Army, a very foolish move at this juncture.

Perhaps it was due to Atwater's illness, or just fatigue from his travels and captivity, or the fact that he desperately wanted to get back to Terryville to the bedside of his sick father. Whatever it was, Dorence Atwater accepted Major Beck's proposition with nothing more than a salute and a handshake to show that the conversation ever took place. Sometimes it is hard for an honorable man to understand that everyone is not as he is.

After the deal was struck, Major Beck arranged for Atwater to quickly sign reenlistment papers and immediately issued him a furlough to return home to Terryville. After the paperwork was completed, Dorence Atwater departed from Washington on the earliest train traveling north through Baltimore and New York. He reached the bedside of his father just a few days before his death on April 25, 1865. It was a hard blow to the young man who always loved and respected both his parents. However, he thanked the Lord for allowing him a few precious days with his father before his death.

His father's death prompted Dorence Atwater to thinking about how much sadder it would have been if his father had passed away never knowing what had befallen him during the war. It also made him reflect on the cemetery at Andersonville. He knew that soon the hard thunderstorms that rolled over Georgia each summer, would quickly wash away all traces of the small wooden headmarkers, and the resulting erosion would expose the shallow buried corpses to the ravages of wild animals.

Atwater pondered what to do. He decided to immediately write down everything he could remember about the cemetery. Atwater wrote a detailed description of how the dead were buried and redrew the map of the cemetery he had first drawn while he were at Andersonville. While this map and description of the cemetery were important in determining where the rows of graves began, without his rolls of the dead prisoners' names and grave numbers the information was useless.

Atwater was scheduled to report for duty in Washington on June 1, 1865. On the way back, he stopped in New York City long enough to send a telegram to Major Beck asking him if his rolls had been copied. He received the succinct reply "not yet."[1]

Dorence Atwater expected to have his rolls returned as soon as he returned to Washington. They had been in the custody of Major Beck for over a month and Atwater felt that was more than enough time to copy them. When he reported to the War Department, Atwater was also surprised to learn that none of the other War Department clerks had been assigned the duty of copying the rolls. He began to suspect that he had been betrayed. Remembering his experience with the Confederate officer in Richmond, Dorence Atwater decided this time to move very cautiously.

Dorence Atwater hoped to gently force the issue by requesting permission from Major Beck to take part of his rolls to his small room in a Washington boardinghouse each night and copy them on his own time. Beck stalled, saying that he first had to consult Quartermaster General E. D. Townsend. After some delay, Major Beck gave Atwater the bad news. General Townsend had decreed that the army had purchased the rolls from Atwater and they were now government property. He said that Atwater had been more than adequately paid for his services and that the rolls were not to be copied "for any traffic whatever."[2]

As soon as this final act of treachery had been exposed, Dorence Atwater initiated a plan he had been hatching in his mind ever since he first suspected that the War Department might try to suppress his rolls. Dorence Atwater spent every spare moment writing letters to friends and relatives who might be able to help him. He also began to arrange private meetings with influential civilians in the Washington area. It was secretive business if the War Department got wind of what Atwater was doing, he could be court-martialled.

The key person in Atwater's plan was a diminutive former school teacher and patient office clerk named Clara Barton. Because she was a woman, Clara Barton didn't even have the right to vote. However, during the Civil War she had risen to a position of unheard of political power and influence.

She had been born in 1821 into a hard-working Massachusetts family. As a girl she had not been allowed to play with toys or dolls. The family belonged to the liberal Unitarian Church and she was taught the importance of thrift, organization, and education by her no nonsense mother.[3]

Clara Barton was a highly intelligent and hard-working young girl, but she was also very shy and hypersensitive, a problem she would have to fight for the rest of her life. She excelled at everything she tried and worked harder than any other child her age. However, her achievements had a dark side. She feared failure and any criticism would bring on a spell of depression and self-loathing.

When Clara was ten years old, her brother was injured in a fall. She spent two years carefully nursing him back to health. She was a caring and gentle nurse, who was skeptical of many of the harsh and painful medical techniques of her day. She convinced her parents to forbid the doctors to apply leeches or hot plasters that caused painful blisters. Clara substituted instead cleanliness, relaxing hot baths, and good nutrition. Once her techniques went into use, her brother, who had been near death, slowly began to recover. This episode was the only medical training or nursing experience she would ever have until the beginning of the Civil War.

Clara Barton was such an intelligent girl she was teaching younger children at age fifteen. Two years later, she passed a rigorous oral exam before an all male committee to receive a Massachusetts teaching certificate. Frustrated by the limitations placed upon her teaching due to her sex, she left Massachusetts and opened her own school at Bordentown, New Jersey. Although the school was a great success, Clara was soon forced to leave because of gossip by local townspeople who disapproved of her unmarried lifestyle. In 1854, she moved to Washington to live with her sister and work as a clerk in the U.S. Patient Office, copying government documents. However, even this prosaic work was to become controversial. She was harassed by her male co-workers until finally President James Buchanan forced Clara to resign because of her strong anti-slavery views. She was not rehired until 1861 when an equally anti-slavery man, Abraham Lincoln, took office.

The start of the Civil War revolutionized Clara Barton's life and made her one of the most famous women in the world. It all began when Clara went to visit soldiers from a Massachusetts regiment who had been injured by a rioting mob as they had passed through Baltimore. Clara Barton was shocked to find the injured soldiers lying on the bare floor of the Senate chamber in the capitol building. The men were receiving no health care other than what they could give each other.

To her horror, Clara Barton found out that the War Department, which was feverishly preparing for war, had not even considered any system for caring for the sick and wounded. The War Department had not made provision for the purchasing of bandages, blankets, surgical equipment, or medicines. It was almost as if the War Department was not expecting there to be any wounded or sick soldiers during the war.

In fact, there wasn't even a system for feeding the wounded soldiers. The men in the Senate chamber had not been fed since the day they were injured. The army system of issuing rations raw and expecting soldiers to cook the food themselves in mess teams simply didn't work once the soldiers were sick or wounded and separated from their messmates.

Clara Barton immediately organized a letter-writing campaign to family and friends in Massachusetts. Soon bundles containing bandages, soap, towels, stationary, needles, and thread began to arrive in Washington. She organized a field kitchen on the front lawn of the capitol building and began preparing hot meals for the injured soldiers.

Clara Barton's humanitarian efforts escalated rapidly after the first battle of Bull Run. She organized well-operated field hospitals in Washington, using every spare foot of unused office space in government buildings as hospital wards. Hundreds of wounded men were treated in the hallways and public areas of government buildings all over Washington.

Clara Barton was everywhere, doing everything she could to relieve the suffering. She bandaged wounds, assisted in surgery, served hot food, and even wrote letters home to worried family members. She once sat perched on a stool reading a home town newspaper to the wounded soldiers gathered around her. Clara Barton worked out a sophisticated supply system with a network of reliable contributors to keep her supplied with all the materials she needed.

By 1862, Clara decided there was only so much she could do from Washington. Wounded soldiers had told her of having lain for hours on a battlefield waiting for medical attention. Many men with treatable wounds had literally bled to death for lack of medical attention. Clara Barton wanted to take her nurse corps to the battlefield itself, but she first had to overcome some powerful prejudices. In the nineteenth century, women were perceived as weak and delicate, totally disregarding the stamina and heroic actions of thousands of pioneer women on the western frontier. Union commanders complained that Clara Barton's nurses would only be in the way and that they would all faint or swoon at the first sight of bloody combat.

During her years in Washington, Clara Barton had cultivated many political friends. She often attended meetings of Congress and the Supreme Court. She knew who to go see and who not to waste her time on. After much lobbying and debate on her behalf, public pressure finally came down on the side of Clara Barton's lifesaving efforts. Under instructions from President Lincoln himself, the Surgeon General of the United States William A. Hammond issued a general pass to "Miss C.H. Barton to travel anywhere she wanted for the purpose of treating sick and wounded soldiers."[4]

In the next three years, Clara Barton would become one of the most respected women in America. At the battles of Fairfax Court House and Chantilly, she bandaged the arm of a young man who had once been one of her students. She also spent the night comforting a delirious soldier who was calling for his sister. At Antietam, she was almost killed by a Confederate bullet that ripped through the sleeve of her dress and killed the soldier she was tending.

By 1865, Clara Barton was a living legend, a woman held in such high regard that not even the highest ranking generals dared deny her anything. Members of Congress sought her out for advise and counsel. Newspaper reporters wrote glowing testimonials to her courage and good works. Abraham Lincoln admired Clara Barton so much she was granted almost instant access to his office, bypassing wealthy and influential men who had been waiting for days to see the president.

Clara Barton first became interested in the plight of prisoners of war when she discovered that her brother, who had moved to North Carolina before the war and joined the Confederate Army when the war started, was being held in a Union military prison. He wrote his famous sister a letter pitifully pleading with her to get him released. At the time, Clara had been appointed superintendent of nurses for the Army of the James and was able to get her brother released immediately, just on her authority. Clara Barton felt that she had seen all the horrors of war. However, when she first viewed her brother Stephen's frail body, it changed her mind. He was ravaged by malaria and diarrhea, and his emaciated body was covered with horrible open sores. She valiantly tried to nurse him back to health, but he died in March of 1865.

Throughout the Civil War, Clara Barton had received hundreds of letters from families seeking information about a loved one who had simply marched off to war never to be heard from again. Many of these missing men where known to have been captured. After the surrender of Robert E. Lee, Clara finally had the time to do something about finding out what happened to these men.

On the day before he was shot in Ford's Theater, Abraham Lincoln had a cheerful visit with Clara Barton. He listened to her plans with interest and signed an executive order authorizing Clara Barton to establish the "Office of Correspondence with Friends of the Missing Men of the U.S. Army." Her title would be "General Correspondent."

Operating from a field tent at Camp Parole, Clara Barton again put her gift of organization to work. She began sorting through the lists of missing men, organizing them by states and units, then listing them in alphabetical order. The lists were printed in newspapers asking anyone with information to write to Clara Barton at Camp Parole. Shortly, Clara's small office was flooded with letters from soldiers providing her with vital information about the missing men. Most of the letters were written in pencil with incorrect grammar and spelling. They told of seeing a missing man fall in battle, or often, they were heart-wrenching stories of how a missing man had died in captivity. As soon as the Office of Correspondence had determined a missing man's fate, a letter was quickly dispatched to the man's next of kin, sharing the information that had been received.

In late June, Dorence Atwater sat in his small Washington room and wrote a letter to Clara Barton at Camp Parole, explaining to her about his register of the dead. Atwater was flabbergasted a few days later when the famous woman showed up at his hotel room to discuss the situation in person. Atwater showed her the map he had made of the cemetery and explained how the summer rains would soon wash away all traces of the graves. Clara Barton proposed that an expedition be immediately sent to Andersonville to preserve the cemetery.

Clara Barton first approached William Hoffman, commissary general of prisons, who was the Union equivalent of General Winder, in total charge of all Union military prisons. He was sympathetic, but doubted if Secretary of War Stanton would approve the expedition. He at first advised Clara Barton to abandon the idea but soon realized that such advise would be wasted on her. He wrote a letter to Secretary of War Stanton giving the idea his enthusiastic endorsement.[5]

A few days later Clara Barton was summoned to the office of the secretary of war.

Secretary of War Edwin Stanton

National Archives

– 12 –

The Barton Expedition

The small woman who sat across from his desk of the powerful secretary of war looked almost childlike next to the commanding and trunk-like girth of Edwin Stanton. Yet, ironically, she was probably the one person in the United States whose political power rivaled his. In the wake of the Civil War, Clara Barton was being heralded to the American people as a true heroine. Her charm and grace, along with her determined courage, had earned her the respect and admiration of millions of Americans in both the North and South. The very fact that she was granted an immediate private interview with the very busy Edwin Stanton, showed the esteem in which he held her opinion.

Secretary of War Stanton had been very vocal in opposition to women being anywhere near the combat zone but had been overridden by President Lincoln. However, the meeting this day in the secretary of war's office was not a test of wills. Edwin Stanton had grown to truly admire Clara Barton, and he was genuinely interested in helping her in any way he could.

She explained that in the prison cemetery at Andersonville, Georgia held the remains of over 12,000 Union prisoners, and that the hard summer rains in southern Georgia would soon wash away the loose soil in the cemetery, exposing the bodies that had been buried only three feet deep. Once exposed, the remains would be disturbed and scattered by farm animals. The combined damage done to the cemetery by the rains and local animals would make it impossible to determine where the individual bodies had been buried and this would make accurate markings of the graves impossible. To halt this desecration, she proposed that an expedition be launched immediately to enclose the cemetery with a fence and mark the graves with headboards. Any exposed bodies would have to be reburied and a national cemetery established.

Stanton listened patiently to Clara Barton as she explained about the cemetery at Andersonville. He had no choice except to grant her requests. He knew from experience that this young woman never took no for an answer, and that if she wasn't given everything she wanted, she would soon be pestering members of Congress and writing letters to influential friends and newspapers across the nation. Stanton had no time to do battle with her.

It took Clara Barton less then twenty minutes to get Secretary Stanton's permission to launch the expedition.[1] He promised her everything she would need to enclose the cemetery and mark the graves. This included Dorence Atwater's lists of dead Union prisoners at Andersonville. He also agreed to allow Atwater to accompany Clara Barton on the expedition as clerk and special advisor, since he was intimately familiar with the prison cemetery. He then surprised Clara Barton by mentioning the existence of the "Confederate lists." What the secretary of war termed the "Confederate lists" were several volumes of handwritten green ledgers seized by Union cavalrymen when they arrested Henry Wirz at Andersonville in May of 1865. These were the same ledgers on which Dorence Atwater had worked while he was a paroled prison clerk. Stanton warned Clara Barton that these "Confederate lists" were incomplete due to water damage. The secretary of war suggested that they be combined with Atwater's rolls to make as complete an accounting of the dead as possible.[2]

Clara Barton's expedition to Andersonville departed Washington, D.C. on July 8, 1865. The entire party was traveling on the propeller steamer *Virginia*. The personnel on the expedition were forty workmen, two clerks, (one of which was Dorence Atwater), and a skilled letterman to print the names on the headboards. The commander of the party was Captain James M. Moore who would supervise the work and make travel arrangements. Clara Barton would be the only woman on the trip. She would act as a special representative of Secretary of War Stanton to offer suggestions and make sure that all work was carried out to her satisfaction.

Loaded aboard the *Virginia* was a large supply of necessary materials to be used when the expedition reached Andersonville. This included all necessary fencing materials, precut to save time at the cemetery site, and almost 13,000 factory cut, military standard, wooden cemetery headboards. Also packed away for shipping were a large supply of carpenter's tools, hammers, saws, drills, and nails that would be needed to build the fence and position the headboards. The supplies also included a large quantity of black and white paint. The fence to be erected around the cemetery was to be painted white, and each headboard would be white with black letters stating the dead man's name, home state, and grave number. Clara Barton also assumed that many of the remains would have to be reburied, so the expedition carried a supply of picks and shovels. Finally there was several sets of gardening tools: hoes, spades, scythes, and rakes, that would be used to beautify the cemetery grounds if time permitted.

Clara Barton had four years of hard-earned experience moving medical supplies to the battle front. She knew that thieves were everywhere along the supply route waiting to steal the contents of her packages and that lazy stevedores often lost or failed to load her supplies. She had worked out a system to thwart theft and immediately let her know when anything was missing. All supplies were to be packed securely in strong wooden crates that would not break open if dropped and could not be opened without a crowbar and hammer. To aid in loading and unloading, no crate was to be too large for two men to carry. Each crate was to be clearly labeled as to its contents and given a loading number. The crates were loaded and unloaded by the numbers stenciled on the crates. Any break in the sequence of numbers on the crates would show that one of the crates was missing.

The steamer *Virginia* arrived at the coastal city of Savannah on July 12, 1865. The party had been warned before leaving Washington that traveling in the South would be difficult. General Sherman's army had passed through the region in the fall of 1864, inflicting total destruction upon the Confederate railroad system. As soon at the war ended, the Union Army began employing hundreds of workmen to labor repairing the wrecked Southern railroads. However, by July, large sections of railroad track in Georgia still lay in ruins. The Barton Expedition was disappointed to find that the railroad between Savannah and Albany, the nearest town to Andersonville, was still under repair. To make matters worse the spring and summer of 1865 had been much drier than usual. This was good for the preservation of the graves at Andersonville but bad for the expedition, since the water in the Savannah River was too shallow to permit boat traffic to move up the river to Augusta, the nearest point where the expedition could switch to railroad cars. The Barton Expedition was becalmed in Savannah. They had little choice except to wait for the repair of the railroad or rains to raise the river. The delay could take weeks.[3]

Luckily, the third week in July produced heavy rainstorms that drenched the area and raised the level of the Savannah River to the point where the Barton Expedition managed to travel by river steamer from Savannah to Augusta.

From Augusta the expedition moved by train to Atlanta, where they found that conditions were chaotic. The city had been badly damaged by the fighting that went on around it during the Civil War. The Georgia capital city was filled with carpetbaggers, scalawags, drunken loafers, thieves, prostitutes, bewildered Freedmen, and every type of corrupt hustler imaginable. Every public official in Atlanta had his hand out, wanting a bribe in return for his cooperation. A railroad conductor refused to allow the members of the Barton Expedition to board the train, claiming the seats were reserved for passengers who had purchased tickets down the line. Captain Moore wasn't about to tolerate this type of extortion. He knew that the conductor was only soliciting a bribe and that no passengers down the line had reserved seats. He invoked the name of Secretary of War Stanton, cowed the obstinate conductor, and ordered the party to board the train.[4]

As the expedition traveled through Georgia, an army courier rendezvoused with the group. He had been dispatched to retrieve the original Atwater rolls, claiming they were needed as evidence in the trial of Captain Wirz. Dorence Atwater was skeptical. He believed that the War Department only wanted the rolls to again suppress them. However, as a soldier in the U.S. Army, he had little choice except to obey orders and surrender the rolls. Atwater was afraid that if he failed to cooperate, the War Department would cancel the expedition and order the group back to Washington.

Originally, Dorence Atwater had his rolls returned to him just before the expedition departed from Washington. As soon as he had the precious pieces of paper back in his hands, Atwater immediately sat down and began making copies. He copied his rolls feverishly while he was sailing south aboard the *Virginia*, and while waiting in Savannah for the river waters to rise. It is unknown how many copies Atwater made of his rolls before the U.S. Army courier arrived. However, he must have compiled at least two complete copies. Because, unknown to anyone but a select few, Atwater had secretly passed a copy of his rolls to a newspaper reporter while in Savannah. The reporter would carry them to New York City, where a very influential person was waiting to receive them.

When Dorence Atwater handed over his original rolls to the army courier, to his total surprise, the courier gave the expedition two copies of Atwater's rolls recorded by War Department clerks. This left the expedition with whatever copies of the rolls Dorence Atwater secretly had in his possession, as well as the captured "Confederate lists" given to the expedition by Secretary of War Stanton. Clara Barton hoped that with these records most of the graves could be identified and properly marked.

After a bone-jarring ride over war-damaged and hastily repaired railroad tracks, the Barton Expedition finally reached Macon. Captain Moore, following proper military protocol, dutifully reported to General Wilson, the commander of all Federal forces in Georgia.

Unlike Atlanta, Macon had been spared the full fury of the Civil War. Sherman's troops had bypassed the central Georgia city, marching farther east in his trek to Savannah. In Macon, General Wilson was firmly in charge, not tolerating the corruption, extortion, and rampant vice so common in Atlanta.

General Wilson received Clara Barton and Captain Moore kindly. He had been forewarned by the War Department of their arrival and was anxious to help. His cavalrymen had arrested Captain Wirz and helped assemble evidence against him to be used at his trial. He was very familiar with the suffering that had been endured at Andersonville and was also familiar with the problems at the prison cemetery. He was anxious to help.[5]

General Wilson felt that the expedition might need some security because of the isolation of the prison site and the hostility of local residents. Also, the heat and humidity in Georgia this time of year was oppressive and the old prison site was not a healthy place. He warned Miss Barton that the shorter the amount of time the group lingered at Andersonville the better. He graciously offered the services of two companies of his men to provide security and help with the work. One company was from the Fourth U.S. Cavalry; the other was from the 137th Regiment U.S. Colored Troops. Clara Barton was thrilled; the approximately 200 men, offered by General Wilson, would greatly speed up the work helping make up for the time lost at Savannah.

The Barton Expedition finally arrived at Andersonville on the scorchingly hot day of July 25, 1865. They were surprised to find that little had changed since the prison had been abandoned three months earlier. The pine log stockade, the hospital sheds, the bakehouse, and numerous minor structures were still standing. However, the area had been looted and every stick of furniture, metal fixture, and pane of glass had been hauled off by the looters.

The earth had already begun to heal itself. Inside the compound where there was nothing but mud and filth a year ago, clumps of grass were now growing thick and green. Wild flowers had sprung up along the pine log wall and squirrels and rabbits could be seen playing in the bushes that had grown up around the old hospital site.

The members of the Barton Expedition were pleasantly surprised to discover that the cemetery was in much better shape than expected. This was due to the hard work of a local citizen, and former Confederate Army officer, named William Griffin, who lived in nearby Fort Valley, Georgia. He had heard reports from local Blacks that the graves in the cemetery were being disturbed by wild animals. Using his own money, Mr. Griffin hired a detail of 20 Black workers who went to work reburying the dead men at a proper depth.

Using lumber salvaged on the site of the old prison, he had begun constructing a crude fence around the fifty-acre cemetery to keep out the cows and hogs from nearby farms that were trampling the graves. The fence was about a third completed when the Barton Expedition arrived.

Mr. Griffin discovered that the cemetery had a serious drainage problem. The rainwater formed long puddles between the rows of graves becoming stagnant and giving off a foul odor. He had dug drainage ditches so that the water could be diverted away from the graves.

To prevent erosion, Mr. Griffin needed to line the drainage ditches with bricks. He had built a brick kiln to attempt to bake bricks made from the red clay deposits found near the cemetery. Next to the kiln was a square trough set into the ground. Here the Black workers mixed the red clay and water by laboriously trudging barefooted back and forth through it. The clay mixture was then placed into rectangular, brick sized, wooden molds to dry. When the bricks were dry, they would be cooked in the kiln until hard. Mr. Griffin then had the workers position the bricks along the sides and bottoms of the drainage ditches to channel away the rain water.

General Wilson had gotten word of Mr. Griffin's work at the cemetery back at Macon. He traveled to Andersonville to inspect the site and was highly impressed. Using his authority as the ranking federal officer in central Georgia, he appointed Mr. Griffin to be the superintendent in charge of the Andersonville Cemetery. Although he had no authority to pay the Black workers, he could offer a salary to Mr. Griffin as superintendent. To further help out, General Wilson also sent surplus army rations to Andersonville to help feed the Black men working on the cemetery.[6]

Work began on repairing the cemetery the same day the Barton Expedition arrived at Andersonville. The work was carried out with clockwork precision. One team of workers began erecting and painting the fence. A second team began painting the precut headboards. The expedition's letterman sat in a field tent patiently cutting and stenciling the dead man's name, grave number and state on each headboard. Dorence Atwater was busy running around the cemetery ensuring that each headboard was positioned at the proper grave site according to his records. Mr. Griffin's team of Black workers continued to dig drainage ditches and line them with the freshly baked red bricks.

When a grave was discovered where the corpse was exposed, or in danger of being exposed, grave diggers would exhume the body and rebury it at proper depth. Clara Barton ordered that each corpse be treated with all due respect and care. To prevent the other graves from being eroded by rainwater, bundles of brown pine straw was collected in the nearby woods and spread over the graves. The pine straw would protect the soil from erosion until the following spring, when grass could be planted in the cemetery.

Clara Barton worked from a headquarters tent erected under the trees near the cemetery. Dorence Atwater shared the tent working with his map of the cemetery and rolls, checking and rechecking the position of each headboard.

The dead prisoners of war had been buried in the order that they died and had been listed in Atwater's rolls and the Confederate lists by their grave number. The Confederate authorities had begun numbering the graves after the first man died, and the practice was continued until the last man was buried over a year later.

When he was working as a paroled clerk at Andersonville, one of Atwater's duties had been to see to it that a flat, wooden stake was driven into the ground next to the grave of the first prisoner of war buried in each trench. Using a sharp nail or small knife, each stake was inscribed with the grave number of the first deceased prisoner of war. When the trench was completely filled with dead prisoners, another stake was driven into the ground at the end of the last grave. This wooden stake had the grave number of the last dead man inscribed on it. Smaller stakes, many times only small sticks, marked each individual grave. Atwater backed up this system with his map using fixed reference points to pinpoint the beginning of each trench. With this system, it was easy to tell what grave numbers lay between the two numbered stakes. With this done, and the numbers determined, the graves could be matched with the names and regiments on Atwater's rolls.

Captain Moore always maintained a small detail of armed soldiers, standing by, in case any local people tried to disrupt the work. There were no hostile incidents, but it was obvious to anyone who visited the small village, that the local citizens were not happy at the presence of the Black Union soldiers.

The owner of the property on which the cemetery was located, Benjamin Dykes, protested that the expedition was trespassing on his property without permission. Captain Moore made short work of the bothersome Mr. Dykes, explaining that his property had been confiscated under the authority of the secretary of war. Captain Moore told Dykes that the entire state of Georgia was under martial law and he would arrest and transport to Macon for trial anyone who tried to interfere with the work in progress or disturb the cemetery after the expedition left.

Disgruntled townspeople were not Clara Barton's chief concern. She was worried about the health of the expedition's workers. They were laboring on the cemetery at the very peak of the hot Georgia summer. Dorence Atwater knew only too well the dangers they faced. Besides the 100 degree heat at midday and very high humidity, the group was plagued by fleas, ticks, red bugs, mosquitoes, and yellow deer flies, whose bites were known to drive farm animals mad.

Clara Barton imposed strict rules of sanitation at the work site. All food was to be thoroughly cooked and eaten in sanitary conditions. Everyone was to eat as many fresh vegetables as possible. Men were sent into the woods to pick blackberries. As when the prison was open, local farmers came by the cemetery peddling vegetables. The water for cooking and drinking came from Providence Springs, the cleanest water around. The workers bathed in water from Sweetwater Creek that was by this time mostly free of all the pollution that had fouled it when the prison was in operation. All expedition members were expected to stay as clean as possible, washing their hands before eating, bathing regularly, and soaking their clothing in boiling water to make sure they were free of fleas and lice.

One of the expedition members Edward Watts, the second clerk assigned to assist Dorence Atwater, was taken ill with typhoid fever during the passage up the Savannah River. Clara Barton kept him isolated from the other expedition members and nursed him personally. However, the traveling was more than Edward Watts' body could take and by the time the expedition reached Andersonville, his condition had become critical. He would eventually die on August 16, 1865, the day before the expedition was scheduled to leave Andersonville. Clara Barton ordered that Edward Watts' body be shipped to Macon to be embalmed and it was eventually returned to his family for burial. He was the only member of the expedition that departed Washington to die. However, six of General Wilson's soldiers also contracted typhoid fever and would eventually die.

Despite all the problems with the heat and humidity, the work went swiftly. By mid-August the small white picket fence had been completed around the cemetery grounds. Each grave had been marked with a regulation white wooden headboard on which was stenciled the dead man's grave number, name, and state. In total, 12,920 graves were marked with headboards. Although the expedition came armed with Atwater's rolls and the captured Confederate ledgers, still over 400 graves still had to be marked "Unknown Union Soldier."

Andersonville had the highest number of dead of any Confederate prison, but it also had the lowest percentage of "unknown" dead. This has been attributed to the fact that at Andersonville the prisoners were buried by their fellow prisoners, while at other prisons the dead were buried by gangs of laborers who cared nothing about them. However, the system of carefully numbering the graves begun by Richard Winder and Colonel Persons, and the diligent work of Dorence Atwater, had much to do with identifying the dead.

While the work was going on, Clara Barton used part of her spare time to speak with the local Black Freedmen who came to the cemetery. While the prison was in operation local slaves were threatened with severe punishments should they be caught anywhere near it. Local whites feared that the sight of the integrated prison population would convey an image of racial equality that might spark a slave revolt. They had protested strongly when Sidney Winder wanted to use local slaves to help build the prison. White masters spread wild tales among their Black slaves about the Yankees locked up in the prison stockade, hoping to frighten them into avoiding the place. Despite the dire warnings and dangers of severe punishments if caught, some Blacks did venture to the prison grounds, curious about the Yankee white men who were chained, whipped, and chased by dogs just as they were.

When word spread through the area about the arrival of the Barton Expedition, with it's guard force of Black soldiers, hundreds of newly freed Blacks flocked to the old prison grounds. They mingled with the Black soldiers, admiring their uniforms and staring in awe at their weapons. Most of the former slaves had never seen a real live Yankee, about which they had heard so much vilification from their white masters. The curious Blacks

The Dedication Ceremony of Andersonville National Cemetery, August 17, 1865
Andersonville National Historic Site

also volunteered to help with the work. They were put to work bringing bundles of pine straw to the cemetery, cutting firewood for cooking, and making hot water to keep everything clean. Their assistance further helped the expedition finish its work on schedule.

The Blacks approached Clara Barton with extreme reverence, seeming to sense from the deference paid her by the Black soldiers and white men that she was a person of some importance, to be spoken to with much respect. At the same time Clara Barton's kind eyes and gentle mannerisms told the poor Blacks that there was nothing to fear. They asked Miss Barton respectfully and honestly if they were truly free and "how massa Lincoln's paper read..." Clara Barton was charmed by their good nature and gentle innocence. The Blacks told her how they wanted to help the Yankee prisoners but dared not do so. This prompted Clara Barton to write:

> Remember mothers, that the pitying tear of the old time slave, whom your son helped to freedom, is the only tear that falls upon his distant grave today.[7]

On the final day of work, the expedition erected a sign near the entrance gate to the cemetery which read:

ENTRANCE
NATIONAL CEMETERY
ANDERSONVILLE, GEORGIA

It would be over two months before Congress would officially designate it as such, but the expedition members felt the sign was appropriate because of the orders they had from Secretary of War Edwin Stanton. The members of the expedition were pleased to know that Superintendent William Griffin and General Wilson would watch over the cemetery, making sure it was kept in good order and the graves would be tended properly. As soon as the Southern railroad system was repaired, it would be fairly easy for family members of the deceased to visit the cemetery and Clara Barton correctly predicted many would. That is, as soon as Dorence Atwater could get his rolls published, so the next of kin of the dead men would know that they lay in the Andersonville Cemetery.

On August 17, 1865, all the expedition members gathered in the cemetery for the dedication ceremony. General Wilson's soldiers donned their dress uniforms and formed ranks in the center of the cemetery. Clara Barton wore a special dress she had brought along especially for this occasion. Dorence Atwater and the civilian members of the expedition stood quietly beside the assembled soldiers, waiting for the dedication ceremony to begin. Atwater's chest swelled with pride. He felt that he had at least in part paid his debt to the poor wretches he watched being so crudely buried each morning. Now their souls could rest in peace. The proper honors had been done them.

Directly in the center of the cemetery the expedition had erected a white painted flagstaff. Ironically, it was only a few feet from the graves of the notorious executed Raiders. Their graves had been suitably marked with white headboards just like all the rest. In the northwest corner of the cemetery was the graves of the Confederate guards who had died while on duty at Andersonville. Clara Barton had ordered the Confederate graves and the graves of the Raiders to be treated no different than the rest. Later, the bodies of the Confederate guards would be exhumed and reburied in a Confederate cemetery.

The dedication ceremony began with an opening prayer and a brief speech by Clara Barton. This was followed by the singing of several patriotic songs and hymns. As the American flag was being slowly hoisted to the top of the flagstaff, General Wilson's soldiers fired a salute. With the singing of more patriotic songs and a closing prayer, the ceremony was concluded. Clara Barton officially turned the cemetery over to Mr. Griffin and returned to her tent to do some final packing as the members of the expedition broke camp and prepared to return to Washington.

The Barton Expedition was able to travel back to Washington completely by rail. It took the group only one week to make the return trip. They arrived in the sticky hot capital city on August 24, 1865. The heat and humidity of the dog days of August and the long journey from Georgia had left Dorence Atwater tired and sick. Clara Barton had worried about his health during the time they were at Andersonville. Despite the length of time he had been free of the Confederate prison system, Atwater was still pale and thin.

He bade Clara Barton goodbye at the Washington train station. She had become Atwater's good friend during the expedition. The two of them had spent many long hours talking about the horrors of Andersonville and what he had endured. She greatly admired the young man who had deeply impressed her with his courage, integrity, and humanity. She worried what the future held for him. Atwater had confided to Clara Barton that he intended to have his rolls published in defiance of General Townsend's order and was prepared to accept the consequences of his actions. She promised him her undying friendship and support as he took his leave to report back to duty at the War Department.

Andersonville National Cemetery in 1867

U.S. Army Military History Institute

– 13 –

Injustice

When Dorence Atwater returned to Washington that hot and humid August day in 1865, he knew he was walking into a hornet's nest. The day he reported back to work at the War Department, he was greeted by blank stares from his fellow clerks. Co-workers who had been friendly when he left were now aloof and cold, avoiding Atwater's friendly morning greetings. Dorence Atwater quickly guessed what the problem was. He knew it would be only a matter of time before he was called before Major Beck or General Townsend.

While he was in Savannah, Atwater had passed a copy of his rolls to a newspaper reporter from the *New York Tribune*. Obviously, word had in some way leaked back to Washington about his actions. Dorence Atwater fully realized the consequences of what he was doing when he turned over the rolls to the reporter, but he couldn't bear to wait any longer to get his rolls published. He knew that all over the United States there were bereaved families of soldiers who were prisoners of war and missing in action who had no idea what had happened to their soldiers. The United States War Department knew what had happened to these brave men, but for some strange reason didn't want to share that information with their families. Dorence Atwater found this mentally torturing. He had lain awake at night agonizing over what to do. His conscience and sense of fair play would not allow him to remain silent. Fate had made him privy to vital information concerning the whereabouts and final resting place of thousands of Union prisoners of war and he could no longer remain silent.

Eventually, Atwater received the dreaded call to report to Major Beck's office. As soon as he entered, Dorence Atwater could tell that his worse fears were confirmed. The look on Major Beck's face told him that his secret plans to have his rolls published had been discovered by the War Department.

Beck, who was livid with anger, felt that he had been tricked by the young clerk and Clara Barton into returning the lists of dead prisoners of war. The rolls were, according to his thinking, now U.S. government property. The War Department had paid good money for the rolls and now they were out in the public where anybody could have access to them. As Dorence Atwater stood at rigid attention, Beck gave him a direct order to immediately hand over all lists in his possession or to return the $300 he had been paid. Dorence Atwater had to reach deep within himself and summon forth all of his courage. He had known ever since that day in Georgia, when he handed over his rolls to the reporter, that this day would eventually come. In a way he was terrified of his future, while at the same time he felt relieved that the matter had finally come to a head.

Even if he had not already spent the $300 paying off debts incurred by his late father, Dorence Atwater had no intentions of complying with Major Beck's order. He had endured his last bit of intimidation from the pompous major. Atwater flatly refused to either turn over his rolls or return the $300.[1]

Major Beck called in a sentry and had Dorence Atwater arrested. Beck ordered that his boardinghouse room and truck be searched for any copies of the rolls. None were ever found. Dorence Atwater was marched in chains and under heavy guard to the Old Capitol Prison where he was incarcerated. He was officially charged with two crimes: larceny of government property and conduct prejudicial to good order and military discipline.[2]

After he saw to it that Dorence Atwater was locked up and properly charged, Major Beck reported to Secretary of War Edwin Stanton, who personally approved of his actions. It was vitally important to the secretary of war that Atwater's list of dead prisoners of war at Andersonville not be released to the public or be published. He hoped that the arrest of Atwater would intimidate any other person, military or civilian, who might have a copy of the rolls to keep them hidden, out of fear of being charged with possession of stolen government documents.

As Dorence Atwater paced back and forth in his cell in the Old Capitol Prison, the question that must have racked his mind was why did the secretary of war so desperately want to suppress his list of dead prisoners of war? The answer was politics.

After the Civil War, just as it would be following the Vietnam War over a hundred years later, the plight of prisoners of war and missing in action had become an emotional and highly charged political issue that transcended all personal loyalties and political alliances.

Secretary of War Stanton was, at the moment of Atwater's arrest, in the process of preparing for the trial of Captain Henry Wirz by military tribunal. Stanton realized that Wirz would be found guilty and hanged. But, would the public accept the death of Captain Wirz as an adequate sacrifice for the brutality inflicted upon the Union prisoners of war at Andersonville. Edwin Stanton feared they would not. Stanton was afraid that the public would ask who in the Federal government was responsible for Union prisoners of war being abandoned to the Confederate prison system, when it was in the Federal government's power to have them released at any time by simply agreeing to prisoner exchanges.

Ever since he assumed the office of secretary of war, Edwin Stanton had been politically allied with the group of militant, Radical Republican congressmen and senators. Stanton knew that the future of the Republican Party, and the success of his reconstruction plans for the South, depended on the Republican Party controlling both Congress and the White House. Stanton also knew that the Republican Party's future was also his future.

In 1868 there would be a presidential election that would also choose a new Congress. The most likely presidential candidate of the Republican Party, and the one favored by Edwin Stanton, would be General Ulysses S. Grant.

It had been General Grant, working under orders from the secretary of war and Abraham Lincoln, who had ordered the halting of prisoner-of-war exchanges in 1863. General Grant vocally defended the halt of prisoner exchanges and his name had become associated with the action in the Northern press.

Edwin Stanton believed that it was in the best interest of the Republican Party that the families of the dead men continue to assume that their loved ones died in glorious combat to save the Union rather than slowly starving to death in a filthy, maggot-infested Confederate prison pen.

Less than two weeks after his arrest, Dorence Atwater was rushed to trial by court-martial. The court was made up of U.S. Army officers appointed by the secretary of war. The court met on five separate days during September of 1865.

With little surprise to anyone, Dorence Atwater was convicted on both charges against him. He was sentenced to eighteen months' hard labor and a dishonorable discharge from the Federal service. He was also fined $300 and was ordered to return all "stolen" property in his possession to the War Department.[3]

On September 26, 1865, Dorence Atwater was delivered to Auburn State Prison to begin serving his sentence. The huge, gray stone prison was located in the Finger Lakes region of western New York state. Auburn was infamous as one of the harshest prisons in the United States.

Auburn Prison was run on a program of strict routine and inflexible rules and regulations. The prison inmates had rules that regulated every aspect of their existence. Inmates were only allowed out of their cells to go eat in the prison's cavernous dining hall, attend mandatory religious services, or to labor in dark, cold, and dirty sweat shops twelve hours a day. When being moved outside their cells, the inmates were forced to walk in a rigid "lock step" with their hands placed on each other's shoulders. They had to be absolutely silent and keep their eyes cast downward at all times. They were not allowed to look up and see where they were going or look around at the other inmates. The inmates were led through the huge prison like well-disciplined sheep, staring constantly at the hard stone floor beneath their feet. Auburn Prison had no exercise yard. The only time the inmates saw the outside world of fresh air and sunshine was a few brief moments each day when they were being marched in "lock step" across a small walled courtyard to their workshops.

Inmates had an appointed time for everything: working, eating, sleeping, and forced religious services. The schedule was the same day after day with absolutely no variations permitted. The inmates only reading materials were Bibles and religious tracts provided by local churches. Letters from home and visits by family members were restricted and all correspondence was censored. The inmates were fed at the same time each day and the diet never varied, it was mostly beans, bread, and just enough vegetables to ward off scurvy. Inmates were given a small measure of meat only on Sundays and holidays. Any inmate found violating the prison routine or regulations was severely punished by being put in a completely dark isolation cell on a bread and water diet.

When not working, the prisoners were locked in one-man cells that were only 3 feet 8 inches wide, 7½ feet long and 7 feet high. These cells were cold, damp cubicles that were poorly ventilated. Each tiny cell had a heavy iron door with one-inch wide, crisscrossed, flat, iron bars forming a small window over the top portion of the door. A guard was able to look in and check on the inmate, but the prisoner could see little looking out. There was no light in the cells except what was admitted through the tiny slits between the flat iron bars. The only toilet facility was a small wooden bucket that was dumped once a day. The prisoners were also provided with another smaller bucket filled with water that was used for drinking and washing. The cells were heated during the winter by coal-burning stoves located in the corridors outside the cells. The stoves were totally inadequate and the cells were always cold and the stone walls were constantly damp to the touch.[4]

Auburn Prison had been opened in 1816 and became the prototype for prison construction in the United States. Newly opened prisons were often referred to as "Auburn Style" institutions. It followed the standard penal philosophy at the time that taught that places of confinement should be a "penitentiary", where a convicted felon did "penitence" for his crime. These "penitentiaries" were specifically designed so that inmates would have many long hours of solitude. It was believed that these long periods of meditation, broken only by periods of extremely hard work, would build character and honesty and rehabilitate the inmates.

The day Dorence Atwater arrived by train at Auburn Prison, wearing heavy chains, he was thin and pale. Atwater's health had not fully recovered from his ordeal at Andersonville and the bout with diphtheria he suffered upon his return home. The three weeks he spent in the July and August heat in Georgia with the Barton Expedition had also taken a heavy toll. He believed strongly that eighteen months of hard labor in the primitive and cruel conditions of Auburn Prison would probably kill him.

Horace Greeley

– 14 –

Vindication

Despite his horrible predicament, Atwater still had some hope. Clara Barton had done all she could to help Atwater during his trial in Washington, but her influence was not enough.

Secretary of War Edwin Stanton was able to pass off the whole incident as a small matter, that consisted only of a low ranking enlisted man who had stolen government property for his own personal financial gain. Clara Barton's opinions were passed over by the highly prejudiced newspaper reporters, who felt that since the Atwater case did not involve medicine or nursing duties, what could she possibly know about it. Women were not supposed to know anything about military discipline, army regulations, or classified government documents. Rumors were started among the snickering reporters and military officers present at Atwater's trial about a possible romantic link between Atwater and Clara Barton, who were both unmarried. It was said that Clara Barton's personal feeling towards the handsome young Atwater had clouded her judgment in the matter.

However, Dorence Atwater had cultivated another ally that would prove to be even more powerful than Clara Barton. He was Horace Greeley, the editor of the famous and powerful newspaper, the *New York Tribune*.

Horace Greeley had been born on February 3, 1811, of British and Scotch-Irish parents in Amherst, New Hampshire. The young Horace grew up in abject poverty on a small New Hampshire hill farm, where his parents worked night and day trying to scratch out a living from the poor New England soil.[1]

Greeley attended the public schools, but was the subject of constant ridicule and bullying by boys who were larger and stronger then he was. He had an unusually pale complexion and very light blond hair. The other children called him "the ghost." Greeley was always small for his age and had a dwarfish appearance even after he was grown. Not being able to run without falling down or catch a ball, no matter how slowly it was pitched, the young Horace was never invited to play with the other children. The pale unathletic Greeley found that it was useless to fight back or return the insults hurled at him by the other children. Horace Greeley grew up in an environment of loneliness and fear, yet he never became bitter or vindictive towards those who had caused him so much pain and grief.

Horace Greeley escaped his tormentors by retreating into books. He read constantly and could recite long passages from memory. His teachers were constantly amazed by his mental brilliance. By age thirteen, he had virtually learned everything his teachers knew how to teach him. They would bring him thick volumes of Byron, Shakespeare, and Shelly which the young Horace would read in only a few days.

Horace Greeley decided as a teenager that he wanted to enter the printing trade. In 1826, with the help of his teachers, he was able to find a job as a typesetter with a nearby newspaper. In his spare time he became involved in local politics, listening intently to speeches and educating himself on the issues. He constantly bombarded his employer with questions and begged to be allowed to report the news. While working at the small New Hampshire newspaper, Greeley was unusually observant, making it a point to find out everything that went on in the newspaper office from setting the type to deciding the editorial policy.

In 1831, with only ten dollars in his pocket, the twenty-year-old Greeley headed for New York City. After many days of pounding the pavement, with all his worldly possessions slung across his shoulder in a hobo pack, Greeley finally found work at a small printing office.

The job was only temporary and very difficult. The company was printing miniature Bibles and the type was very small. The young Greeley had an almost photographic memory, and in his childhood he had memorized large sections of the Bible. Unlike the other typesetters, Greeley did not have to keep referring back to the original text when positioning the type. Greeley astonished his employers at his speed in setting the type.

News of Greeley's abilities spread and soon he was offered a new job as a news composer. Even though he did a good job, his employer was reluctant to give him a reporter's position because of his unusual appearance. Greeley was full of energy and after his work day ended, he became a man about town, being seen frequently in the city's finest restaurants and night spots. Instead of being shunned for his small body frame, pale complexion, and light colored hair, men of prominence found Greeley to be a fascinating dinner companion and women found him charming. Greeley seldom drank and all his off-duty social activities were purely business; he were learning the ins and outs of New York City politics and making valuable news contacts.

He was able to parlay his confidential news sources into better and more important positions on rival newspapers. With each job change his salary increased, allowing him to spend more time and money building up his social contacts. However, Horace Greeley was getting tired of the frequent arguments he was having with his superiors about editorial policy and journalist standards. He wanted his own newspaper so he could print the news as he saw fit.

In 1841, ten years after arriving in New York City, Horace Greeley was finally able to secure enough financial backing to start his own newspaper. It was named the *New York Tribune* and was an instant success.

In Greeley's *Tribune*, the news was solid and accurate, but at the same time Greeley included enough backstairs gossip and titillation to make his newspaper interesting reading. Horace Greeley had an uncanny knack for muckracking, and he kept his readers well supplied with stories about crooked politicians and scandals. By 1860, the *Tribune* had a circulation of over 200,000 loyal readers and Horace Greeley was a wealthy man.

The *Tribune* became the voice of Horace Greeley. Because of the prejudices he had encountered in his youth, Greeley had an active social conscience. He used his newspaper to champion social causes. He was an ardent abolitionist and wanted slavery abolished even if it meant disunion. He was so vocal on the issue that once during a visit to Washington, he was attacked and beaten by an irate Southern congressman. He also endured threats and boycotts by New York businessmen with strong financial ties to the South.

In the election of 1860, the *Tribune* was solidly behind Abraham Lincoln of Illinois. After the election, Greeley was an honored guest at the inauguration.

When the Civil War began, Horace Greeley was caught in a moral quagmire: while Greeley was strongly opposed to slavery, he was just as strongly opposed to war as a method of solving disputes. Greeley felt that the South should be allowed to peacefully leave the Union. When the casualty figures began arriving in his office, Greeley went into a deep depression. The idea of Americans killing other Americans was pure torture to him. He began firing off letters to Abraham Lincoln urging him to immediately open negotiations with the South and arrange for a cease-fire. This alienated Secretary of War Edwin Stanton and antagonized the Radical Republicans in Congress who had been his strong allies before the war. Lincoln was so concerned with Greeley's opposition to the war, he had a special cubbyhole in his desk reserved exclusively for correspondence concerning Horace Greeley.

In July of 1864, Horace Greeley made the biggest mistake of his life. He attempted to arrange a "peace conference" at Niagara Falls between representatives of Confederate President Jefferson Davis and agents of Abraham Lincoln. The entire matter blew up in Greeley's face. Abraham Lincoln rejected the proposed meeting as an attempt by the South to stir up antiwar feeling in the North, and the Confederate representative leveled a propaganda barrage against Lincoln for being unreasonable. The whole idea of a "peace conference" collapsed with widespread criticisms being leveled against Horace Greeley for meddling. The Radical Republicans in Congress turned upon Greeley with a vengeance, describing his actions as "Niagara tomfoolery" and "cuddling with traitors."

Greeley was highly embarrassed by the Niagara disaster and wanted to mend fences with the Lincoln administration. Lincoln likewise wanted Greeley's support for his reelection. After carefully evaluating the situation, Greeley decided that no one could have managed the affairs of the nation better then Lincoln had done, even though he often disagreed with him. In an editorial published on September 6, 1864, the *Tribune* officially endorsed Abraham Lincoln for reelection.

After Lincoln was reelected, a bond of friendship was established between the two men. Greeley was deeply impressed with Lincoln's second inaugural address where he said "with malice towards none and charity towards all." The *Tribune* strongly endorsed President Lincoln's humane and tolerant plan for Southern reconstruction. Abraham Lincoln invited Horace Greeley to the White House, where the two men held a long private meeting. Neither Lincoln nor Greeley ever recorded what was said that day, but it was obvious that they departed as good friends and strong allies.

After the end of the war and the tragic assassination of President Lincoln, Greeley continued to be a thorn in the side of the Radical Republicans and the new Johnson administration, especially Secretary of War Edwin Stanton. Greeley was outraged at the arrest and imprisonment of former Confederate President Jefferson Davis. He called for his immediate release. Horace Greeley had a deeply rooted sense of fair play that was just as strong toward the defeated South as it had been for the unfortunate slaves before the war. Greeley believed that any type of harsh reconstruction plan would only embitter the South and the newly freed Blacks would be the worst for it.

It is unknown for certain when, and under what circumstances, Horace Greeley and Dorence Atwater first made contact. However, Horace Greeley was as powerful an ally as a man could want. As Dorence Atwater was wasting away the tomb-like cells of Auburn Prison, Horace Greeley was doing what he could to have him released.

Clara Barton had also been busy during the time Atwater was in prison. She had won the support of a number of high-ranking Union officers the most prominent of which was Major General Benjamin F. Butler. Atwater's family was also active. They were very successful in lining up political leaders from Connecticut to petition the secretary of war for Atwater's immediate release.

For Edwin Stanton, the Dorence Atwater affair was rapidly becoming more trouble than it was worth. He simply had too many irons in the fire. The trial of Henry Wirz was going poorly and there was still growing national and international opposition to the continued imprisonment of Jefferson Davis. Stanton was still being vigorously criticized for his brutal treatment of the Lincoln conspirators, especially Mary Surratt. On top of all this, he was now doing battle with the new president Andrew Johnson over the plan of reconstruction for the South. Stanton simply had to compromise somewhere to silence the growing opposition against him. He decided that Dorence Atwater was the least of his problems. After two months of intense political pressure, the secretary of war ordered Dorence Atwater released from prison. Stanton's order gave Dorence Atwater the dubious distinction of being the only man released from Auburn Prison without a discharge order by a court or an executive pardon.[2]

When Dorence Atwater was released from the dungeons of Auburn Prison, he was weak and ill, but at the same time jubilant to be free. However, after several weeks of recuperation at home, he was advised by attorneys that he was again in a peculiar legal situation created by the master lawyer Edwin Stanton.

Dorence Atwater had been freed from prison by the direct order of the secretary of war. His conviction and sentence had not been overturned by any court, neither did he have any type of pardon or parole agreement. In other words, Secretary of War Stanton could return him to prison as easily as he had released him. The implications of this action were obvious—remain quiet about the lists of dead prisoners of war and Atwater could remain a free man, cause any more trouble about publishing the lists and go back to Auburn Prison. It was a brilliant legal and political move. Stanton had quieted the growing political pressure to release Atwater, while at the same time creating a legal quagmire to silence the young clerk.

However, Secretary of War Edwin Stanton had once again underestimated the personal courage of Dorence Atwater. Despite the fact that he was a penniless convicted felon, in bad health, dishonorably discharged from the U.S. Army, and deeply humiliated and disgraced, Atwater felt he had come too far to turn back now. He would go ahead and publish his rolls even if it meant a return to incarceration and maybe his own death in the cold, wet cells of Auburn Prison.

In Atwater's home state of Connecticut, family and friends were rallying to his cause. One of the key players in Atwater's struggle was his brother Francis, who was a New Haven publisher and would later become a Connecticut senator. During the entire year of 1866, Francis Atwater worked tirelessly on behalf of his brother attempting to get a general pardon from the president of the United States. Several Connecticut newspapers and many state politicians also called for a general pardon for the young clerk. In an effort to help Atwater get a pardon, the state of Connecticut officially honored Dorence Atwater on July 11, 1867, with a memorial for "courageous and patriotic service to the United States."[3]

President Andrew Johnson had been approached several times by friends and supporters of Dorence Atwater seeking a presidential pardon. The president was sympathetic, but also cautious. At the same time he was being pressured for a pardon for Atwater, he was also considering a pardon for convicted Lincoln assassination conspirator Doctor Samuel Mudd, who had set the broken leg of John Wilkes Booth during his flight south through Maryland.

The president was also having serious problems with the secretary of war and the Radical Republicans in Congress concerning the reconstruction of the South. Johnson, a pro-Union Southerner from Tennessee, wanted to follow Lincoln's conciliatory plan of reconstruction, while the Radical Republicans wanted harsher treatment for the defeated South. Under the circumstances, the president felt that he couldn't expend valuable political capital at this crucial time by pardoning Dorence Atwater.

Dorence Atwater spent two years working to clear his name, depending upon the generosity of family and friends for financial support. During that time he testified about his situation before the powerful *Joint Congressional Committee on Reconstruction*. Atwater's testimony was badly twisted by the committee, that was more interested in recording atrocities against Union prisoners of war than learning about Atwater's mistreatment at the hands of Union officials. President Johnson was distressed at the testimony, feeling that it only gave more ammunition to those who wanted to force a harsh reconstruction on the South.

Late in 1867, President Johnson finally discovered a way to help Atwater, and at the same time, keep him from testifying before any more congressional committees. President Johnson would appoint Dorence Atwater as U.S. Consul to the remote Seychelles Islands in the Indian Ocean. The appointment would provide Atwater with much needed employment, remove him from the reach of the vindictive Edwin Stanton, and provide him with at least partial vindication.

In New York City, Horace Greeley waited patiently until Dorence Atwater was safely en route to the Seychelles Islands before making his move. Ever since Atwater had secretly passed his list of dead prisoners of war to Greeley, the publisher had guarded them carefully, waiting for the right moment to print them. He could not possibly jeopardize Atwater's life and freedom by printing the rolls while he was in Auburn Prison or at the mercy of the Federal government. But now with Atwater safely out of the country, he could finally publish the rolls.

In 1868, the Tribune Publishing Company printed Atwater's list of dead prisoners of war. The lists which were officially called *The List of the Union Dead at Andersonville*, more commonly called the "Death Register" or "List of the Dead," sold for only twenty-five cents, barely enough to cover the cost of printing and handling. Dorence Atwater and Horace Greeley had decided among themselves that it would be improper to make any monetary profit from the lists. Printing the lists at such a low cost to the consumer brought Atwater and Greeley much support from the families of the dead prisoners of war buried at Andersonville and made a lie out of the claim by the War Department that Atwater copied the rolls only for financial gain.

The *List of the Dead* was an immediate best seller. Thousands of copies were sold. Any person with a missing loved one in the Civil War quickly grabbed a copy, hoping to find their name on Atwater's list. Civil War veterans purchased copies hoping to find out what had happened to a missing comrade in arms. Some of these people found who they were looking for in the *List of the Dead*, others were disappointed.

Civil War veteran's groups lined up solidly in support of Dorence Atwater and reevaluated their position towards Horace Greeley, who had been criticized by many Union Civil War veterans for his pacifist attitudes during the war. After the lists were published, Horace Greeley was seen by many veterans as a friend of the fighting man and an ally of all veterans.

The *List of the Dead* contained a forward written by Dorence Atwater where he laid out all his troubles with Major Beck and Secretary of War Edwin Stanton and their efforts to suppress the promulgation of the lists. When Edwin Stanton read the forward, he was livid with anger and immediately set about attempting to get Dorence Atwater's consulate canceled. He wanted to have him brought back to the United States and returned to Auburn Prison to finish his sentence.

Dorence Atwater had become a minor pawn in a tremendous struggle for political power between Edwin Stanton and President Andrew Johnson. Neither man liked each other personally nor politically. The two men violently disagreed on several important issues such as the fate of Jefferson Davis and other Confederate leaders, the rights of the newly freed Blacks, and how the former Confederate States should be readmitted to the Union.

It had become common knowledge that Johnson wanted to replace Stanton as secretary of war. To prevent this from happening, Congress passed the Tenure of Office Act that would require the president to get the approval of the Senate before removing any cabinet member. Johnson felt the law was unconstitutional and decided to challenge it by replacing Stanton in defiance of Congress. The House of Representatives responded by voting articles of impeachment against Andrew Johnson. Johnson's impeachment trial before the Senate was a stormy affair. The final vote was taken on May 25, 1868, and it fell one vote short of the number needed to remove Johnson from office.

After Johnson's acquittal, Edwin Stanton resigned as secretary of war. His resignation removed the pressure to have Dorence Atwater returned to the United States. President Johnson's acquittal also allowed him to grant a full pardon to Dorence Atwater for any crimes committed in relation to *The Register of Dead Union Soldiers Buried at Andersonville.* During this same period of time, Johnson also pardoned Dr. Samuel Mudd, who had been sentenced to life imprisonment for his alleged involvement in the Lincoln assassination, and Jefferson Davis was released from prison on bond.

Andrew Johnson did not seek reelection and was replaced in the White House by Ulysses S. Grant, the candidate supported by Edwin Stanton and the Radical Republicans.

The same sailing vessel that brought Atwater news of his pardon, also brought word that his consulate was canceled by order of the new Republican President Ulysses S. Grant. Since the post of U.S. Consulate was a political patronage position, Dorence Atwater had no recourse. The cancellation left Atwater with a crucial dilemma. Johnson's pardon made it safe for him to return to the United States, where no doubt he would receive a hero's welcome from supporters and the families of the men buried at Andersonville; but, for reasons personal to himself, Atwater chose to remain in the Seychelles Islands living as an expatriate American, a permanent exile from the nation that had mistreated him. Atwater wrote to his brother Francis: "The word soldier makes me mad, while the sight of a uniform makes me froth at the mouth."[4]

The Seychelles Islands were a remote and minor part of Great Britian's Colonial Empire. Located about 1,000 miles off the coast of Africa, just north of Madagascar, the islands guarded the sea lanes connecting Great Britian and India, the largest jewel in Queen Victoria's Imperial Crown of foreign possessions. There was ample employment available for an intelligent young man with clerical skills. The Seychelles Islands were the leading exporters of copra (dried coconuts), patchouli oil (used in the manufacturing of perfume), and the important spice cinnamon. Dorence Atwater was probably attracted to the warm climate of the islands and the relaxed lifestyle of the inhabitants. After all he had endured in the Civil War, the warm tropical waters and bright silver sands of the Seychelles Islands were a balm for Atwater's troubled soul.

For three years Dorence Atwater remained in the Seychelles Islands, thriving both physically and mentally in the warm tropical climate.

On Christmas Eve 1869, Edwin Stanton died suddenly under mysterious circumstances at his home in Washington. There were rumors that he had committed suicide by cutting his own throat like his older brother had done. His family's actions in declining an offer for a state funeral in favor of a hasty burial only fueled the rumors that Stanton had taken his own life.

President Grant had frequently been urged to help Dorence Atwater and being a decent man he certainly had a great deal of sympathy for the brave young man. However, Edwin Stanton and his powerful Radical Republican friends were just as adamant against any help for Atwater and the president demurred.

Grant had appeased the Radical Republicans by appointing Edwin Stanton to the Supreme Court, thus giving him a lifetime income and a respectable position. Grant also generally supported the Radical Republican reconstruction plan. So, with Stanton dead, there was no one left to violently oppose any action he took to help Dorence Atwater. However, the president felt he should wait a respectful period of time before taking any action.

Two years after Stanton's death, at the urging of Clara Barton and Dorence Atwater's family and friends, President Grant appointed Dorence Atwater to be U.S. Consulate to the island of Tahiti in the Society Islands. Atwater was at first reluctant to leave the Seychelles Islands, where he had built up a good financial situation and had made many friends. However, Atwater had listened intently to tales of the beauty of Tahiti told by sailors, and finally decided to take the diplomatic assignment.

It is impossible to tell what Dorence Atwater was thinking when he stood on the bow of the ship taking him to Tahiti. However, when the beautiful, verdant island finally came into view on the horizon, Atwater must have been struck by the irony of how things turned out. After all the suffering and death he had witnessed in the Civil War, after all the horrors of Andersonville, after the cold and loneliness of Auburn Prison, after all the slander and humiliation he had endured at the hands of the War Department, Dorence Atwater, like a man rewarded by God for his good works, would be destined by fate to live the rest of his life in the nearest place to paradise on this earth.

Dorence Atwater instantly fell in love with the gentle and beautiful island of Tahiti. Atwater was literally intoxicated with the tropical beauty of the island. He was also quite taken with the almond-eyed charms of the raven haired Tahitian women. Atwater was immediately attracted to Moetia Salmon, a princess of the Tahitian Royal Family, renowned for her great beauty. Atwater, in his polite and gentlemanly manner, successfully courted and eventually married her. It turned out to be a very happy union. The young couple got along well and the marriage made Dorence Atwater a member of the Tahitian Royal Family.[5]

As part of his duties as U.S. Consulate to the island of Tahiti, Atwater received a diplomatic pouch from the United States twice a year by ocean steamer. The pouch contained his diplomatic instructions, letters from home, and New England newspapers.

Atwater was saddened when he heard of the death of Horace Greeley. The eccentric publisher had helped him greatly in his legal troubles with the War Department, and he had grown quite fond of the peculiar looking little man.

After the Civil War, Greeley had continued publishing his beloved *New York Tribune*. Even though he had made many bitter enemies during the Civil War, he would not be silenced. Greeley became a vocal critic of reconstruction policies in the South and the scandal ridden Ulysses Grant administration. He also became a champion of a variety of social causes: feminism, vegetarianism, better treatment for the mentally ill, slum removal, and health care for the poor. He also became an advocate for a variety of new inventions released after the Civil War. It excited Greeley to think of all the wonderful new inventions the future of the United States would produce.

Horace Greeley always had a secret desire to be elected to high public office. For years he considered a bid for the U.S. Senate. In 1872, Greeley was able to obtain the Democratic Party's nomination to be its candidate for president of the United States.

It seemed that everyone knew that Greeley didn't have a chance, including him. He once confided to his daughter that he felt like David fighting Goliath. During the bitterly fought election campaign many of Greeley's old friends and allies abandoned him to support Grant. They loved and respected Horace Greeley but doubted seriously if the unpredictable and often contradictory publisher would make a suitable president.

Fourteen days before the election, Horace Greeley received a shattering telegram from his daughter—his wife Mary had been taken seriously ill and would probably die. Greeley quietly gave up the presidential campaign and went home. His wife died on October 30, 1872, six days before the election. Greeley was a crushed and broken man, suffering from clinical depression and chronic insomnia. On election day, Horace Greeley was solidly defeated by a coalition of eastern money interests, pro-Reconstruction Republicans, and veterans of the Union Army who remained loyal to their old commander.

After the election, Horace Greeley tried to return to work at the *Tribune*, but was so psychologically and physically ill he couldn't perform. He was taken to a private sanitarium where he died on November 29, 1872.[6]

Ulysses Grant remained in office for another four years. In 1877, after serving two terms as president, he retired to his home in New York City. Grant was followed in the White House by another Republican, Rutherford B. Hayes. That same year Dorence Atwater learned that his consulate in Tahiti had been canceled by the new administration.

Atwater had always known that his consulate was a political patronage appointment, and eventually he would be replaced. Dorence Atwater had carefully prepared for the day he would no longer be an employee of the United States government.

Shortly after he had arrived in Tahiti, Atwater had begun to involve himself in several business ventures. These ventures turned out to be so successful that he soon was making so much money, that his salary as U.S. Consulate looked like a pittance.

Dorence Atwater had become totally fixated with his life in Tahiti. He learned the Tahitian language to a degree that he could read and write it like a native. He became an expert in Tahitian religions, folklore, and culture. He often wore native dress and took part in traditional Tahitian ceremonies, an honor never before bestowed on a non-Tahitian. Atwater was held in such high regard by the Tahitian Royal Family, that he was given the Tahitian name "Tupuatooroa" which means "wise man."[7]

The Tahitian Royal Family refused to do any business with foreigners without the advise of Dorence Atwater. Any foreign company wishing to conduct business in Tahiti had to first employ the services of Dorence Atwater as a liaison with the Royal Family.

There was much business for foreigners to conduct in the tropical islands. Tahitian farmers grew and exported breadfruit, taro, yams, copra, vanilla, coconuts, bananas, and papayas. Part of the profits from all these exports was diverted to Dorence Atwater and the Tahitian Royal Family. Atwater was careful to insure that the Tahitian farmers were treated fairly in any financial dealings.

Atwater also organized expeditions to nearby islands where he employed native divers to look for pearls. It was a highly successful undertaking. The once insolvent and disgraced ex-prisoner of war became a wealthy man with tremendous power and prestige.

Atwater met and became friends with another expatriate on the island of Tahiti, the famous writer Robert Lewis Stevenson, author of *Treasure Island*, and *Doctor Jeckyl and Mister Hyde*. Stevenson featured Dorence Atwater as a fictional character in his book, *The Ebb Tide*. Together, the two men founded the first steamship line to operate between Tahiti and San Francisco. Atwater also knew the eccentric French artist Paul Gauguin who lived in Tahiti between 1891 and 1893. Gauguin's artwork acquainted the whole world with the beauty of Tahiti.

His life in Tahiti had totally transformed Atwater's appearance. He had regained all his lost weight on a diet of fresh tropical fruits and fish and took on a healthy distinguished appearance.

Robert Louis Stevenson described Atwater as a man with "a dash of the epicure." An invitation to dine at the Atwater home was highly coveted in Tahiti. Robert Louis Stevenson describes a meal at the Atwater home in *The Ebb Tide:*

> They sat down to an island dinner remarkable for its variety and excellence; turtle soup and steak, fish, fowls, a sucking-pig, a coconut salad, and sprouting coconut roasted for desert.

Dorence Atwater, a self-educated man, learned French, German, and Spanish, so he could deal with the foreign companies doing business in Tahiti without using an interpreter. He also read volumes of Shakespeare, Byron, and the works of the American transcendentalists such as Ralph

Waldo Emerson and Henry David Thoreau. When Atwater entertained foreign visitors at his home near the Tahitian capital city of Papeete, he charmed his guests with refined after dinner conversations on various subjects.

Atwater had ample financial resources to return to the United States and retire, but he was totally satisfied with his life in Tahiti, and any discussion of returning to the United States was cut short by Atwater, who ordered the subject dropped. He apparently visited San Francisco on business when he was setting up his steamship line but never returned to his home town. Atwater carried on a correspondence with his family and they urged him to return home, at least for a visit. Dorence Atwater loved his family and missed them greatly. He was especially close to his brothers. He never forgot that his family had nursed him back to health when he was sick, and had stood by him in all his troubles. However, Atwater felt that as long as he was a dishonorably discharged, convicted felon, he could not return home.

Back in the United States, a group of prominent citizens, led by Clara Barton and Atwater's brother Francis, were lobbying Congress to clear Atwater's name. A presidential pardon was just what the name implied, forgiveness for a wrongdoing. Atwater's supporters maintained that he had never committed any wrongdoing to be pardoned. Only Congress had the power to overturn a court-martial verdict and it had never done so before. Congress debated the issue until 1899, thirty-three years after the original verdict, before it finally took action. Both Houses of Congress passed a special resolution overturning the verdict of guilty and granting Dorence Atwater an honorable discharge from the United States Army. The Congressional action described Dorence Atwater's conviction as a "great wrong."[8]

The news of the congressional action was greeted with great rejoicing in Atwater's hometown of Terryville, Connecticut, where the effort to clear Atwater's name had become a *cause célèbre*. The city's leaders immediately planned a memorial to Dorence Atwater. An opposition group was formed in the neighboring town of Bristol that vowed to fight the spending of public funds for a memorial to Dorence Atwater. They pointed to Atwater's dishonorable discharge and his imprisonment for theft of government property.

The opposition group was directly challenged by another of Dorence Atwater's brothers, Richard. In a open letter to the opposition group Richard challenged them to a debate on the issue. The opposition group refused to meet and debate and the challenge to the memorial failed.

The Dorence Atwater memorial was dedicated on Memorial Day 1907 with Clara Barton and many other prominent people present, but not Dorence Atwater, who chose to remained in Tahiti and not attend the ceremony.

Only after strong persuasion by friends in Tahiti, and impassioned letters from his brothers, did Dorence Atwater finally decide to return to the United States. Accompanied by his lovely Tahitian wife, Dorence Atwater sailed to the United States in 1908.

Dorence Atwater was given a hero's welcome when he arrived at the train station in Terryville. He was honored at a moving ceremony at the memorial built in his honor. Tears filled Atwater's eyes, and long suppressed memories swept over him. The Grand Army of the Republic honored Atwater with a special ceremony for his service in helping to locate missing prisoners of war.

Atwater was gracious and humbled by all the praise and honor bestowed upon him. He quietly reminded people that during the Civil War he was only a clerk and a messenger for Union officers. He felt that he had not done anything particularly heroic. He reminded the assembled veterans that he had never led any heroic charge against the Confederates; neither had he ever captured any important enemy objective. However, heroism, like love, is in the eye of the beholder. To the citizens of Terryville

Dorence Atwater in Later Life
Andersonville National Historic Site

and millions of other Americans, Dorence Atwater's name would always be synonymous with quiet, dignified courage.

Everywhere Atwater went in Terryville, he was swamped by people eager to meet the town's most famous citizen, who most had never met. Atwater was bombarded with invitations to speak to civic groups in Terryville and surrounding towns. Prominent citizens asked his advise in business matters and constantly solicited Atwater to join their business ventures.

In 1910, Dorence Atwater again returned to the United States. This time, he traveled to San Francisco for medical treatment. He was preparing to return to his Tahitian home when he suddenly turned ill and died in a San Francisco hotel room. Dorence Atwater was 65 years old.[9]

On his death bed, Dorence Atwater had requested that his body be returned to his beloved island of Tahiti for burial. Dorence Atwater had become well known in San Francisco where his steamship company had an office. He was greatly admired by the city's Union Civil War veterans, who had established a post of the Grand Army of the Republic in San Francisco named for Abraham Lincoln. When news circulated through the city of Dorence Atwater's death, the members of the Grand Army of the Republic assembled an elaborate funeral cortege that carried Atwater's body through the streets of San Francisco to the pier where a steamship was waiting to return him to Tahiti. The cortege was escorted by a fifty-member honor guard made up of Union Civil War veterans. At a ceremony at the pier, Dorence Atwater's flag-covered coffin was rendered full military honors and a tribute was read from President William Howard Taft, honoring the service of the deceased former U.S. Consul.[10]

After an eleven-day voyage, the steamship carrying Dorence Atwater's body arrived at Tahiti on January 22, 1911. The entire island went into morning. Dorence Atwater's body was born off the ship by tribal pallbearers, wearing full Tahitian ceremonial dress. Dorence Atwater was laid to rest in a simple grave in a lovely Tahitian setting.

Some time in the years after his death, Atwater's grave site was decorated with a simple granite marker, that makes no reference to Andersonville Prison or his famous *Register of the Dead Union Soldiers Buried at Andersonville.*[11]

Clara Barton read of Atwater's death at her home in Glen Echo, Maryland. She was 88 years old and was living a quiet but productive retirement.

After the Civil War, she traveled the world, rendering assistance to the victims of wars and natural disasters. On May 21, 1881, Clara Barton and a group of dedicated followers established the American Red Cross, a non-governmental private organization to render assistance during any type of disaster in the United States. Using the same gift for organization and fund raising she had used during the Civil War, Clara Barton stockpiled food, clothing, and medical supplies. She also put together a top-notch organization to deliver the supplies wherever they were needed.

She also strongly supported the International Red Cross and in 1882 helped convince Congress to sign the International Red Cross Treaty.

Clara Barton served as president of the American Red Cross until 1903, when she retired at age 83 to return to her home in Glen Echo, Maryland.

After her retirement, Clara Barton created the National First Aid Society. It was an organization designed to teach people what immediate medical procedures to follow in the event of an accident or sudden illness until a trained professional's services could be obtained. Clara Barton was convinced that thousands of lives could be saved if only enough people knew basic first aid. The group taught first aid classes in schools, churches, and public meeting halls. The group introduced the emergency medical kit, more commonly called the "First Aid Kit", to the American scene. Schools, colleges, police stations, fire stations, courthouses, and millions of businesses and homes harbored the famous "First Aid Kits" with the symbol of the American Red Cross prominently displayed on the outside.

During the final years of her life, Clara Barton lived quietly at her retirement home in Glen Echo. Even though she was afflicted with all the physical ailments common to a person of her age, she remained alert and active. She pursued her interests in astronomy, religion, and spiritualism. When she heard of the death of Dorence Atwater, she wrote a note of condolence to his family in Connecticut. Clara Barton died of pneumonia on April 12, 1912, two years after the death of Dorence Atwater; she was 90 years old.

PART FOUR

"Grant our brother may sleep in peace."

Former Andersonville Prisoners, Taking a Drink from Providence Springs during a Reunion in 1897

U.S. Army Military History Institute

– 15 –

An Adherence to Truth

The execution of Henry Wirz did not bring an end to the saga of Andersonville Prison. In many ways it was only the beginning of one of the most controversial chapters in the history of the South's most notorious prison, and the man who paid the price for what happened there.

The decades after the end of the Civil War were in many ways as important as the war itself in determining the future of the South. Between 1865 and 1877, a political and social struggle would be waged in the South that would become known as the Reconstruction period.

While the forces of slavery and secession had lost the Civil War, they were victorious in their twelve-year battle against the Reconstruction policies that the Radical Republicans in Congress hoped to impose upon the defeated Confederacy. When the shady political deal was struck in 1877, that removed Union troops from the South in return for Southern support for the presidential candidacy of Rutherford B. Hayes, the fate of the region was sealed for almost a century.

The South would wrap itself in what it saw as its "past glory," with the belief that an agrarian semi-feudal society produced a superior class of statesman in the mold of George Washington, Thomas Jefferson, and James Madison. The South seldom reflected on the laziness, bickering, and absenteeism of the Confederate Congress or of the failures of Jefferson Davis to forge a unified Confederate nation.

The Civil War would be the first war in American history to produce politically powerful veterans' organizations. Over three million men had served at one time or another in the Union Army. In 1865, over 800,000 men had been mustered out of the Northern armies. Union veterans had fought in 10,450 major and minor engagements and had suffered more than a million casualties. Aside from the dead, 360,222 from the North and 258,000 from the South, hundreds of thousands more from both sides bore the marks of the war. According to the *Official Records*, at least 280,000 Union veterans returned home with wounds of varying severity; it is estimated that the Confederate wounded were about half that number.[1]

In the North, the largest and most powerful Union Army veterans' organization was the G.A.R., the Grand Army of the Republic. At its peak, the G.A.R. had a membership of over 450,000 Union veterans. The Southern counterpart of the G.A.R. was the U.C.V., the United Confederate Veterans. After the end of Reconstruction, it gained as much respectability in the South as the Grand Army of the Republic had in the North.[2]

Not only did the G.A.R. and the U.C.V. have impressive membership lists, but the general public hailed the veterans as heroic survivors of a noble cause. Besides their well-attended reunions, they also marched in parades, set up educational programs in schools, and lobbied for veterans' causes in Congress and state legislatures. Because of the activities of the G.A.R. and U.C.V., Civil War veterans were given tax breaks and preference for public jobs. Employers were pressured to hire veterans whenever possible, and pension disputes were quickly resolved by politicians anxious to have the support of the veterans' groups in the next election.

Besides the parades, reunions, and political clout they wielded, the G.A.R. and the U.C.V. also embarked on a massive crusade to see that the Civil War would forever be memorialized in stone and bronze. Within only a few short decades after the end of the Civil war, every town or village that had sent young men off to fight in the Civil War had a statue, stone marker, or bronze tablet erected to honor their service. Memorial halls, museums, city parks, bridges, libraries and other public buildings were built and dedicated to the veterans of the Civil War. Congress established the Memorial Day holiday as a time to clean and decorate the graves of fallen soldiers. Veterans' groups aided by state and local governments established "Soldier's Homes," also called "asylums," where crippled, destitute, or aged veterans could live out their lives in peace and dignity free from worry. Northern and Southern groups worked together to ensure that Civil War battlefields were preserved and covered with appropriate statuary.[3]

Eventually, the passage of time began to take its toll on the membership rolls of the Grand Army of the Republic and the United Confederate Veterans. As the veterans of the Blue and Gray aged and died off, the Grand Army of the Republic would eventually be replaced by the American Legion, formed by veterans of World War I. The American Legion based its membership criteria, charter, and activities on the precedent established, by the Grand Army of the Republic.

The United Confederate Veterans was also replaced as its membership aged and died, but not by another veterans' organization. The U.C.V.

was be succeeded by two elitist and hereditary groups separated by the sex of its membership. They were the United Daughters of the Confederacy (U.D.C.) and the Sons of Confederate Veterans.

In the latter decades of the nineteenth century, the South began to deal emotionally with its slave-owning past and bitter defeat in the Civil War. Southern scholars and traditionalists began to forge a revisionist history of the Civil War, and the events that led up to it. In the South, and in much of the rest of the nation, this revisionist history would stand unchallenged as factual for almost a century. The United Daughters of the Confederacy and the Sons of Confederate Veterans were in the vanguard of the movement that was redefining what the slave-owning South, the Civil War, and the Reconstruction period were all about.

In all-white Southern classrooms children were taught that the Civil War was really the "War Between the States", and that it was not fought over the issue of slavery, but for a nebulous concept Southerners referred to as "states' rights." The institution of slavery was romanticized and depicted as a time of bojangles, banjos, jolly mammies, and happy singing darkies' stereotypes.

The music and literature of the South portrayed a time and place that in reality never existed. Blacks were depicted in minstrel shows and plays as child-like innocents, happy in their bondage, and joyful in the institution of slavery that protected rather than exploited them. Masters were always gentle and paternal men who never resorted to the whip or chain.

The rest of the United States also bought into the myth of the "Old South" with as much vigor as the heart of Dixie itself. Minstrel shows, lavish Broadway productions, and serious drama all perpetuated the myth of a romantic, semi-feudal, Southern society built upon chivalry and a deeply rooted Southern code of honor. The average citizen of the North, trying to deal with the pollution, crime, and poverty-ridden slums that unchecked industrialism created, were quick to believe in the romantic myth of the "Old South." To these beleaguered Northern city dwellers, tales of a warm and enchanted land, filled with stately, moss-draped oaks, and beautiful Southern belles were impossible to resist.

The adoption of the romantic myth of the "Old South" by the Northern states allowed the former Confederacy to celebrate its secession and war of rebellion without appearing unpatriotic or treasonous. In the South the old Confederacy became the "Noble Lost Cause." Confederate generals such as Robert E. Lee, Stonewall Jackson, Nathan Bedford Forrest, and J.E.B. Stuart were turned into Southern national heroes. City parks, town squares, state capitals, and county courthouses, all became shrines to the "Noble Lost Cause." They were festooned with all types of heroic statuary and bronze plaques honoring Confederate heroes and the "glorious dead". In the South, counties, public schools, bridges, parks, and streets were named for famous Confederate military and civilian leaders. The states of

Georgia and Mississippi were even so bold as to include the Confederate flag as part of their state flag. All over the South the familiar sight of the Confederate battle flag could be found flying as proudly as if the South had won the war.[4]

While all this revisionist history was being spread throughout the North and South, Blacks in the South were rendered politically powerless, economically impoverished, and culturally mute by segregation laws and outright terrorism. Their poverty was shared by millions of poor whites who were likewise trapped in the Southern tenant farm system. These poor whites were also rendered politically powerless by the same poll taxes and literacy tests that kept Blacks away from the voting booths on election day.

The South became a region with strange social norms and peculiar political institutions. The South would continue to exist with grinding rural poverty, widespread illiteracy, and political and economic backwardness until the Civil Rights laws of the 1960s freed the region from its semi-feudal and over-romanticized past.

In the midst of all this revisionist history of the "Noble Lost Cause" of the Confederacy there suddenly arose the almost forgotten name of Henry Wirz.

The person who reached into the obscurity of history to lift out the name of Henry Wirz, and again thrust it into the public spotlight, was none other than the former president of the Confederate States of America, Jefferson Davis himself.

Since his release from imprisonment at Fortress Monroe, Davis had spent some time traveling in Canada and Europe before finally settling down at the home of a wealthy Mississippi widow named Sarah Anne Dorsey. The widow Dorsey had remodeled a lovely "cottage pavilion," named Beauvoir, especially for the use of Jefferson Davis while he was collecting materials for his memoirs. Sarah Dorsey idealized the former Confederate president and saw to it that his every whim and want was granted. This was something not lost on the local gossips and Davis' wife Varna, who often flew into wild rages of jealousy over the relationship between Jefferson Davis and Sarah Dorsey.

Jefferson Davis
Author's Collection and the
National Archives

Jefferson Davis enjoyed the beauty and quiet of Beauvoir and the hospitality of Sarah Dorsey, despite the fact that his wife refused to join him in his Mississippi home. Jefferson Davis used his time at Beauvoir to write his great apologia of the "Lost Cause," *The Rise and Fall of the Confederate Government*, which was published in 1881. To revisionist Southern historians of the "Lost Cause," the writings of Jefferson Davis were like sacred scripture. They took his work to heart, even though it was severely criticized by other prominent Confederates, especially former Confederate General Joseph E. Johnston.

With his great literary work on the Confederacy completed, Jefferson Davis now became the grand spokesman of the "Lost Cause" writing and making speeches, defending what he saw as the South's noble struggle to protect its way of life.

Most of what Jefferson Davis wrote and said was ignored outside the South. The rest of the nation was too busy settling the West and building industrial empires to pay much attention to Jefferson Davis' belabored justification for the late Confederate States of America.

However, that radically changed in January of 1890 when the first of two articles by Jefferson Davis defending Henry Wirz appeared in *Belford's Magazine.*[5] In his article Davis called Henry Wirz "a martyr to a cause through adherence to truth."

The publication of Davis' magazine article caused a storm of controversy in the North. United States Army General N. P. Chipman, the judge advocate of the military court that prosecuted Wirz, was particularly inflamed by Davis' writings. He was so angry, he wrote a heated and well-documented reply that defended the trial and execution of Henry Wirz.[6]

Jefferson Davis' article knocked the lid off what had been a long quiet, but slowly simmering, pot of controversy in the South. Southerners detested the notion that one of their soldiers was a "war criminal," the very term insulted Southern honor. Davis' article started a national debate over what had exactly happened at Andersonville, and who really was to blame. To Southerners the case of Henry Wirz suddenly became a *cause célèbre*. The cry went up across the South that Wirz was a "scapegoat," and that the deaths at Andersonville were more of a result of the Union's naval blockade of medicines and the North's refusal to exchange prisoners than any deliberate acts of cruelty by Confederate authorities.

Just as Jefferson Davis' article was beginning to be forgotten by the public, another event occurred which again raised the debate over Andersonville and the fate of Henry Wirz.

As early as 1864, the United States government had begun collecting all available Union Army records, reports, orders, and memorandums issued, posted, filed, or printed during the Civil War. After the war ended, the compilation increased and was expanded to include Confederate records. In 1874 Congress voted an appropriation of money to allow the

War Department to speed up the compiling of the records.[7] However, even with the extra money it still took over fifteen years to fully collect the thousands of war records that were scattered all over the United States.

It proved much more difficult to obtain Confederate records due to the chaotic conditions under which records were maintained in the Confederacy, especially in the final years of the war, when many Confederate records were either lost or destroyed.

It was not until 1881 that the monumental task of indexing and printing the huge mass of Union and Confederate documents was begun. It took nineteen years before all the records were finally published. When the momentous task was finally completed in 1901, the United States government had published 28 volumes, containing 138,000 pages of Union and Confederate documents. This massive work was titled the *Official Records of the Union and Confederate Armies in the War of the Rebellion*, or the *Official Records* or *OR* for short. Later, another thirty-one volumes of naval records would also be published and titled the *Official Records of the Union and Confederate Navies in the War of the Rebellion*. This second collection of naval records would be quickly shortened to the *Navy Records* or *ORN*.

The publication of the *Official Records* insured that future historians or any public citizen would have ready access to the most important documents related to the Civil War. Almost every major library in the United States managed to eventually obtain a set of the *Official Records*. Public interest in the documents was high all over the United States, but it was particularly high in the South, especially among young people born after the Civil War who were eager to learn more about the great national conflict in which their fathers and grandfathers had done battle.

The publication of the *Official Records* presented a fresh view of what had actually transpired at the Confederate prison at Andersonville, Georgia, that was in sharp contrast to the press coverage presented during the trial of Henry Wirz. The *Official Records* provided to ordinary citizens Union and Confederate military documents that were not available to the general public when Henry Wirz stood trial in 1865.

The documents found in the *Official Records* helped dispel many of the old myths about the alleged brutality and cruelty of Henry Wirz and General John H. Winder. During the Wirz trial these men were depicted as sadistic brutes who deliberately brutalized Union prisoners of war. The *Official Records* showed that Henry Wirz, General Winder, and Captain Richard Winder had all done far more than their duty required to try and relieve the suffering of the Union prisoners of war. Instead of being part of a sadistic conspiracy to torture and kill Union prisoners of war, these men had written strongly worded letters to their superiors informing them of the horrible conditions at Andersonville, and they sincerely attempted to procure better food and decent lodgings for the prisoners.

Some of the letters written by Confederate officials at Andersonville were so filled with emotion they actually bordered on insubordination. In one letter written on April 11, 1864 by Captain R. B. Winder to Major J. G. Michaeloffsky, the quartermaster at Macon, Captain Winder complained about a load of lumber at Gordon, Georgia that had been awaiting transportation to Andersonville for the past twelve days. In the letter Captain Winder states: "The very great emergency, as far as the need of it here requires safely excuses me in requiring you to act in this matter. I am burying the dead with out coffins. I shall rely entirely upon you. If it is not here in a reasonable period, I shall be compelled to report the matter to the authorities at Richmond."[8]

Another document was written by Henry Wirz on June 6, 1864 to Captain R. D. Chapman, acting adjutant of the post of Andersonville. In this letter, Wirz complains bitterly about the nature of the rations issued to the prisoners and the deficiency of buckets without which the rations of vinegar, rice, beans, and molasses could not be issued to the prisoners. Henry Wirz clearly states that the cornmeal being issued to the Union prisoners was unfit to eat, and requests that Chapman do something immediately to correct the situation.[9]

The *Official Records* also showed that Union officials were well aware of the conditions in Andersonville, and the suffering of their soldiers imprisoned in the South. On August 11, 1864, a delegation of sergeants, commanding detachments of prisoners at Andersonville, were allowed to send the minutes of their meeting to President Lincoln by way of a delegation of released prisoners of war. The sergeants fully informed the president of the conditions at Andersonville and asked that prisoner exchanges be resumed. The records also document the reaction of General Grant who wrote: "We have got to fight until the military power of the South is exhausted and if we release or exchange prisoners captured it simply becomes a way of extermination."[10]

At the same time as the sergeant's petition was being drawn up, a frustrated and angry General Winder wrote to Inspector General Cooper: "I do beg that you will give the officer at Millen full authority to press everything including land, houses, slaves, teams, wagons, sawmills, etc. to enable him to press the work forward so that we may relieve this prison."[11]

The *Official Records* show that the Confederate officers in charge of the prison did what they could to obtain more and better food for the prisoners and did attempt to get tools and lumber to build shelters inside the stockade, but they were hampered by a lack of support from Georgia officials, especially Governor Brown, and the general shortcomings of the Confederacy in transportation, men, and resources. One particularly angry letter was written by Captain Richard B. Winder on September 3, 1864 requesting delinquent funds to keep the prison operating. "If I do not get this money, I really do not know what I shall do, except to ask to be relieved from this post."[12]

The *Official Records* do not exonerate Henry Wirz and the other Confederate officers by any stretch of the imagination. Clearly, there were serious mistakes made and much incompetence. One of the greatest unanswered questions about Andersonville will always be whether commanders more efficient at obtaining supplies, better organized in allocating the limited resources available, and better skilled in handling men might have averted much of the death and misery at the prison.

However, the *Official Records* do not show any evidence that there was any type of organized brutality on the part of the officers commanding Andersonville. There were incidents of theft and brutality, including the unnecessary shootings of prisoners by undisciplined guards. However, there is adequate documentation that General Winder, Henry Wirz, and others did in fact complain in the strongest possible terms about the undisciplined nature of the guard force. In his consolidated report for the month of August 1864, Henry Wirz writes after referring to the large number of escapes: "The worthlessness of the guard force is on the increase day by day."

The information made public in the *Official Records* was very important to those people who had steadfastly defended the name of Henry Wirz since his hanging in 1865. This was especially true of his daughter Cora, who was only ten years old when her father was tried and hung in 1865. When the *Official Records* were finally published in 1901, she was 46 years old and married to James Sessions Perrin of Natchez, Mississippi.

Cora had risen far above the abject poverty she endured in western Kentucky after the hanging of her father. She had watched her mother laid to rest in a pauper's grave, but she had grown up to marry a well-respected man and improved her financial situation substantially. She became a strong and respected member of the United Daughters of the Confederacy, crusading to clear her late father's name.

The controversy began with the publication of the Jefferson Davis article in 1890, and was fueled by the publication of the *Official Records* in 1901, and became a raging inferno in 1908 when the Georgia Division of the United Daughters of the Confederacy voted at their 14th annual convention, held in Savannah, to erect a monument to Captain Henry Wirz.[13]

The Wirz Monument, Andersonville, Georgia

– 16 –

To Rescue His Name

The news of the United Daughters of the Confederacy's proposed monument to Henry Wirz hit like a bombshell in the North, where memories of the Wirz trial were still fresh, and many Andersonville veterans and court officials were still alive. The Northern press sought them out for comments on the proposed monument and most were in bitter opposition.

Wirz's prosecutor, General N. P. Chipman, became so furious when he read of the proposed monument that he wrote and self-published a 500-page book titled *The Tragedy of Andersonville*. Chipman would spend the rest of his life defending the verdict in the Wirz trial and decrying the attempts to picture Henry Wirz as a hero and martyr.

Father Henry Clavreul, one of the heroic Catholic priests, who braved the filth of the muddy Andersonville stockade, to minister to the sick and dying men, and who testified for Henry Wirz during his trial, wrote in his diary:

> Not long ago a friend wrote me from Savannah that Wirz's admirers in Georgia intended to erect a monument in his honor. Now, I think the poor man is no more worthy of a monument now then he was at the time deserving of being hanged. His name should be forgotten.[1]

The decision to erect a monument to Henry Wirz at Andersonville was not made in a social and political vacuum. At the time the U.D.C. voted to erect the monument, the South was embroiled in the most important struggle for power since the end of the Reconstruction era. The Wirz monument and hundreds of other Confederate monuments would actually become weapons in that struggle.

Following the end of the Reconstruction period, the area of the United States that had made up the rebellious Confederate States of America had sunk deep into poverty and backwardness. The dawn of the twentieth century beheld the South as a land of dirt roads, sharecropper's shacks, illiteracy, and intestinal parasites. Few children, black or white, ever saw the inside of a school or a doctor's office. In a survey done in 1919, it was estimated that people in the South had an income 40 percent lower than the national average.[2] The economic panic of 1893 had driven the price of land in the South so low, it could no longer be mortgaged. This situation was aggravated by the fact that Southern banks had very little money to lend. Each growing season saw more and more small farmers being driven off their own land and into the tenant farming system.[3] Closely related to the region's poverty was a lag in literacy, education, public health care, libraries, and standard of living.

The South had also been humbled politically as well as economically by the Civil War. In the seventy-two years between Washington and Lincoln, Southerners held the presidency for fifty years and the title of chief justice of the Supreme Court for sixty years. The region furnished more than half the justices of the Supreme Court and half the diplomatic representatives to the major world powers; nearly half of the men who held cabinet rank in the pre-Civil War presidential administrations had been Southerners and half the Speakers of the House of Representatives came from Southern states. During the half century after the Civil War, by contrast, no Southerner, except Andrew Johnson, served as either president or vice president. Only 14 of the 133 presidential cabinet members in post-Civil War administrations were Southerners and only seven of the justices of the Supreme Court came from the South. In Congress the loss of political power was just as great. Of the twelve Speakers of the House of Representatives after the end of the Civil War, only two were from the South.[4]

Not everyone in the South was willing to accept this loss of political power and abject poverty. A strong social movement began in the late nineteenth century to free the South from its semi-medieval past. It was led by transplanted Northerners, who had remained in the South to live and work after the end of the Civil War and Reconstruction, along with progressive-thinking native-born Southerners. Inspired by the Populist movement that had begun in the farming regions of the mid-west and the Progressive social reform movements in the urban areas of the northeast, they began in the South what would become known as the "New South Movement."

The "New South Movement" advocated the abandonment of the old Southern economic traditions, primarily the almost total reliance on agriculture, and the start of Northern-style industrialization.

Everyone associated with the "New South Movement" fully realized that industrial development in the South would, by necessity, bring with it urbanization and increased immigration both from Northern states and overseas. Such immigration and shifting of populations from rural farms to urban areas would, by necessity, fundamentally change what traditional Southerners referred to as the "Southern way of life."

To Southern traditionalists, such as the United Daughters of the Confederacy and the Sons of Confederate Veterans, the "New South Movement" was an insult to those who had fought and died in the Civil War for Southern nationhood. Southern politicians and wealthy landowners decried what they saw as a movement to rob the South of its glorious agricultural heritage. Southern ministers preached long-winded sermons warning their congregations of the dangers of selling one's birthright for worldly gain. The traditionalists pointed to the crime-ridden slums of Northern cities as to what lay in store for the South, should it embrace the "New South Movement." White racists proclaimed that the "New South" would be a mongrelized place, full of strange smelling foreigners, speaking in unrecognizable tongues. The sacred vessel, the holy Anglo-Saxon race itself, would become polluted with intermarriages between Southern whites and European immigrants. Religious bigots cried that immigrants would bring "Romanism," the religion of the Pope, to the South. With the influx of Catholics would come parochial schools, threatening the traditional Southern Protestant faiths.

The United Daughters of the Confederacy and the Sons of Confederate Veterans allied together to begin a massive campaign to remind Southern whites of their noble heritage and their duty to the glorious "Lost Cause" of Southern independence. Victory meant swaying the sentiments of poor whites. Blacks had little political power, thanks to the poll taxes and literacy tests needed to vote. Wealthy and middle-class whites had for the most part already chosen sides.

The problem faced by traditionalists was how to persuade a largely illiterate and uneducated population of their noble heritage and the dangers of the "New South Movement."

The answer was heroes and holidays. The traditionalists turned the Confederate Decoration Day holiday, which had been started to clean and decorate the graves of Confederate soldiers, into a type of Confederate Fourth of July with parades, picnics, speech making and fireworks. Other celebrations were held on the anniversary of the firing on Fort Sumter, the founding of the Confederate Congress, and the birthdays of Jefferson Davis and Robert E. Lee.

Ancient civilizations, such as those of Egypt, Greece and Rome, had learned the tremendous impression made on an uneducated populace by monuments, pageantry, and statuary. Egyptian pharaohs, Greek kings, and Roman Caesars legitimized their power and right to rule with bronze statues, ornate columns, and elaborate processions under triumphant arches. The United Daughters of the Confederacy was steeped in the traditions of ancient times in their rituals and beliefs. It is therefore no surprise that the U.D.C. would rely on this tried and true method to halt the "New South Movement."

It was during this period of cultural struggle between the "New South Movement" and the traditionalists that the Ku Klux Klan was formally reborn with a secret nighttime ceremony atop Georgia's Stone Mountain. This new post-Reconstruction Klan was dedicated to the preservation of "Americanism" and what it saw as "American values." The newly reborn Ku Klux Klan was after what it saw as the new carpetbaggers: Catholics, Jews, foreign-born immigrants, and supporters of Black rights.

The United Daughters of the Confederacy and the Sons of Confederate Veterans formally denounced the Klan and would actually work to prevent the formation of a Klan chapter in Virginia in 1921.[5] The United Daughters of the Confederacy and the United Sons of Confederate Veterans were part of the genteel upper crust of Southern society and wanted nothing to do with midnight rides, lynchings, and mutilations. They considered the revised Klan to be an organization whose leaders were low-class barbarians out to make money and build political power. To the United Daughters of the Confederacy the Ku Klux Klan was actually doing a disservice to the reputation of the South as a peaceful and refined land that bred Southern gentlemen in the mold of Thomas Jefferson and Robert E. Lee.

Despite the intense and often bitter struggle between the "New South Movement" and Southern traditionalists, the decision to erect a monument to Henry Wirz was probably not done deliberately to provoke controversy. However, the United Daughters of the Confederacy did feel justified in their move to erect a monument to Henry Wirz, since they felt they were responding to an act of provocation by forces from the North.

In 1899, the state of New Jersey had dedicated a monument in the national cemetery at Andersonville to honor the men from that state who had died in the Confederate prison. Other Northern states immediately followed with plans to erect suitable monuments for their dead prisoners of war. The United Daughters of the Confederacy, long aggravated by signs in the cemetery telling of the terrible events that had occurred at the prison, now felt they had been pushed too far. Since the United Daughters of the Confederacy could do little to halt the construction of Northern monuments at Andersonville, they felt their only alternative would be to erect a counter-monument to the memory of Captain Henry Wirz.

The United Daughters of the Confederacy announced that the monument would be erected at a prominent spot inside the small village of Andersonville. This decision caused almost as much acrimonious debate as the decision to erect the monument in the first place.

The Grand Army of the Republic let it be known in no uncertain terms that they considered the monument to be a direct insult to the groups of aging Andersonville veterans who made the long pilgrimage to Georgia each year to visit the cemetery and hold reunions on the old prison grounds. But more importantly, the proposed monument would desecrate the graves of the Union soldiers who lay beneath the white headstones in the cemetery. Very persuasively, they argued that Union veterans had never done anything to desecrate the grave of any Confederate soldier, or try to make a political statement against the Confederacy, or anyone who served the Confederacy, at any of the preserved battlefields or national cemeteries.

The fire storm of opposition to the Wirz monument by Northern veterans caused a wave of unease to settle over the South. While no one wanted to challenge the right of the United Daughters of the Confederacy to erect the monument, it violated some type of long-held Southern sense of good manners and decency to offend the dead. The city officials in Macon negotiated to allow the monument to be erected on the grounds of Wesleyan College. Savannah also offered to find a site for the monument in one of their city's many parks. Richmond proposed that the capital of the old Confederacy would be a better site for the proposed monument than a small and remote railroad village. In a magnanimous act of compromise, the city of Americas, the nearest city of any size to Andersonville, also offered to find an appropriate site for the Wirz monument.

The controversy over the Wirz monument, and the hints by many prominent Southerners that putting the monument at Andersonville, so near the Union cemetery, would be in bad taste, took the United Daughters of the Confederacy off guard. Its membership was badly split on the issue. More pressure was put on the U.D.C. to change the location of the monument by the officials at the national cemetery at Andersonville. They offered to remove any signs at the cemetery or prison site the United Daughters of the Confederacy found offensive. The U.D.C. wanted assurances that no other Northern monuments would be erected at Andersonville. This was something that could not be done since such matters were in the hands of Congress.

While the pressure not to erect the Wirz monument at Andersonville was intense, the United Daughters of the Confederacy was not about to cave in easily. They knew the amount of political clout they held in the region. The vast majority of white Southerners highly approved of the U.D.C.'s projects. The year before the Wirz monument had been announced, over 200,000 people had flooded into Richmond from all over the United States and several foreign countries to attend the dedication of a monument to Jefferson Davis. The United Daughters of the Confederacy was so pleased with the public support for its monument building program that already the group was planning their most grandiose project: to turn Georgia's Stone Mountain into the largest monument ever conceived, all to the honor of the glorious "Lost Cause" of the Confederacy.

After an intense closed door debate, the United Daughters of the Confederacy voted to accept the offer of the city of Richmond and build the monument there. However, at the last minute, after intense lobbying by the hard-liners who wanted the monument put at Andersonville, the U.D.C. changed its mind and voted to erect the monument at Andersonville.

Part of the controversy surrounding the Wirz monument was speculation over what would be inscribed on the stone. Any words praising or defending Henry Wirz would, by necessity, attack those who sent him to his death on the gallows. In an attempt to prevent future controversy within its own ranks, the United Daughters of the Confederacy appointed a committee to write the monument's inscription. The committee was instructed to keep their deliberations secret.[6]

The Wirz monument was to be an unimaginative structure of a standard design commonly found on Civil War battlefields and courthouse squares throughout the South. The lower half of the monument would be a huge square of granite carved in what was known as the Richardsonian Romanesque style, where the rock is left rough-hewn much as it looked when it came out of the earth, except for the smooth face where the inscriptions were located. Sitting atop this square pedestal would be an obelisk shaft, that brought the total height of the monument to 45 feet. The obelisk shaft would be made from smooth cut stone without any further adornment or inscriptions. The monument would cost $2,000, which was a considerable sum in 1909, when $400 was considered a good yearly wage for a factory worker.

At the 1909 meeting of the Georgia Division of the United Daughters of the Confederacy, the inscriptions that would adorn the Wirz monument were first read to the members present. The inscriptions would, after minor modifications, be published in most Southern newspapers.

Separate inscriptions would be visible on all four sides of the rough-hewn pedestal. The front side would face directly east towards the old prison site. On it would be inscribed:

In memory of Captain Henry Wirz, C.S.A. Born Zurich, Switzerland, 1822. Sentenced to death and executed at Washington D.C., Nov. 10, 1865.

"To rescue his name from the stigma attached to it by embittered prejudice, this shaft is erected by the Georgia Division, United Daughters of the Confederacy.[7]

On the second side of the Wirz monument:

Discharging his duty with such humanity as the harsh circumstances of the times, and the policy of the foe permitted, Captain Wirz became at last the victim of a misdirected popular clamor.

He was arrested in a time of peace, while under the protection of a parole, tried by a military commission of a service to which he did not belong and condemned to ignominious death on charges of excessive cruelty to Federal prisoners. He indignantly spurned a pardon, proffered on condition that he would incriminate President Davis and thus exonerate himself from charges of which both sides were innocent.

On the third side was a quote taken from a letter, written by General Grant and found in the *Official Records*:

It is hard on our men held in Southern prisons not to exchange them, but it is humanity to those left in the ranks to fight our battles. At this particular time to release all rebel prisoners North, would insure Sherman's defeat and would compromise our safety here. August 18, 1864

Ulysses S. Grant

The fourth side contained a quote from Jefferson Davis, speaking of Henry Wirz:

When time shall have softened passion and prejudice, when reason shall have stripped the mask of misrepresentation, then justice, holding even her scales, will require much of past censure and praise to change places. December, 1888

Jefferson Davis

The monument had lain for over a year in an Americus warehouse, carefully packed in strong wooden shipping crates, while the leadership of the United Daughters of the Confederacy made the final decision on where it would be placed. After the decision was made, the dedication was again postponed for several months while workmen erected the monument and it was postponed again, waiting for the advent of warm spring weather. Finally, after all the delays it was time for the big event.

The Wirz monument was officially dedicated on May 12, 1909. The dedication was a gala affair. Special trains were needed to ferry all the newsmen and political dignitaries to the monument site. Local people also flocked to the small village of Andersonville in order to be present at this historic event and the promise of free food. Local newspaper reporters estimated the crowd in excess of 4,000 persons.

The guest of honor and the center of everyone's attention was Henry Wirz's daughter Mrs. J. S. Perrin and her small daughter Gladys. The two had traveled from their home in Natchez, Mississippi as the special guests of the Georgia Division of the United Daughters of the Confederacy, who had paid their expenses. While at Andersonville, Mrs. Perrin and her daughter resided at the nearby Hodges Plantation. The June 1909 edition of the *Confederate Veteran* reported the dedication this way:

Over the hushed throng scarcely a sound rippled and tears sprang to hundreds of eyes as Mrs. Perrin of Natchez, Mississippi, daughter of the dead commander, loosened the veil from the straight, white monolith.

Springtime flowers were heaped upon the monument and speakers who loved and respected the Confederate cause stood near its base under the once rival flags and told many incidents in the career of Wirz, stories of kindness to Northern prisoners and of attempts to secure for them food and shelter which he could not get.

President A. Stovall, editor of the Savannah Press, said that the dedication was not intended to reopen questions long since settled, but to do an act of justice too long delayed. Of the difficulties under which Wirz was commanding many desperate men, some of them brave and good; but others were recent arrivals from abroad who barely spoke the English language, who were without understanding of the causes of the war-merely mercenaries. He was hampered by the exigencies of his own government.

Dr. J. C. Olmsterad, of Atlanta, related an instance of Wirz going personally to Macon, Georgia., to solicit food and medicine for the prisoners at Andersonville.

It was learned that a report had been spread through many sections of this state that the National Cemetery and the prison park would be closed to-day. Both were open as usual and there was no foundation for the report.

Scattered among the three thousand or more Southerners, mostly Georgians, from near by towns, was a sprinkling of men and women from the North, some of whom have relatives at rest in the national cemetery near by. There was not a single incident to mar the exercises, those from beyond Mason and Dixon's line looking on in silence, while those who gathered to pay tribute to the memory of the prison commander performed that service with enthusiasm and a spirit of marked devotion.

The invocation at the opening of the exercises was delivered by Rev. Father McMahon, of Albany, Georgia. The singing of Maryland, My Maryland by the large chorus (and) the firing of a salute by the military company of Americus, Georgia., and the sounding of taps brought the exercise to a close. [*sic*]

The day of the dedication of the Wirz monument was unusually chilly for May in central Georgia. Photos taken of the event show ladies well bundled against the unexpected cold. Despite the low temperatures, most of the crowd remained after the dedication to attend an outdoor barbecue in a pecan grove near the monument.[8]

Following the dedication of the Wirz monument, the small village of Andersonville more or less returned to normal. As the years passed, the yellowish-red clay soil of southwestern Georgia turned the pinkish gray granite of the monument a pale yellow.

Union Army veterans who had survived the prison continued to gather each year over the Memorial Day weekend, camping on the old prison grounds. By 1909, the Union veterans were well along in years and attendance at the reunions was much lower than it had been in years past. The old veterans could clearly see the Wirz monument from the Andersonville train depot, when they arrived for the reunion. It must have been a hateful thing for these old veterans to see a monument erected to the man they felt was responsible for their suffering and the deaths of thousands of their comrades.

Members of the United Daughters
of the Confederacy Pose at the Wirz
Monument, May 12, 1909
                                    Peggy Sheppard

Aside from the annual veterans' reunions, nothing unusual happened in relation to the Wirz monument until 1919, when local residents awoke to find the monument defaced with yellow and black paint. Members of the community immediately blamed Northern airmen stationed at Souther Army Airfield, located between Andersonville and Americus, Georgia. The airfield had been opened during World War I to train Army Air Corps pilots. Many of the young pilots in training often traveled to Andersonville to visit the national cemetery and prison site when they had a weekend pass. Friction soon developed between local citizens and the Northern airmen, who often made unfriendly remarks about the Wirz monument and the glorious "Lost Cause." They soon found that they were no longer welcome in the small town of Andersonville.[9]

At the strong urging of local citizens, military officials conducted an investigation into the vandalism of the Wirz monument and eventually charged three soldiers with the act of painting the monument. However, only one of the men charged with the crime was still in the service when the investigation was completed. This lone soldier was given an administrative punishment that had little effect on his career. The army considered the defacing of the monument a minor offense and treated it as such. The other three soldiers had already been discharged and had returned to their homes in California where they were out of the reach of military justice.[10]

Shortly after the incident with the Wirz monument, the army closed Souther Army Airfield. While there had been some friction between the aviation cadets and local citizens, civic leaders in Americus knew the army payroll would be badly missed by local merchants. In an effort to deflect some of the negative economic impact the base closing would have on local merchants, Sumter County officials managed to get control of the old air base and turned it into a civilian airport serving southwestern Georgia.

The old army airfield near Andersonville would have one small burst of fame before it became a totally civilian airport. After the air base was closed, the army posted for sale most of the old World War I biplanes assigned to Souther Field.

One day, a young man named Charles A. Lindbergh heard of the sale and traveled by motorcycle to Georgia to take flying lessons and purchase his first airplane. The young pilot, destined to become the most famous aviator in American history, took his first solo flight over the old prison grounds at Andersonville.

This isolated act of vandalism, allegedly by Northern airmen, was not to be the worst thing to happen to the Wirz monument. The site for the monument, directly in the middle of Andersonville, might have been prominent, but it was also hazardous. During the decades after the monument was dedicated, it was involved in several automobile accidents, which caused serious cracking in parts of the monument. At that time the main highway between Macon and Americus passed directly through the small village of Andersonville, where the monument was actually sitting in the middle of the busy road. The community placed strong concrete posts and rails around the monument to prevent vehicles from hitting it, but road grime and auto exhaust had so discolored the granite that the inscriptions were hard to read. Eventually the road would be relocated to the east of town, bypassing the small village of Andersonville altogether, but by that time the damage had already been done.

In 1958, the Georgia Division of the United Daughters of the Confederacy tried to get the Georgia Historical Commission to pay for cleaning and repairing the Wirz monument. The proposal to use public monies to fix the controversial monument ignited a debate in the news media that forced the historical commission to defer the matter to the state legislature. A seventy-year-old Georgia legislator from Jones County, named U. S. Lancaster, led the opposition to using public funds to clean and repair the monument. His uncle had been a guard at the prison and had often told his nephew gruesome stories of Wirz's cruelties. Primarily because of Lancaster's opposition, an appropriation's bill to finance the cleaning and repair of the Wirz monument was defeated.[11]

Andersonville National Cemetery, Looking West Towards the Entrance Gate Erected by the Women's Relief Corps

Andersonville National Historic Site

– 17 –

The Peaceful Rest

The early battles of the Civil War had created more casualties than anyone had expected. The combination of modern weapons' technology and outdated military tactics caused battles, such as Shiloh and The Seven Days, to create more casualties than all the previous wars in which the United States had fought up until that time put together. For the first time, unburied bodies created serious sanitation problems for civilians who lived near battlefields. Vultures and wild hogs frequently could be seen feasting on the dead bodies. But, most importantly, more than the sanitation problems was not giving soldiers a decent burial which was bad for the morale of the troops and it eroded public support for the war effort.

To deal with the problem, in 1862 Congress quickly passed the National Cemetery Act. It was originally designed to be only an emergency wartime measure to get dead soldiers buried as quickly as possible. It gave busy military commanders the authority to commandeer the land necessary to bury their dead, without having to enter into troublesome negotiations with local civilians and to purchase the needed property. Hardly anyone realized at the time what ramifications this piece of quickly enacted wartime legislation would have, and how these cemeteries, hastily laid out with no regard for esthetics, would one day become neatly manicured national shrines.

The largest national cemetery created during the Civil War was on the grounds of the Curtis-Lee mansion, across the Potomac River from Washington. This former home of Robert E. Lee was taken over by the Federal government and turned into a military hospital when Secretary of War Edwin Stanton discovered that corpses were being stored in one of the mansion's outbuildings. He ordered that the bodies be buried on the

231

lawn near the house. This hateful act by the secretary of war insured that Robert E. Lee would never again live in his pre-Civil War home, and created Arlington National Cemetery, which today contains the grave of President John F. Kennedy and the tomb of the Unknown Soldier.

By the 1870s, veterans' groups and charitable organizations had adopted the national cemeteries and were busy planting flowers, trees, and hedges to make the grounds more beautiful. They also were tending the graves, erecting suitable monuments, and conducting patriotic services on national holidays and battle anniversaries. They also began the custom of decorating each grave with a small American flag on important holidays.

After the Civil War, the job of maintaining national cemeteries fell to the Department of the Army, which was poorly equipped and not particularly motivated to do the job. Luckily, the Women's Relief Corps, the female auxiliary of the Grand Army of the Republic, volunteered to help. The army was more than happy to turn over its control of the cemetery to the Women's Relief Corps.

The Women's Relief Corps had been founded in Portland, Maine in 1869. At first, it was only a state organization, but in 1883 a national convention was held in Denver, Colorado. Unlike the United Daughters of the Confederacy, membership in the Women's Relief Corps did not depend on kinship to any Civil War veteran, only a desire to serve with hard work with sympathy and an observance of the rules of the order.

The Women's Relief Corps was established for the purpose of assisting all needy and sick soldiers, sailors, marines, and the widows and orphans of deceased soldiers. It maintained soldiers' home for aged or disabled veterans, staged memorial services for the dead, and assisted Civil War veterans and their widows and orphans in obtaining pensions.

When the national cemetery at Andersonville was offered to the Women's Relief Corps, the organization sent Elizabeth Ann Thompson, a Boston widow, to inspect the site.

Elizabeth Ann Thompson had been born on February 1, 1829, in East Windsor, Connecticut. Following her father's death and the remarriage of her mother, she was adopted by Miss Hannah Abbe of Warhouse Point, Connecticut. Elizabeth grew up to be a well-respected young lady, who was deeply religious, caring, and profoundly patriotic. In 1849, she married Francis F. L. Turner, a native of Georgia. She spent much of her married life in Georgia with regular trips back to New England to visit family and friends. In 1853, her husband suddenly died, leaving her a widow without any means of support. Being highly motivated, intelligent, and hard working, she entered into a business career in Portland, Maine, and did very well. In 1901, she retired from her business and moved to New Britain, Connecticut, which became her retirement home.[1]

Andersonville National Cemetery, Looking East
Andersonville National Historic Site

Elizabeth Ann Thompson had no close relatives in the Civil War, but she felt a deep need to do what she could to help relieve the suffering of the conflict. When wounded Union soldiers first arrived in Boston in 1861, she immediately began caring and comforting them during their hospital stay. After the war ended, she became a leading member of the Women's Relief Corps, helping to open the Massachusetts Soldiers' Home. It was while she was serving with the Women's Relief Corps in Massachusetts, that she began meeting with members of the Ex-Prisoners of War Association and the Andersonville Veterans Association. From them she developed an interest in the Georgia prison. She volunteered to lead a delegation to Georgia to inspect the cemetery and prison site.

When Elizabeth Thompson first arrived at Andersonville, she immediately saw there was much work to be done. She enjoyed being back in the warm climate of the South and immediately made plans to stay, buying a winter home near Andersonville. Elizabeth Thompson loved the long growing season that the mild Georgia winters allowed. She was an avid gardener who was most happy when she was tending to her flowers and trees. Elizabeth Thompson was particularly fond of growing roses and also loved the shade and nuts provided by pecan trees.

Under the direction of Elizabeth Ann Thompson, using money raised from donations in the North, the Women's Relief Corps set about enclosing the entire park with a strong wire fence to keep out wandering cows and wild hogs. An ornate iron gate was placed at the entrance and crowned with an arched sign reading "Andersonville Prison Park". A paved walkway was laid down in the cemetery, and a bold program of planting shade trees, flowering plants, and shrubs was begun. All total, the Women's Relief Corps, under the tireless direction of Elizabeth Ann Thompson, planted over 200 pecan trees and 300 rose bushes, plus hundreds of other plants and bushes.[2]

The actions of the Women's Relief Corps did not meet with universal approval. The United Daughters of the Confederacy strongly objected to the wordings of many of the signs the Women's Relief Corps erected telling the history of the prison from a decidedly Northern point of view.

Most of the women who served with the Women's Relief Corps at Andersonville were Northern born and educated. They often clashed violently with local white residents, who resented their attitudes towards the late war and what the Southern women considered the Women's Relief Corps "too friendly" relationship with local Black people, who were employed tending the cemetery.

Because Elizabeth Ann Thompson had lived in Georgia before the Civil War and was familiar with Southern attitudes towards race and history, she attempted to avoid antagonizing the local citizens, but was firm in her duty to the thousands of Union dead who were in her care.

While most important, and many relatively minor, Civil War battlefields have been set aside and covered with appropriate memorial statuary,

Andersonville is the only Civil War prison to be preserved. It was almost as if both sides were anxious to rid themselves of these places where war puts on its least heroic and most barbaric face. However, the preservation of the cemetery at Andersonville was not done without considerable controversy.

Many in the North claimed that the state of Georgia was attempting to cover up the terrible events that had occurred at Andersonville. One of them was Benjamin F. Gue, an Iowa newspaper editor, former state senator, and lieutenant governor of Iowa. He made a shocking claim in an article published in the *Iowa State Register* of May 30, 1884. Gue claimed that while traveling through Georgia in 1884, he discovered that the small village of Andersonville had been removed from all state maps published after the war. Even though Andersonville was a regular refueling stop for the Central Georgia Railroad, no mention of the town could be found in any railroad guides or timetables. Gue also claimed that local citizens feign no knowledge of such a place, and were of no help to travelers.[3]

Benjamin Gue's claims, while seemingly inconceivable, probably have a lot of credence. Shortly after the Civil War ended, former prisoners of Andersonville began to have annual reunions at the national cemetery and the old abandoned prison grounds. The Andersonville Veterans Association had been founded in September 1865, just before the beginning of the Wirz trial. It was dedicated to keeping alive the memory of the men who had died in Andersonville and to help survivors of Andersonville and their widows and orphans obtain pensions. The Andersonville Veterans Association organized the first reunions shortly after the end of the war. The first were held in the North, but later, as rail transportation to the South improved, the reunions began to be held at Andersonville over the Memorial Day weekend. After the Women's Relief Corps took over the management of the national cemetery, the veterans became their guests.

The ladies of the Women's Relief Corps were determined to do everything in their power to assist the veterans and make their visit to Andersonville as pleasant as possible.

Elizabeth Thompson ordered that the thick underbrush that covered the old prison grounds be cleared away, and that the cleared area be seeded with Bermuda grass to prevent erosion. A roadway was built around the old prison site and two strong wooden bridges were built over Sweetwater Creek. Gangs of Black workers, employed by the Women's Relief Corps, braved poisonous snakes and knee-deep water to clear the creek bed of the tangled undergrowth of weeds and vines that had grown up since the end of the war. Large bonfires consumed what was left of the rotting logs that had made up the old stockade walls. Stone markers were set into place to indicate the location of the North and South Gates, and smaller stones marked the perimeter of the stockade. Later, small white stakes would mark the location of the deadline.

The Union veterans who gathered at Andersonville each year would stage prayer services in the cemetery, listen to patriotic speeches, sing hymns, and place flowers on the graves of their fellow prisoners who would never go home. After the various ceremonies were finished, the veterans would wander in small groups down a narrow dirt road to the old prison site, where they would attempt to locate the spot where their she-bang had been pitched. Many veterans would bring their families with them, and as the afternoon shadows fell, the family groups could be seen wandering over the old prison grounds, listening attentively as harrowing tales of life inside the Confederate prison pen were passed on to a new generation.

The veterans would always end their visit with a symbolic toast to fallen comrades with water drawn from Providence Springs. Many of the veterans would proudly drink from the same tin cups they had carried during the Civil War.

Most Civil War reunions were racially segregated. Blacks did not enter the Union Army until 1863, and were then placed in all black regiments commanded by white officers. Since veterans' reunions were usually organized by regiments, they were almost always separated by the color line. However, the military prison at Andersonville had held all races, nationalities, and religions. They suffered as equals, so they insisted that during their annual reunions each veteran without regard to race, religion, or nationality be treated as an equal.

This did not set well with the local citizens of Macon, Americus, or Andersonville. They dreaded the annual gathering of former prisoners of war in their midst and did everything in their power to make the returning veterans feel unwelcome. Apparently, based on Benjamin Gue's account, to the point of deleting the name of Andersonville from maps and railroad timetables. The train depot at Macon, where returning veterans had to change trains to go to Andersonville, was particularly unfriendly. Sometimes conductors refused to stop at Andersonville passing on to Americus, forcing the veterans to walk the ten miles back to Andersonville. Local newspapers decried the annual reunions as drunken affairs, filled with all forms of lewdness and bawdy behavior.[4] Wives and daughters who accompanied the veterans to Andersonville were assumed to be "loose women" or outright prostitutes until proven otherwise.

The newspapers also protested the fact that the veterans ignored local and state laws prohibiting the mixing of the races. They editorialized that the integrated gathering each year at Andersonville would have a bad influence upon local Blacks and young people, who might be led to challenge long held social practices.

Despite all the local resistance, the veterans continued to hold their racially integrated reunions each year, seemingly unconcerned with the local opposition. Apparently, after enduring all the hardships and dangers

Entrance to Andersonville National Cemetery, Circa 1910

Andersonville National Historic Site

of the Civil War, the former prisoners of Andersonville would not be deterred by the resentments and fears of local citizens.

The Association of Ex-Prisoners of War and the Andersonville Veterans Association lobbied Congress to have the old prison grounds set aside as an historical landmark. While approximately 13,000 prisoners lay buried in the Andersonville cemetery, experts believe that twice to three times that number died on the way home or shortly after reaching the North. Even more died weeks and months later from diseases directly attributed to their imprisonment. As many as 30,000 men probably died as a direct result of the conditions in the Confederate prison at Andersonville, Georgia. This was a death rate on a par with many of the more famous Civil War battles. The Andersonville Veterans Association argued forcefully that the United States government owed it to the dead, and surviving veterans, to preserve the prison grounds at Andersonville, just as it had the important battlefields of the Civil War.

The notion that the Andersonville Prison site should be preserved was bitterly opposed in the South. Southern congressmen felt it would be unfair to preserve the prison site at Andersonville, when no Union prison had been likewise preserved. No where was the sentiment against preserving the prison site at Andersonville stronger than in the state of Georgia. State officials were willing to do whatever they could to see that the old prison grounds did not fall into Federal hands. However, unknown to Georgia officials, events had already transpired shortly after the Civil War that would result in the old prison grounds being preserved.

The legal owner of the property on which the prison was located was Benjamin Dykes, Andersonville's station master and the small community's largest landowner and wealthiest citizen. It was Benjamin Dykes who had misled Sidney Winder about local opposition to the prison and had convinced him to locate the prison on the banks of the small creek.

During the war, Dykes had been a hardcore Confederate sympathizer; and while the prison was open, he had entertained General Winder and Captain Wirz in his home, soliciting their favors. He had probably made a considerable amount of money doing business with the Confederate guards and Union prisoners of war.

Despite his friendship with General Winder and Captain Wirz, Dykes had protested strongly when he discovered that Union prisoners were being buried on his property. General Winder quickly dismissed his protests, claiming that Dykes had being adequately compensated for the use of his property. Dykes became even more angry when the Federal government seized the cemetery grounds and turned it into a national cemetery, without paying him for the land.

In 1866, after the prison had been abandoned for almost a year, Dykes penned a letter to Secretary of War Edwin Stanton. In the letter, Dykes stated that during the war he had leased the land to the Confederate government for the purpose of building a prison supposedly to house only

10,000 prisoners of war. He had been paid in Confederate money which was now worthless. Dykes had been trying to sell the land since the war ended, but could find no buyers. He offered to sell to the Union War Department 990 acres for $5,000.[5]

The 990 acres Dykes offered for sale included much more than the eighteen acres of the prison site, and the price that Dykes asked for the land was exorbitant. Following the Civil War, land prices in the rural South fell so low that land unsuitable for farming, such as the pine woods around Andersonville, was almost worthless and good farm land was worth little more. There is no record of Edwin Stanton ever responding to Dykes' letter, but apparently the secretary of war could see no reason to buy the land.

At this point, exactly what happened becomes unclear. Apparently, there were some type of secret, off and on, negotiations between Dykes and the War Department, that took place over a period of the next nine years.

Pressured by the Andersonville Veterans Association, the Association of Ex-prisoners of War, the Grand Army of the Republic, and the Women's Relief Corps, members of Congress began a low-key lobbying effort to get the War Department to purchase and preserve the old prison site. War Department officials wanted to keep the negotiations secret to keep from angering Georgia officials who might take steps to sabotage the land sale. Benjamin Dykes, hoping to get rid of his basically worthless land at a good price, certainly did not want to alert his Georgia neighbors that he was attempting to sell his land to the War Department.

Finally, in 1875, a deal was struck. The land records of Macon County, Georgia show that 120 acres of land was transferred from Benjamin and Elizabeth Dykes to the United States government for $3,300. The deed was dated February 9, 1875.[6]

While he still owned the property, Dykes apparently had made money by selling small hermetically sealed bottles supposedly containing water from Providence Springs. He also built a small wooden shelter over the spring, and charged a fee for visitors who wanted to visit it. When the prison site transferred to the control of the Women's Relief Corps, they replaced Benjamin Dykes' shelter with a much larger and more stable structure, that included a basin made from stones and mortar to collect the spring water. They also halted the practice of charging a fee to visit the spring and selling bottled water, although bottles supposedly containing Providence Springs' water could be purchased in various parts of Macon and Sumter county as late as 1896.[7]

In 1901 the Women's Relief Corps, using money made from selling pecans raised on the property, built a granite Greek Revival building over Providence Springs. The Andersonville Veterans Association also raised money through donations, and added a catch basin to the new spring house.

In 1910, the Women's Relief Corps was forced to return control of the Andersonville cemetery and prison grounds back to the Department of the Army. With the death of Elizabeth Thompson, and the advancing age of the other women available to take over her duties, the Board of Trustees of the Women's Relief Corps felt it could no longer perform their duties at Andersonville in an adequate manner. The Department of the Army would administer the park for sixty years, until 1970, when it was given over to the National Park Service who still operates it today as Andersonville Historical Site.

Today, Andersonville, Georgia is a quiet and pleasant little village. With the exception of the paved roads, automobiles, and electric lights, it probably looks little different today than it did before the Civil War. Its population today is only slightly larger, and the buildings found in the historic area are all of the style one would find during the Civil War era.

The countryside around Andersonville is gently rolling hills covered with a mixture of pine forests, pecan groves, and cotton fields. The state of Georgia, now hungry for tourist dollars, no longer tries to keep out-of-state visitors away from Andersonville. Each year, an estimated 150,000 visitors from all over the United States, and many foreign countries, come to Andersonville Military Park which includes the national cemetery and the old prison site.

When a visitor tours the old prison grounds or walks reflectively through the cemetery, one thought keeps recurring: time heals all wounds. It is physically impossible to have any glint of what a horrible place Andersonville was during that terrible summer of 1864. The grounds today are adorned with pecan trees, azalea bushes, sweet smelling magnolias and dogwood trees that bloom each spring in an explosion of white and pink blossoms.

Summer turns the park a dark lush green; in the fall early frosts bring on a wash of golden-red foliage; and even in the winter, when the trees are barren, and the grass is brown, the grounds have a somber beauty.

After the end of the Civil War, the remains of Union soldiers killed in fighting in other parts of Georgia were moved to the Andersonville cemetery and are buried separate from the prison camp dead. The bodies of Confederate guards, who had died when the prison was in operation and had been buried near the prisoners, were removed to Confederate cemeteries in other locations.

Many visitors are surprised to find that only part of the cemetery holds the graves of Civil War dead. Veterans of later wars are also buried at Andersonville. It is not uncommon for a visitor to encounter a funeral in progress. Military honor guards from nearby Fort Benning, Georgia and the Marine Corps base at Albany, Georgia, smartly render military honors to veterans of World War II, Korea, and Vietnam. The sharp crack of musketry and the soft sound of Taps often float over the cemetery as another veteran is laid to rest.

The change from wooden to marble headstones did not occur at Andersonville until 1877, and it took over three years before the work was completed. The marble for the graves at Andersonville came from a north Georgia quarry and was shipped to the small depot by rail. The marble was already cut into headstone-sized slabs, that were inscribed on the site. Each marble headstone contains only the name and unit of the dead soldier.

Of all the graves in the cemetery at Andersonville, the one that attracts the most attention is that of Corporal Lewis S. Tuttle, Company F, 32nd Maine Infantry. Corporal Tuttle's grave lies in Section H, a remote part of the cemetery near the western perimeter wall. Each year thousands of visitors seek out grave number 12,196 to photograph Corporal Tuttle's unique headstone, that is topped by a small white dove, obviously carved by a skilled stonecutter, out of the same piece of marble as the headstone. Corporal Tuttle's headstone is the only one in Andersonville so adorned and why it is so uniquely decorated is still a mystery.

Historians have sought Corporal Tuttle's military records for some clue as to why his headstone is different from all the others. The records show that he was from Saco, Maine, and that his pre-war career was that of a barrel maker. He was married and had two children. His wife was named Lydia and his two daughters were named Clara Ella and Addie Cora. Lewis Tuttle had two brothers Loren and David, also in the 32nd Maine Infantry. Loren was wounded and discharged from the Union Army as disabled; however, no records have ever been found concerning what happened to Loren Tuttle after the war. David Tuttle was also captured and was confined at Andersonville with his brother. Lewis Tuttle died of diar-

rhea on November 30, 1864, a little more than a month before his brother David died of scorbutus (scurvy) on December 20, 1864. David Tuttle lies near his brother, also in Section H, grave number 12,322. His headstone contains no unusual decorations or markings.[8]

There are many speculations as to why Lewis Tuttle's headstone would be specially adorned with a white dove. The white dove has long been a symbol of peace, the Holy Spirit, and God's love. The white dove was a common object of sacrifice in ancient Israel for poor people who could not afford to sacrifice a lamb. Tradition has it that Mary and Joseph offered two white doves as a sacrifice when the Christ child was presented in the temple, a long-standing Jewish tradition.

Grave of Lewis Tuttle
Author's Collection

Some have speculated that Tuttle's surviving brother, or his wife, or one of his children, who would have been grown by 1877, may have arranged for Lewis Tuttle's gravestone to be adorned with the dove. There are several holes in this theory. The first is why wasn't Lewis Tuttle's brother's grave also adorned with a dove? It would not be logical for a family to honor one brother and not the other. Secondly, at the time Tuttle's stone was installed, all headstones in national cemeteries were paid for by the government and had to be uniform. That meant that Lewis Tuttle's headstone was illegally adorned with the small dove. The big question is: how did it pass inspection, either at the stonecutter's workshop, or when it was installed in the cemetery?

The most probable theory is that one of the stonecutters simply became bored with the repetition of cutting stone after stone in the same manner and decided to add a flourish. Lewis Tuttle's headstone was probably chosen at random for the honor. How such a headstone passed inspection is a mystery that will probably never be solved. Barring the discovery of some unknown documentation on the subject, the secret of Corporal Lewis Tuttle's stone dove will probably remain a mystery and a part of the unique mystique of Andersonville National Cemetery.

During a heavy rainstorm in 1899, two bodies were washed out of their graves. The skeletal remains were widely scattered by the flooding before the accidental disinterment was discovered by cemetery workers. It was impossible to determine which of the bones belonged to which body; so the remains were gathered together and buried in a single grave, number 13,718. The inscription reads simply "Two U.S. Soldiers."

Another of the thousands of soldiers buried in the national cemetery at Andersonville is Sergeant James Wiley, Company B, 59th New York Infantry. James Wiley was an Ohio blacksmith with a powerful body, forged strong by long hours of hard work. He enlisted in the Union Army in 1861 at the age of 23, then reenlisted when his original 90-day term expired. The highly patriotic young man was determined to see the Civil War through to its completion. Quickly promoted to sergeant, he campaigned with the Army of the Potomac, fighting in its many failed attempts to capture the Confederate capitol of Richmond. At the Battle of Gettysburg, the 59th New York's position on Cemetery Ridge came under heavy assault by Confederate forces, led by Major General Richard Anderson. During the bloody and fierce battle, James Wiley captured the regimental flag of the 48th Georgia Infantry. For this heroic act, Wiley was promoted to first sergeant and was placed into consideration for a new military decoration that had been authorized by an act of Congress on March 3, 1863. The new decoration was to be called the Medal of Honor.

While military authorities in Washington were mulling over Sergeant Wiley's act at Gettysburg, he continued to face death in the Union Army. First Sergeant Wiley was captured on June 22, 1864 by Confederate forces who overran his position in the Union trenches before Petersburg. Sergeant Wiley was in the stockade at Andersonville on December 1, 1864, the day he was formally awarded the Medal of Honor. He would never see or learn about the great honor his nation had bestowed upon him. Confederate records show that Sergeant James Wiley died of chronic diarrhea on February 7, 1865; he was 26 years old. Today, Sergeant James Wiley, winner of the Congressional Medal of Honor, lies in Section H, grave number 12,607. He is the only known Civil War Medal of Honor winner buried at Andersonville.[9]

The first recorded burial in Andersonville Cemetery was Adam Swarner of the 2nd New York Cavalry, which was the same unit in which Dorence Atwater served. Swarner had contacted pneumonia during the long train ride to Andersonville, and died within forty-eight hours after he arrived.

Compared to the thousands who came after him, Adam Swarner had a luxurious funeral. Richard Winder had a makeshift coffin built from some rifle cases, and even arranged to have a chaplain conduct a brief funeral service.

In July, Adam Swarner's brother Jacob joined him in the prison cemetery. He had died of Anasarca, a horrible affliction where the joints fill with fluid and swell to grotesque proportions with a constant draining of the fluid. Caused by acute malnutrition, Anasarca almost always leads to death if not treated immediately with proper nourishment. Dorence Atwater knew both of the Swarner brothers, having served with them in the 2nd New York Cavalry before their capture. In his *List of the Dead*, Atwater begins his numbering system with the grave of Adam Swarner, listing his final resting place as grave number one. Next to Jacob Swarner's name, Atwater notes that he was the unit's bugler. This small personal note, by a friend to a dead comrade, gives Jacob Swarner's death a touch more humanity than most of the other names in his famous death register. Jacob Swarner lies in Section Q, grave number 4,005.

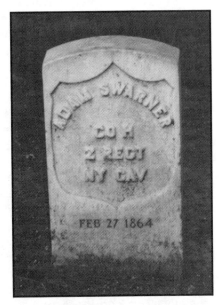

Grave of Adam Swarner, Andersonville's First Victim
Author's Collection

In 1899 the state of New Jersey decided to erect a monument in the national cemetery at Andersonville, Georgia; it would be the first state to do so.[10] The New Jersey monument is more or less representative of the types of monuments commonly found on Civil War battlefields and court-house squares across the United States. Located near the center of the cemetery, it shows a well-dressed, well-fed and armed Civil War soldier in winter dress, standing atop an ornate square pedestal. The New Jersey monument bears the inscription "DEATH BEFORE DISHONOR", as if the men at Andersonville were engaged in some type of ferocious battle. There was no "honor" in the way men died inside the muddy and disease-ridden Andersonville stockade.

Between 1900 and 1904, Massachusetts, Ohio, Rhode Island, and Michigan also erected monuments. All four of these states chose to place their monuments on the old prison grounds, instead of the cemetery. They were short, squat, tombstone-like structures that honor the men from their states who perished in the prison.

In 1905, the states of Pennsylvania and Iowa placed well-designed monuments in the national cemetery. In the years ahead, these two monu-ments would draw more attention, and favorable comment, than any erected before or since. The Pennsylvania monument is a covered archway, topped by an eight-foot high bronze statue of a youthful looking Union soldier. However, unlike the soldier atop the New Jersey monument, this young man is unarmed. He appears to be a recently captured prisoner of war, his head is bowed, and appears to be staring down at the rows of graves. The original plan was for the statue to be facing northward towards the prisoner's home states. However, since the Pennsylvania monument was on the north side of the cemetery, it appeared as if the soldier atop the monument was turning his back on the graves, an impression the designers did not wish to convey. Therefore, the design was altered and the statue faced the south, toward the rows of dead prisoners' graves.

Within the archway of the Pennsylvania monument are a series of bronze plaques, one of which gives a remarkably accurate depiction of soldiers dipping their tin cups, attached to end of long poles to avoid cross-ing the deadline, into the pool of water formed by Providence Springs.

The Iowa monument also pays homage to Providence Springs. On the monument is inscribed "GOD SMOTE THE HILL AND GAVE THEM DRINK, AUGUST 16, 1864".

In 1907, the state of Connecticut constructed its monument in the cemetery. This long, low, work was also topped by an eight-foot high statue of a youthful-looking, Union soldier, hat in hand, looking reflectively at the graves. Sculpted by Boston artist Bela Lyon Pratt, the monument's inscrip-tion tells of the artist's intention when he modeled the work. Pratt wished to depict a typical New England lad, of teenage years, who had been recently taken prisoner and disarmed. The youth's face reflects the worry of what lies ahead, while at the same time showing courage in the face of his adversity.

The Indiana monument, erected in 1908, is a beautiful gray marble slab, flanked by four Corinthian columns. Its inscription reads: "TILL THE MOUNTAINS ARE WORN OUT, AND THE RIVERS CEASE TO FLOW, SHALL THEIR NAMES BE KEPT FRESH WITH REVERENCE UPON THE BOOK OF NATIONAL REMEMBRANCE." On the side of the Indiana monument appears a second inscription: "NOT THEIRS THE MATCHLESS DEATH BY SWORD OR SHOT: INSTEAD THE AGONY OF MARTYRDOM".

Altogether, nine states placed monuments in the national cemetery, and five others placed monuments on the prison grounds. Tennessee was the first of the former Confederate states to place a monument at Andersonville. The state of Tennessee, although formally allied with the Confederacy, recognized that many of its sons had fought for the North during the war.

Located on the prison grounds, the Tennessee monument is an unimpressive structure: a simple rectangular slab, of rough cut granite, that bears an unimaginative inscription: "IN MEMORY OF HER UNION SOLDIERS AND LOYAL SONS WHO DIED IN CONFEDERATE PRISONS. WE WHO LIVE MAY FOR OURSELVES FORGET, BUT NOT FOR THOSE WHO DIED HERE."

The modest Tennessee monument is in sharp contrast with the huge stone structure erected on the prison grounds by the state of Wisconsin. It is the largest monument at Andersonville. Topped by a huge bronze eagle, it bears the name "WISCONSIN" in large letters above the state seal. It is dedicated "TO HER SONS, WHO SUFFERED AND DIED IN ANDERSONVILLE PRISON, MARCH 1864-APRIL 1865". Engraved on the base of the monument are the words "LET US HAVE PEACE".

In 1907 the Women's Relief Corps erected a monument on the prison grounds to its late leader Elizabeth Turner. The granite work bears a likeness of the medal worn by members of the Women's Relief Corps, with the entire monument sculpted to look as if it is topped by a funeral shroud. In 1934, the Women's Relief Corps placed another granite monument near the one honoring Elizabeth Turner. This simply designed monument honors the dead from Andersonville from states that did not see fit to erect a monument honoring their dead. The monument lists, almost punitively, the states without monuments, and the number of dead from each. They are: Delaware, Kansas, Kentucky, Maryland, Missouri, New Hampshire, Vermont, and West Virginia.

Another small monument honoring the work of the Women's Relief Corps stands nearby. It is topped with a bronze sundial and bears a lengthy bronze plaque, honoring the role played by the Women's Relief Corps in preserving the Andersonville cemetery and prison grounds. The plaque is badly pitted by oxidation and very difficult to read.

A pink granite monument, near the "sundial" monument, pays homage to Clara Barton and her work to preserve the cemetery. The monument to Clara Barton is the least impressive stonework at Andersonville. The stone slab is dominated by a red cross, that is actually larger than the bronze plaque. Like the "sundial" monument, this plaque has become very hard to read due to bronze oxidation. When Clara Barton made her expedition to Andersonville in 1865, she was not yet affiliated with the International Red Cross, nor had she yet founded the American Red Cross, so some would argue that the Red Cross symbol on this monument is inappropriate. Also, the Clara Barton monument makes no mention of Dorence Atwater and his contributions to saving the cemetery.

The monuments erected at Andersonville are, in most part, different from those found on most Civil War battlefields. There are no equestrian statues of brave generals, astride noble steeds, sabers drawn for the charge. No representations of men locked in mortal combat, rushing the enemy breastworks. Only the New Jersey and Maine monuments show armed figures, and on the Maine monument, the muzzle of the weapon is pointed downward, a traditional military symbol of mourning. At Andersonville the statuary is more somber than heroic, more anti-war than militaristic. More reflective and sad than one would normally find in a typical Civil War military park.

In the fall, after the weather turns cool, and the early winter rains fall, a strange phenomena occurs with the monuments at Andersonville. The differences in the temperature of the granite, and the air that surrounds it, make the rainwater cling to the stone and drip in dark, straight lines. It looks as if the monument itself is weeping. The combination of cool air, misting rain, and the history of Andersonville make for an eerie sensation, when one first sees the weeping stones.

When the foundation for one of the monuments in the prison grounds was being dug, a gruesome discovery was made. Human remains were found only a few feet below the surface of the earth. It confirmed the rumors, circulated by Andersonville veterans, that many dead prisoners were never carried out to the "dead house," but were buried in shallow graves inside the stockade. Many of the she-bangs were little more than grave-like holes in the ground. When a prisoner with no remaining friends died, sometimes his neighbors would simply shovel dirt into the dug out she-bang, covering the body with only a few inches of topsoil. Other dead men were shoved down abandoned wells and partially collapsed escape tunnels. During the winter of 1864–1865, the prisoners were allowed to dig small caves into the side of the creek bank for shelter. When one of the prisoners died, instead of carrying him down to the North Gate, or the dead house, his fellow prisoners simply knocked in the roof of the small tunnel, letting the soil fall and cover the corpse. Exactly how many men lay buried in this manner inside the old prison grounds will probably never be known. It would take an extensive archaeological excavation to even get a rough idea.

In 1976, a resident of Sumter County, Georgia was elected president of the United States. Jimmy Carter had grown up twenty miles from Andersonville in the small town of Plains, Georgia. As a youth, he had often visited the prison and cemetery, and had a fine regard for its history. President Carter believed strongly that the state of Georgia, on whose soil Andersonville lay, should erect a monument in the cemetery in the spirit of healing the wounds of the Civil War.

It was decided that the Georgia monument would become a memorial, not only to the thousands who had died in the filthy Confederate stockade at Andersonville, but "to all American prisoners involved in all American wars from our country's birth up to the present."[11]

Sculptor William Thompson was commissioned to develop the memorial, and in 1976 it was formally unveiled. The monument showed three gaunt and emaciated figures, one of which was on a crutch. It is impossible to determine if they are Civil War soldiers caught in a summer rainstorm inside the Andersonville stockade, or World War II soldiers in the Bataan death march, or American paratroopers taken prisoner in the Battle of the Bulge, or the crew of a B-52 bomber shot down over North Vietnam. The Georgia monument bears an inscription taken from the Old Testament, Book of Zechariah: "TURN YOU TO THE STRONGHOLD YE PRISONERS OF HOPE".

While the Georgia monument is the most recently unveiled, it is not the one that draws the most attention from average cemetery visitors. The Iowa monument, erected in 1905, is a beautiful and tastefully designed stone structure, that appears to be rising from a sea of white marble headstones. It is topped with a weeping female figure kneeling in her grief. It could be some dead soldier's mother, sister, wife or sweetheart. On the side of the Iowa monument is a verse from the New Testament's Book of Revelation that more than any other inscription at Andersonville Historical Site personifies the sacrifice, courage, and most of all the faith of the men who suffered and died here.

The Book of Revelation deals with the vision of an early Christian martyr, identified only as John. He, like the prisoners at Andersonville, was also imprisoned under horrible conditions on a small Greek island, awaiting execution for his faith. During his imprisonment, John had a vision from God of the world to come, and a view of heaven itself. In his vision, John saw special persons, dressed in white, who were actually allowed to approach the throne of God. He asked his guide who these special persons were, and he was told: "These are they which have come out of great tribulation." The rest is found engraved in the beautiful stone of the Iowa monument:

"THEY SHALL HUNGER NO MORE, NEITHER THIRST ANY MORE: NEITHER SHALL THE SUN LIGHT ON THEM, NOR ANY HEAT. FOR THE LAMB WHICH IS IN THE MIDST OF THE THRONE SHALL FEED THEM, AND SHALL LEAD THEM UNTO LIVING FOUNTAINS OF WATER: AND GOD SHALL WIPE AWAY ALL TEARS FROM THEIR EYES."

REVELATION 7:16–17

(Untitled) Grave of an Unknown Union Soldier
Author's Collection

APPENDIX

A Word About Historical Sources

No historical researcher can author a book about a subject as complex and controversial as Andersonville without considerable assistance from others. The modern writer obviously could not have experienced all the events that occurred at Andersonville. Therefore, dependence upon other people's work is absolutely necessary.

The worrisome dilemma about the events that transpired at Andersonville is that the researcher cannot afford to take anything found on the subject at face value; exaggeration, understatement, myths, and outright lying are all part of the historical record. Very few events in history are recorded without the writer's bias, and in the case of Captain Henry Wirz and the Confederate prison at Andersonville, Georgia, the temptation to create heroes and villains, to reflect values and perceptions, and to reduce a historical event to its lowest common denominator seems to overwhelm everyone who ever wrote on the subject.

Avoiding this pitfall is the tiresome and sometimes frustrating duty of the modern day historical writer. The situation is made worse by the fact that certain persons, in both the North and the South, have in the past attempted to sanitize or cover up the events that occurred at Andersonville, and even today there is a general reluctance on some quarters to openly discuss the issue and share information.

No event that occurred during the Civil War stirs so much controversy and heated passion as the terrible events that occurred at Andersonville. Even today, over a century and a quarter after the events transpired, tempers still flare when Andersonville is mentioned. Almost everything recorded about the Confederate prison called Camp Sumter was written with the intention of either damning or defending Henry Wirz and the Confederate States of America.

Nothing recorded about Andersonville can be considered the absolute truth except the obvious: There was a Confederate prison at Andersonville, and that over 12,000 Union prisoners of war died and were buried there, and that the survivors endured terrible hardships. Anything else, who was at fault, could it have been prevented etc., is open for interpretation by the reader. Healthy skepticism and an open mind are a must for the Andersonville researcher.

In preparing any historical work, certain sources are much more important than others. Also, some sources are very reliable for accuracy while others are not, and still others are in between. This cannot be determined when a writer follows the standard format taught in writing classes of listing sources in alphabetical order by the last name of the author. Therefore, we must have a candid analysis of the sources used to discuss their relevance and accuracy.

The transcript of the trial of Captain Henry Wirz can be found in the library at Andersonville Military Park. This voluminous work of more than a thousand pages contains almost all the important testimony presented at Wirz's trial, both by the prosecution and the defense. From this lengthy transcript the reader will get an accurate picture of the conditions at Andersonville prison, as seen by both the prosecution and defense. A more workable, and surprisingly objective, account of Wirz's trial is General N. P. Chipman's *The Andersonville Prison Trial, the Trial of Captain Henry Wirz*. It was first published by the author in 1911, and has recently been republished by the Notable Trials Library.

One of the most informative, and sometimes entertaining, sources of information is the diaries written by Andersonville prisoners. It is absolutely amazing that a prisoner fighting to survive while living inside the muddy, filthy, and overcrowded Andersonville stockade could maintain a diary, much less that the diary should survive to the present day. However, several of them did. These diaries run the gamut from brief descriptions of the weather and major events to fascinating in-depth accounts of life in the prison and the personalities of the prisoners themselves.

Without doubt, John Ransom's *Andersonville Diary* is the most entertaining to read. John McElroy's dairy is another rich source of information, except that it is badly tainted with bias against Captain Wirz and the Confederacy in general. Other diaries worth reading are by Ira S. Petit, published as *The Dairy of a Dead Man*, as well as the diaries of James Denison and Charles Hopkins to name a few. A good account of conditions in Andersonville from a source other than a prisoner is the diary of Father Clavereul, the Catholic chaplain who visited the prison.

Union prisoners of war at Andersonville were allowed to write letters home, and many of these have survived. The prisoners would address their letters in the usual way with the name and address of the person whom they wished to contact, then write "via flag of truce and

Washington." The letters were censored by Rebel authorities before being forwarded, but this censorship seems to have been a sporadic off and on thing. Many of the letters were censored by either Captain Wirz or General Winder and bare their initials. Most of the letters were short and sad, informing family members in the North of the death of a loved one in Andersonville.

Some Andersonville prisoners wrote accounts of their captivity later in life. William W. Glazier, brevet captain of the New York Volunteer Cavalry, wrote *The Capture, Prison Pen and Escape* in 1867. Another example is *Life and Death in Rebel Prisons* by Robert H. Kellogg, sergeant major of the 16th Connecticut Volunteers, also published in 1867.

These accounts are often very critical of Captain Wirz, General Winder, and the Confederacy in general. This should be expected from a former prisoner of war who is writing about the people he considers responsible for his misery during his captivity.

As far as the life of Henry Wirz is concerned, it is extremely difficult to find Civil War period information that is not written by either a defender or prosecutor of the unfortunate Confederate officer. Many fine articles have been written by modern authors. One of the best is by Katherine and Robert Morsberger titled "The Judgment and Execution of Henry Wirz" which was first published in *Civil War Times Illustrated*. Wirz's dealings with the Andersonville Raiders is dealt with in an article by David L. Mallinson "The Andersonville Raiders" also found in *Civil War Times Illustrated*.

There are three areas of the Henry Wirz strange saga where little or no information is available. Exactly what Wirz's life was like in Europe before he came to the United States, and why he had to leave his native land is unclear. Henry Wirz's trip to Europe in 1863 is the second unsolved mystery about his life. The fate of Wirz's wife and children after he was executed is also clouded with uncertainty. The only evidence is the oral history passed down to the living descendants of Henry and Elizabeth Wirz, and census records.

After Henry Wirz was executed, his wife and children returned to Kentucky, apparently, where Elizabeth Wirz lived out her life in extreme poverty and died sometime in the late nineteenth century. She is buried in an unmarked pauper's grave near Cadiz, Kentucky.

Colonel Heinrich L. Wirz of the Army of Switzerland, the great-grand-nephew of his famous namesake, regularly visits the United States to attend ceremonies at Andersonville on the anniversary of his great-granduncle's execution. Colonel Wirz is an authority on the life of Henry Wirz and was a most valuable source of information about Wirz's life and personality.

Colonel Wirz is frequently accompanied at the ceremonies at Andersonville by Mr. Perrin Watkins of Baton Rouge, Louisiana, who is Henry Wirz's great-grandson. Mr. Watkins and the rest of his family regularly make the eight-hour drive from Louisiana to attend ceremonies staged at Andersonville by the Sons of Confederate Veterans to honor Captain Wirz. All the members of the Watkins' family willingly provided valuable information that helped clear up some of the mysteries concerning the events in the life of Captain Wirz.

The first scholarly and complete account of the events at Andersonville was written by Ovid L. Futch and was titled *A History of Andersonville Prison*. From this beginning, others have also written about the prison, some defending, others condemning, Henry Wirz.

Some modern writers have attempted to analyze the events that occurred at Andersonville objectively. These works form the last literary line in the winding thread that a researcher must follow in attempting to separate fact from fiction in the story of Andersonville. Ken Drew, a local resident, has written a brief but highly informative history of Andersonville titled *Camp Sumter, The Pictorial History of Andersonville Prison*. David E. Roth and Robin Roth have compiled a fascinating history of the cemetery titled "The Human Interest Side of Andersonville" which was featured in *Blue and Gray Magazine*, Volume III, Issue 3, which deals almost exclusively with Andersonville. Without doubt, the best book about the town of Andersonville, and the local history of the region, is Peggy Sheppard's *Andersonville U.S.A.* It is an excellent book that could not have possibly been written by someone who had not spent a lifetime living and working at Andersonville.

Government documents concerning Andersonville are found in a variety of places, the most useful being the *Official Records of the War of the Rebellion*. Most of the information about Andersonville can be found in Series 2, Volumes 7 and Volume 8. Information about the cemetery can be found in Series 1, Volume 47. Other sources of government documents concerning Andersonville are the *U.S. National Archives and Records Administration*, Washington D.C.; Compiled Military Service Records, (Record Group 94); Consolidated Correspondence File, Office of the Quarter Master General (Record Group 92), Pension Records (Record Group 15). These records contain information about individual soldiers and regiments. The deed books of Sumter County, Georgia record the passing of ownership of the prison site to the United States government.

The *Sumter Republican*, the nearest newspaper to Andersonville during the Civil War, was printed in Americus, and is available on microfilm in the Sumter County Public Library. The *Sumter Republican*, at the time of the Civil War, was more of an advertising sheet than a true newspaper.

There is one last source of information about Andersonville that must be mentioned and that is the place itself. No one can write about Andersonville without first feeling its spirit. The knowledge one obtains from a visit to the small Georgia community, goes far beyond the exhibits in the museum and the inscriptions on the monuments. Clara Barton, who journeyed to Andersonville in 1865 to mark the graves of the dead, wrote in her dairy that she could feel the spirits of the dead prisoners calling to her.

Others, including this writer, have also felt their spirits speaking. The nearly 13,000 men who died in the filthy prison stockade have baptized this small corner of Georgia clay with their blood, and the stain will remain forever. Their souls rest in the arms of a just and merciful God, but their spirits still walk the grounds of the old prison, and their sacrifice hangs over the cemetery like the mist on an early spring morning.

NOTES

Introduction

1. Edward Ayers, *The Promise of the New South, Life After Reconstruction*, pp. 55–57.
2. Steven A. Channing, *Confederate Ordeal, the Southern Home Front*, p. 8.
3. Mary Elizabeth Massey, *Ersatz in the Confederacy, Shortages and Substitutes on the Southern Home Front*, p. 8.
4. Ronald H. Bailey, *Battles for Atlanta, Sherman Moves East*, p. 21.
5. Robert C. Black III, *The Railroads of the Confederacy*, accompanying map insert.
6. Ibid., p. 22.
7. Ibid.; Massey, p. 24.
8. Colonel Knox Livingston, "Florida Girl Gave Her Shoes to a Soldier," *Confederate Veteran*, 15, 1907, p. 458.
9. Massey, p. 29.
10. Ibid., p. 21.
11. Ibid., p. 10.

PART ONE

Chapter 1

1. Walter Angst, "Henry Wirz, Commander of Andersonville," *Swiss American Review,* November 14, 1990. Also, *Historisch-Biographisches, Lexiken des Schweiz*, Volume 8, pp. 569, 571.
2. Katherine and Robert Morsberger, "The Judgment and Execution of Henry Wirz," *Andersonville*, pp. 26–27.
3. Interview with Colonel Heinrich L. Wirz, November 10, 1993.
4. Olivid L. Futch, *History of Andersonville*, pp. 16–17.
5. Elizabeth Leonard Parker, *The Civil War Career of Henry Wirz, and its Aftermath*, pp. 1–3.
6. Charles E. Rosenberg, "What it was like to be sick in 1884," *American Heritage*, October–November 1984, pp. 89–90.
7. David Armstrong and Elizabeth Metzer Armstrong, *The Great American Medicine Show, being an Illustrated History of Hucksters, Healers, Health Evangelists, and Heroes from Plymouth Rock to the Present*, pp. 31–35.
8. Eli N. Evans, *Judiah P. Benjamin, the Jewish Confederate*, p. 6.
9. Eugene D. Genovese, *Roll Jordan Roll, the World the Slaves Made*, pp. 224–225.

10. Morsberger, p. 26.
11. *The Trial of Henry Wirz*, 40th Congress, House of Representatives, House Document 23, Washington D.C., p. 704, statement of Henry Wirz. Hereafter referred to as the *Wirz Trial.*
12. Parker, p. 2. There has recently been some doubt as to the truth of the claim that Henry Wirz was actually wounded at the Battle of Seven Pines. William Marvel in his book, *Andersonville, the Last Depot*, p. 37, claims that Wirz's commissioning as a captain, only eleven days after the battle, indicated that he could not have possibly been wounded at Seven Pines. He quotes Wirz detractors who claimed that he was injured in a stagecoach accident. However, after careful checking with physicians and Vietnam veterans who had also been shot in the arm and shoulder, I have come to the conclusion that Wirz's stated symptoms are consistent with that of a severe gunshot wound. Where he was wounded may be arguable. However, Henry Wirz's injuries were clearly related to a gunshot wound, and not the result of a broken arm in a stagecoach accident.
13. Ibid., p. 3.
14. Ibid.

Chapter 2

1. Herbert Langer, *Thirty Years War*, pp. 56–60, 103–112.
2. Jack Coggins, *Ship and Seamen of the American Revolution*, pp. 79–84.
3. E. Milby Burton, *The Siege of Charleston 1861–1865*, pp. 56–57.
4. James I. Robertson Jr., *Tenting Tonight, the Soldier's Life,* p. 111.
5. The Dix-Hill Cartel, negotiated between Major General John A. Dix, U.S.A., and D. H. Hill, C.S.A., found in Denney, *Civil War Prisons and Escapes*, pp. 9–12, 375–376; U.S. Army Regulation 36, p. 378.
6. William Marvel, *Andersonville, the Last Depot*, p. 26.
7. Frank E. Moran, "Escape from Libby Prison," *American History Illustrated*, November 7, 1985, pp. 38–39.
8. Ibid.; Marvel, p. 26.
9. *OR*, Series 1, Volume 6, pp. 455–456.
10. Patricia L. Faust, ed., *Encyclopedia of the Civil War*, pp. 146–149.
11. *OR*, Series 1, Volume 6, pp. 455–456.
12. *OR*, Series 2, Volume 6, p. 558.
13. Ibid.; Faust, pp. 83–84.
14. Ibid.; Marvel, p. 14. The name Plains of Dura probably referred to the city of Dura Europus on the Euphrates River in Eastern Syria. It was the home of an early group of Christians, who founded a church there around 232 A.D.
15. Ibid., p. 15.
16. Ibid.; Faust, pp. 16–17.
17. Arch Frederic Blakey, *General John H. Winder, C.S.A.*, p. 181.
18. *OR*, Series 2, Volume 6, p. 965; *Sumter Republican*, January 22, 1864.
19. *OR*, Series 2, Volume 53, p. 279; *OR*, Series 2, Volume 6, pp. 797, 925, 966.
20. *OR,* Series 2, Volume 6, p. 965.
21. Ibid., p. 966.
22. Ibid.; Moran, pp. 38–39.
23. Ibid.; Faust, pp. 202–417.

24. Ibid.; Marvel, p. 23.
25. *OR*, Series 2, Volume 6, p. 965.
26. Blakey, p. 176.
27. "Cracker Cowboys of Florida", *The South, A Collection from Harper's Magazine* (New York: Gallery Books, 1990), pp. 120–125.
28. Massey, pp. 38–41.
29. *OR*, Series 2, Volume 6, pp. 976–977, 985, 1000.
30. *Wirz Trial*, pp. 244–247, report of Colonel D. T. Chandler.
31. *Wirz Trial*, p. 687, testimony of Edward Wellington Boate, *Macon Daily Telegraph*, February 27, 1864.
32. Ibid.; Marvel, pp. 28–29.
33. *Wirz Trial*, p. 455, testimony of A. W. Persons; *OR*, Series 2, Volume 6, pp. 244–247.
34. *Wirz Trial*, pp. 99–100, testimony of Colonel A. W. Persons; Norton P. Chipman, *The Tragedy of Andersonville*, pp. 53–54.
35. Ibid.; Marvel, p. 19; McElroy, *This Was Andersonville*, p. 32.
36. Dorence Atwater, *List of the Prisoner's Who Died at Andersonville*, p. 42.
37. *OR*, Series 2, Volume 8, p. 625, report of Surgeon Thornburg.
38. *Report of Clara Barton*, p. 6.
39. *Wirz Trial*, pp. 117, 176, 512–513, testimony of Frank Maddox; Chipman, pp. 219–220, testimony of Vincenzo Bardo and Andrew J. Spring.
40. *Wirz Trial*, pp. 177–179, testimony of Archibald Boyle.
41. There were two Civil War era maps made of Andersonville and surrounding area. The first was drawn in August 1864 by a Confederate topographical engineer, who was not allowed to accurately represent certain aspects of the prison for security reasons. The second was an actual survey done after the war which accurately represented the dimensions of the stockade and earthwork defenses. Both maps have been widely reproduced in a variety of places, many times altered in various ways to illustrate a point. Another good source of information about the layout of the prison, and probably the most accurate, is a drawing done by Thomas O'Dea, Company E, 16th Maine Infantry. It shows the prison as it appeared on August 1, 1864 with 35,000 prisoners of war.
42. Map of Andersonville that accompanied the testimony of Dr. Amos Thornburg, *Wirz Trial*, p. 322, and Chipman, p. 113. The term "pigeon roosts" is found in a number of private diaries of Andersonville prisoners.
43. Ibid.
44. *Wirz Trial*, p. 557, testimony of George W. Fechtner.
45. Ibid.
46. John L. Ransom, *Andersonville Diary*, p. 94. Hereafter referred to as *Ransom Diary*.

Chapter 3

1. *Wirz Trial*, p. 99, testimony of Alexander W. Persons; Chipman, pp. 52–54.
2. *Wirz Trial*, p. 455, second testimony of Alexander W. Persons; Chipman, p. 211.
3. *OR*, Series 2, Volume 7, p. 165.
4. John McElroy, *This was Andersonville*, p. 40; *OR*, Series 2, Volume 6, General Order No. 6, p. 1054.

5. *Wirz Trial*, p. 577, et seq, testimony of George W. Fechtner; Chipman, p. 236; OR, Series 2, Volume 7, pp. 1040–1041.

6. *OR*, Series 1, Volume 33, pp. 296–300. The Confederate attack on the defenses of New Bern, N.C. failed.

7. Ibid.; Marvel, p. 57; *Wirz Trial*, p. 560. John McElroy, writing in *This was Andersonville*, estimated that the Plymouth Pilgrims had between ten thousand and one hundred thousand dollars in reenlistment bounty and back pay. During the Civil War, a Union Army private made only thirteen dollars a month. This was probably equivalent to approximately one million dollars in modern money.

8. Ibid.; McElroy, p. 40.

9. Ibid., p. 41.

10. B. A. Botkin, *A Civil War Treasury of Tales, Legends, and Folklore*, pp. 451–453.

11. *Wirz Trial,* p. 81; McElroy, p. 73; David L. Mallinson, "The Andersonville Raiders," *Andersonville*, p. 2.

12. Ibid.; McElroy, p. 76.

13. Ibid., p. 75.

14. Ibid.; Chipman, p. 84; *OR*, Series 2, Volume 8, p. 596.

15. *OR*, Series 2, Volume 8, pp. 730–735.

16. *OR*, Series 1, Volume 39, Special Orders No. 129, p. 634.

17. *OR*, Series 2, Volume 8, pp. 730–755.

18. *Wirz Trial*, pp. 76–77, testimony of Boston Corbett.

19. The day of the assault on the Raiders is recorded in two independent accounts: McElroy's *This was Andersonville*, p. 82, and Ransom's *Andersonville Diary*, pp. 112–113.

20. This plot was discovered sometime around June 7. One of those put in irons for being part of the conspiracy was George Hendryx, a friend of John Ransom. See *Ransom Diary*, p. 87.

21. *Ransom Diary*, pp. 112–113, maintains that the Raiders entered the stockade about 10:00 A.M. McElroy, p. 89, says only that Wirz entered a little after noon. Amos E. Stearns in his diary, p. 70, says only that the hanging occurred in the afternoon. Robert E. Kellogg in his *Life and Death in Rebel Prisons*, p. 170, lists the time of the entrance of Wirz as 4:30 P.M. All the diarists agree that the gallows was built the morning of the execution.

22. McElroy, p. 89. McElroy was apparently referring to a well-known painting, "Death on a Pale Horse," by Asher B. Durand. testimony consistently showed that Henry Wirz always rode a brownish-red roan horse. Therefore, this bit of over dramatic hyperbole must be viewed with skepticism. Henry Wirz was such a fastidious dresser that it is hard to imagine him wearing a dirty or wrinkled uniform on such an important occasion.

23. The account of the execution of the Raiders is found in a variety of sources already cited. They are all fairly consistent except that some have Wirz's speech made in his heavy German accent: "May Gott hap mercy on ya souls." See *Ransom Diary*, pp. 112–117; McElroy, *This Was Andersonville*, pp. 87–95; Mallinson, "The Andersonville Raiders," *Andersonville*.

24. Ibid.; Morsberger, p. 34.

25. Ibid.; McElroy, pp. 90–91.

26. Munn's tombstone at Andersonville National Cemetery is inscribed only as A. Munn. Ovid L. Futch, *History of Andersonville Prison*, reports that he was also known as "Muir" and "Murray." However, U.S. Army Quartermaster reports list him as "Munn." The first name Andrew comes from Consolidated Morning Reports, Entry 3, RG 29, quoted in Marvel, *Andersonville the Last Depot*, p. 143. See also, *Wirz Trial*, pp. 426–428, testimony of Father Whelan.

27. Munn's plea of innocence is totally unbelievable. The fact he had so many aliases indicates that he was an experienced bounty jumper. The fact that he was sentenced to die shows he was a major Raider leader with many crimes to his credit.

Chapter 4

1. Ransom, *Ransom Diary*, p. 114; McElroy, pp. 90–91. The final words of the Raiders vary in minor detail from one account to the other.
2. Ibid.; Morsberger, p. 34.
3. *OR*, Series 2, Volume 8, p. 596.
4. Ibid.; Marvel, pp. 82–83.
5. Ransom, *Ransom Dairy*, p. 84.
6. *OR*, Series 2, Volume 7, p. 138.
7. Ibid.; Marvel, p. 53.
8. Ibid., pp. 80–81.
9. Ibid.; Futch, p. 36.
10. *OR*, Series 2, Volume 7, pp. 499–500.
11. Ransom, *Ransom Diary*, p. 54.

Chapter 5

1. Ibid.; Morsberger, p. 27.
2. Alan Axelrod, *The War Between the Spies*, pp. 35–36.
3. Biographical information about the life of General John H. Winder comes from Blakey, *General John H. Winder, C.S.A.* See also John K. Mahon, *The War of 1812*, pp. 289–305.
4. James Dunwoody Jones, "A Guard at Andersonville," *Andersonville*. From a manuscript owned by Jones' daughter Mary J. Hillyer of New York City.
5. *Ransom* Diary, pp. 233–236.
6. Ibid.; Marvel, pp. 60–61; *Ransom Diary*, p. 79. John Ransom claimed that the festivities occurred on Sunday, May 14, 1864.
7. Riddle's photographs have been widely reproduced and can be found in the National Archives, Washington D.C., and the U.S. Army Military History Institute, Carlisle Barracks, Pennsylvania. Biographical information on A. J. Riddle comes from Marvel, *Andersonville, the Last Depot*, p. 289.
8. *OR*, Series 2, Volume 7, pp. 588–589. The rumor of Captain Wirz's death found in *Ransom Diary*, p. 130.
9. *OR*, Series 2, Volume 7, pp. 623–624.
10. Ibid., p. 565.
11. Ibid., p. 869.
12. Ibid., p. 590.
13. Ibid., pp. 503–504.

14. *OR*, Series 2, Volume 7, p. 590. This is an extremely idealized view of the defenses. However, remains of the earthworks can still be seen at Andersonville Military Park. See also Thomas O'Dea Map, Andersonville National Historic Site.
15. *OR*, Series 2, Volume 7, p. 589.
16. Ibid.; McElroy, p. 144.
17. Ibid.

PART TWO
Chapter 6

1. Lee Kennett, *Marching Through Georgia*, pp. 23–25.
2. William O. Bryant, *Cahaba Prison and the Sultana Disaster*, p. 30.
3. *OR*, Series 2, Volume 7, pp. 1075, 1083.
4. Kennett, p. 33.
5. Ibid., p. 114; D. Mark Katz, *Witness to an Era, the Life and Photographs of Alexander Gardner*, pp. 194–195.
6. *OR*, Series 2, Volume 8, p. 515.
7. Bryant, pp. 113–114.
8. Robert C. Black III, *The Railroads of the Confederacy*, pp. 13–14.
9. Op cit., p. 115.
10. *Harper's Weekly*, June 17, 1865.
11. Bryant, p. 119.
12. Ibid., pp. 123–124.
13. Ibid., pp. 129–138.

Chapter 7

1. Drew, *Camp Sumter*, p. 28.
2. *Wirz Trial*, testimony of Major N. E. Noyes, also Chipman, pp. 45–47; *OR*, Series 1, Volume 47, Part 2, p. 800.
3. United Daughters of the Confederacy, *Facts and Figures vs Myths and Representations*, p. 5.
4. *OR*, Series 2, Volume 8, pp. 537–538.
5. United Daughters of the Confederacy, *Facts and Figures*, p. 5.
6. *OR*, Series 2, Volume 8, pp. 537–538.
7. Ibid., p. 538.
8. *Harper's Weekly*, June 17, 1865.
9. Pvt. Alfred Bellard, *Gone for a Soldier*, pp. 251–253.
10. From a sketch of the interior of Wirz's room in the Old Capitol Prison by Frank H. Schell, published in *Frank Leslie's Illustrated Newspaper*, reprinted in Morsberger, p. 35.

Chapter 8

1. The personality of Edwin Stanton and the politics of the nation during the time of the trial of Henry Wirz, the comparisons to the trial of the Lincoln conspirators, and the imprisonment of Jefferson Davis may be found in several works. However, I recommend Burke Davis' *The Long Surrender* (New York: Random House, 1985).
2. Ibid., Davis, *The Long Surrender*, p. 193.

3. Ibid., pp. 178–179.
4. Ibid., p. 204.
5. Ibid.
6. Chipman, *The Andersonville Trial*, p. 31.
7. Ibid., pp. 28–30.
8. Ibid., pp. 45–50.
9. Ibid., pp. 189–191.
10. Ibid., pp. 65–76; *Wirz Transcript*, pp. 224, et seq.
11. Ibid., pp. 83–98.
12. Ibid., pp. 150–155.
13. Ibid., p. 153.
14. McElroy, p. 20.
15. Chipman, p. 272.
16. McElroy, pp. 56–57.
17. Chipman, pp. 280–288.
18. Ibid., pp. 265–269.
19. Ibid., pp. 219–220.
20. Ibid., pp. 286–287; *OR*, Series 2, Volume 7, p. 403.
21. Ibid., pp. 290–291.
22. Ibid., p. 280.
23. Ibid., p. 293.
24. Ibid., p. 270.
25. *Wirz Trial*, p. 711.
26. Ibid., p. 712.
27. Ibid., p. 716.
28. Michael V. Gannon, *Rebel Bishop*, pp. 103–104. In Gannon's book Father Clavreul's name is spelled as in this text. It is also spelled "Clavreul" in "The Prison Ministry of Father Peter Whelan, Georgia priest and Confederate Chaplin" by Peter J. Meaney O.S.B., printed in the *Georgia Historical Quarterly*, Volume 81, Number 1, Spring 1987. However, in Chipman's *The Andersonville Prison Trial* the name is spelled "Clavereul."

Chapter 9

1. Morsberger, p. 35.
2. Katz, pp. 195–201.
3. Morsberger, p. 35.
4. *Procedure for Military Executions*, U.S. Department of the Army, Army Regulations, 633–15, Section 2.
5. Ibid.
6. Autopsy photo of Henry Wirz by Alexander Gardner from the Western Reserve Historical Society.
7. *Blue and Gray Magazine*, Volume 3, p. 61; Norman and Betty Donaldson, *How Did They Die*, pp. 40–41. The War Department had reported that Booth's body had been dumped into the Potomac River, when in reality it had been secretly buried in the Arsenal grounds. This type of deceit by the War Department served to fuel many of the rumors circulating around Washington concerning the remains of Henry Wirz and Mary Surrat.
8. Dorothy Meserve and Phillip Kunhardt, *Twenty Days*, p. 54.

9. Sheppard, *Andersonville Georgia U.S.A.*, p. 12.
10. *The Macon Telegraph and News*, November 11, 1990, pp. 1, 10.

PART THREE

Chapter 10

1. Francis Atwater, *Dorence Atwater*, a defense of Dorence Atwater written by his brother. Hereafter referred to as *Atwater Defense*.
2. Ibid., p. 1.
3. Terry E. Baldwin, "Clerk of the Dead," *Andersonville*, p. 13.
4. Foreword to *A List of Union Prisoners Buried at Andersonville* by Dorence Atwater. Hereafter referred to as the *Atwater Foreword*.
5. Robert H. Kellogg, *Life and Death in Rebel Prisons*, pp. 255–282.
6. The procedure for burying the dead at Andersonville can be found in Charles F. Hopkins, Company I, First New Jersey Volunteers, "Hell and the Survivor," *American Heritage*, October–November 1982, pp. 78–93. See also, *OR*, Series 2, Volume 7, p. 40.
7. Ibid.; Kellogg, pp. 247–271.
8. Ibid., pp. 259–260.
9. Kennett, pp. 115, 141.
10. Ibid., pp. 262–263.
11. *Atwater Defense*, p. 4.
12. *New York Tribune*, February 1, 1865, and March 21, 1865. For an excellent description of the Confederate prison at Salisbury, North Carolina, see Louis A. Brown, *The Salisbury Prison, A Case Study of Confederate Military Prisons*.
13. Military Service Records of Dorence Atwater, National Archives and Records Administration, Record Group (RG) 94, Compiled Military Service records.
14. Steven B. Oates, *A Woman of Valor, Clara Barton and the Civil War*, pp. 296–297.

Chapter 11

1. *Atwater Foreword*, p. 1.
2. Ibid.
3. All biographical information on the early life of Clara Barton comes from Leni Hamilton, *Clara Barton* (New York, Philadelphia, Pa.: Chelsia House Publishers, 1988).
4. Information concerning Clara Barton's Civil War career is found in note 3 as well as Stephen B. Oates, *A Woman of Valor, Clara Barton and the Civil War*.
5. Ibid., pp. 315–316.

Chapter 12

1. All information, except that noted, comes from Clara Barton's report on the expedition to Andersonville titled: "*Report of an Expedition to Andersonville, Georgia, July 1865, for the Purpose of Identifying the Graves and Enclosing the Grounds of a Cemetery Created of that Place as a Prison for Union Soldiers in Rebel Hands.*" Hereafter referred to as the *Barton Report*.
2. Stanton to Meigs, June 30, 1865, National Archives, RG 92.

3. *OR*, Series 2, Volume 5, pp. 319–322.
4. *Barton Report*, p. 3.
5. *OR*, Series 2, Volume 47, p. 1051. A man who identified himself as J. R. Griffin, of the 8th Georgia Cavalry, testified at the trial of Henry Wirz. During his testimony he said he was the brother of a man who was working to restore the cemetery. This was obviously William Griffin, *Wirz Trial*, p. 384.
6. *OR*, Series 2, Volume 47, p. 1054.
7. *Barton Report,* p. 3

Chapter 13

1. *Atwater Foreword*, p. 1.
2. Baldwin, "Clerk of the Dead," p. 17.
3. Ibid., p. 16.
4. The description of Auburn Prison can be found in a book by Norman Johnson, *The Human Cage, A Brief History of Prison Architecture*, pp. 38–41.

Chapter 14

1. All biographical information concerning Horace Greeley comes from *Horace Greeley, Fighting Journalist,* by Julian Messer.
2. Ibid.; Baldwin, p. 17.
3. Ibid.
4. Ibid.
5. Julian Messer, *Horace Greeley, Fighting Journalist*, p. 181.
6. *Atwater Defense*, p. 4.
7. Ibid.; Baldwin, p. 18.
8. Ibid., p. 19. Much of the background on the lifestyle of Dorence Atwater in Tahiti comes from Robert Louis Stevenson's *The Ebb Tide, A Trio, A Quartet*; the "a dash of epicure" quote is found on page 144. The description of the meal at Atwater's home can be found in various places in chapters nine and ten. It must be emphasized that *The Ebb Tide* is a work of fiction based on Stevenson's real life experiences in the South Pacific. Stevenson significantly changes certain facts about Dorence Atwater's life to protect his privacy. These changes included changing the spelling of Atwater's name to "Attwater." He portrayed his good friend as an eccentric pearl hunter who was a British subject.
9. Ibid.; Baldwin, p. 19.
10. Ibid.
11. Ibid.

PART FOUR

Chapter 15

1. Richard W. Murphy, *The Nation Reunited*, p. 25.
2. Ibid., p. 160.
3. Ibid., pp. 160–171.
4. Charles Wilson Reagan, *Baptized in Blood, the Religion of the Lost Cause*, contains an in-depth analysis of the prevalent attitudes in the South following the Civil War.
5. *Belford's Magazine*, January 1990. See also Peggy Sheppard, *Andersonville, Georgia U.S.A.*, p. 23.

6. Ibid.; Sheppard, p. 23.
7. Foreword to the *Official Records* by Major Robert N. Scott, approved by Alex Ramsey, Secretary of War, War Department, Washington, D.C., August 23, 1880.
8. *OR*, Series 2, Volume 7, p. 40.
9. Ibid., pp. 617–618.
10. Ibid., p. 589.
11. Ibid., p. 615.
12. Ibid., p. 762.
13. Minutes of the Fourteenth Annual Convention of the Georgia Division of the United Daughters of the Confederacy, Savannah, Georgia, October 1908.

Chapter 16

1. *Diary of Father Clavereul* published in 1908 by the Connecticut Association of Ex-Prisoners of War. Reproduced in part in Chipman's *Andersonville Prison Trial*, p. 198.
2. F. B. Simkins, *A History of the South*, 1953, quoted in *The National Experience*, John M. Blume, Bruce Catton, Edmund S. Morgan, Arthur M. Schelesinger Jr., Kenneth Stampp, and C. Vann Woodward, p. 392.
3. James West Davidson, William E. Gienapp, Christine Leigh Heyrman, Mark H. Lytle, and Michael B. Stoff, *Nation of Nations*, pp. 759–773.
4. *The National Experience*, p. 392.
5. Davis M. Chalmers, *Hooded Americanism, the History of the Ku Klux Klan*, p. 230.
6. Minutes of the Fifteenth Annual Convention of the Georgia Division of the United Daughters of the Confederacy, West Point, Georgia, 1909.
7. Ibid.; Also found on the Wirz monument.
8. "Shaft to Wirz," *Americus Weekly Times-Recorder*, Thursday, May 13, 1909.
9. Sheppard, p. 69.
10. Ibid., p. 65.
11. Ibid., p. 65.

Chapter 17

1. William G. Burnett, *Our Lizabeth*, p. 7, an unpublished manuscript.
2. Ibid., p. 26.
3. Sheppard, pp. 43–44.
4. Ibid., p. 59.
5. Dykes to Stanton, National Archives, RG, 92.
6. *Records of Deed's Book*, Sumter County, Georgia, pp. 293–294. During the Civil War the Andersonville Prison site was located in Sumter County. Today it is just outside the boundaries of Sumter County in Macon County.
7. John L. Maile, *Life in Andersonville*; Sheppard, p. 43.
8. Steve Davis, "Monumentation and the National Cemetery at Andersonville," *Blue and Gray Magazine*, Volume 3, Issue 3 (1985), pp. 51–52.
9. Sharpe and Dunnigan, *The Congressional Medal of Honor*, 1984; Davis, "Monumentation at Andersonville," *Blue and Gray Magazine*, Volume 3, Issue 3 (1985), pp. 51–52.
10. Ibid. See also information found on the monuments themselves.
11. Quote from the monuments. Information about sculptor William Thompson, see Davis, "Monumentation at Andersonville," p. 52.

BIBLIOGRAPHY

Andrews, W. H., First Sergeant, Company M. *Footprints of a Regiment, a Recollection of the 1st Georgia Regulars*. Annotated and with an introduction by Richard M. McMurry. Atlanta, Georgia: Longstreet Press, 1992.

Atkinson, Rick. *The Long Gray Line*. New York: Simon and Schuster, 1989.

Atwater, Dorence. *List of Union Soldiers Buried at Andersonville*, Tribune Publishing Company, 1866. Also found in *Official Records*, Series 2, Volume 8, pp. 837, 869–870, 960, 1051, 1193.

Atwater, Francis. *Dorence Atwater*. New Haven, Conn. Found in the *Andersonville Monument Commission Report*.

Ayers, Edward L. *The Promise of the New South, Life After Reconstruction*. New York, Oxford: Oxford University Press, 1992.

Balwin, Terry. "Clerk of the Dead," *Andersonville*. Eastern Acorn Press, 1983. First Published in *Civil War Times Illustrated*, 1976.

Barton, Clara. *Report of an Expedition to Andersonville, Georgia, July, 1865, for the Purpose of Identifying the Graves and Enclosing the Grounds of a Cemetery Created There During the Occupation of That Place as a Prison for Union Soldiers in Rebel Hands*. New York Tribune, February 14, 1866.

Bearss, Edwin. *Andersonville National Historic Site*. Office of Historic Architecture, Department of the Interior, Washington D.C., July 31, 1970.

Botkin, B. A. *A Civil War Treasury of Tales, Legends and Folklore*. New York: Promontory Press, 1981.

Brown, Louis A. *The Salisbury Prison, A Case Study of Confederate Military Prisons 1861–1865*. Washington, N.C.: Broadfoot Publishing Co., 1992.

Burton, E. Milby. *The Siege of Charleston, 1861–1865*. Columbia, S.C.: University of South Carolina Press, 1970.

Black, Robert C. *The Railroads of the Confederacy*. Wilmington, N.C.: Broadfoot Publishing Company, 1987.

Blakey, Arch Frederic. *General John H. Winder, C.S.A.* Gainesville: University of Florida Press, 1990.

Blume, John M., Bruce Catton, Edmund S. Morgan, Arthur M. Schlesinger Jr., Kenneth Stampp, and C. Vann Woddward. *The National Experience.* Burlingame, N.Y.: Harcourt, Brace, and World Inc., 1993.

Burnett, William G. *Our Lizabeth,* Copyright number TXU 462170, (self-published) 1991.

Byre, Frank L., ed. "A General Behind Bars: Neal Dow in Libby Prison." *Civil War History,* June 1862.

Chalmers, David M. *Hooded Americanism, The History of the Ku Klux Klan.* New York, London: New Viewpoints, 1951.

Channing, Steven A. *Confederate Ordeal, the Southern Home Front.* Alexandria, Va.: Time Life Books, 1984.

Chipman, General N. P. *The Andersonville Prison Trial, The Trial of Captain Henry Wirz.* Notable Trials Library, Special Edition, Birmingham, Alabama, 1990. First published in 1911 by Blair-Murdock Company, San Francisco.

Chipman, General N. P. *The Tragedy of Andersonville.* San Francisco, Ca.: Blair-Murdock Company, 1911.

Clavereul, Father H. *Diary of Father Clavereul.* First published in 1910 by the Connecticut Association of Ex-Prisoners of War. Reprinted in part within General N. P. Chipman's *The Andersonville Prison Trial.*

Coggins, Jack. *Ships and Seamen of the American Revolution.* Harrisburg, Pa.: Promontory Press, 1969.

Davidson, James West, William E. Gienapp, Christine Leigh Heyrman, Mark N. Lytle, and Michael B. Stoff. *Nation of Nations.* New York, N.Y.: McGraw Hill, 1990.

Davis, Burke. *The Long Surrender.* New York, N.Y.: Random House, 1985.

Davis, Steve. "Monumentation and the National Cemetery at Andersonville." *Blue and Gray Magazine,* Volume 3, Issue 3, 1985.

Davis, William C. *Brother Against Brother, the War Begins.* Alexandria, Va.: Time Life Books, 1983.

Davis, William C. *Jefferson Davis, The Man and His Hour.* New York, N.Y.: Harper Perennial, 1991.

Denney, Robert E. Foreword by Edwin C. Bearss. *Civil War Prisons and Escapes.* New York, N.Y.: Sterling Publishing, 1995.

Dennison, James H., Company K, 113th Illinois Volunteer Infantry. *Dennison's Andersonville Diary.* Kankakee, Ill.: Kankakee Historical Society, 1987. Notes and transcripts by Jack Klasey.

Dick, Everett. *The Dixie Frontier, A Social History.* Norman, Okla.: University of Oklahoma Press, 1993.

Domschuke, Bernhard. *Twenty Months in Captivity, Memoirs of a Union Officer in Confederate Prisons.* Edited and translated by Frederic

Trautmann, Dickinson University Press. London and Toronto: Associated University Presses. Originally published in German in 1865. Republished in 1987.

Donaldson, Norman and Betty. *How Did They Die*. New York, N.Y.: Greenwich House, Crown Publishers Inc., 1980.

Dow, Neal. *The Reminiscences of Neal Dow, Recollections of Eighty Years*. Portland, Maine: The Evening Express Publishing Co., 1898.

Drew, Ken. *Camp Sumter, The Pictorial History of Andersonville Prison*. Self-published by Ken Drew, Andersonville, Georgia, 1989.

Dunlop, W. S. *Lee's Sharpshooters; or the Forefront of Battle*. Little Rock, Ark.: Tunnah and Pittand, 1899.

Foust, Samuel L., Company I, 149th Pennsylvania Volunteers. *Diary of Samuel L. Foust*.

Futch, Ovid L. *History of Andersonville Prison*. Gainesville, Fla.: University of Florida Press, 1968, (reprint).

Gannon, Michael V. *Rebel Bishop*. Milwaukee, Wisc.: Bruce Publishing Co., 1964.

Genovese, Eugene D. *Roll Jordan Roll, the World the Slaves Made*. New York, N.Y.: Pantheon Books, a division of Random House, 1972.

Glazier, Willard W. *The Capture, the Prison Pen and Escape*. Hartford, Conn.: H. E. Goodwin Publisher, 1867.

Gooding, James Henry, Corporal, 54th Massachusetts Volunteer Infantry. *On the Altar of Freedom, A Black Soldier's Letters from the Front*. Edited by Virginia M. Adams. Foreword by James M. McPherson. New York, N.Y.: University of Massachusetts Press, Warner Books, 1991.

Hyde, Solon, 7th Ohio Volunteer Infantry. *A Captive of War*. Columbus, Ohio: McClure Phillips and Company, 1900.

Hemmerlein, Richard F. *Prisons and Prisoners of the Civil War*. Boston, Mass.: Christopher Publishing Houser, 1934.

Hesseltine, William B., ed. *Civil War Prisons*. Kent, Ohio: Kent State University Press, 1962.

Hopkins, Charles, First New Jersey Infantry. *The Andersonville Diary and Memoirs of Charles Hopkins*. Edited by William B. Styple and John J. Fitzpatrick. Foreword by Roger Long, Kearny, N.J.: Belle Grove Publishing Company, 1988.

Hopkins, Charles. "Hell and the Survivor." *American Heritage*, October–November 1982.

James, David G., president and compiler. *Andersonville Monument Commission Report*. This report contains a copy of Francis Atwater's defense of his brother referred to as the *Atwater Defense*.

Johnson, Norman. *The Human Cage, A Brief History of Prison Architecture*. Published for The American Foundation, Incorporated, Institute of Corrections. Philadelphia, Pennsylvania by Walker and Company, New York, 1973.

Jones, Charles Edgeworth. Formerly Historian Camp 435, United Confederate Veterans (U.C.V.), *Georgia in the War, 1861–1865*, unpublished.

Jones, James Dunwoody. "A Guard at Andersonville." *Andersonville*. Eastern Acorn Press, 1983. First published in *Civil War Times Illustrated*, 1964.

Katz, Mark D. *Witness to an Era, the Life and Photographs of Alexander Gardner*. New York, N.Y.: Viking Penguin, 1991.

Keegan, John, and Joseph Darracott. *The Nature of War*. New York, N.Y.: Holt, Rinehart and Winston, 1981.

Kellogg, Robert H. *Life and Death in Rebel Prisons*. Hartford, Conn.: L. Stebbins, 1867.

Kennett, Lee. *Marching Through Georgia. The Story of Soldiers and Civilians During Sherman's March*. New York, N.Y.: Harper Collins, 1995.

Kunhardt, Dorothy Meserve, and Phillip H. Kunhardt Jr. *Twenty Days*. New York, N.Y.: Harper and Row, 1965.

Larson, Rebecca D. *Blue and Gray, Roses of Intrigue*. Gettysburg, Pa.: Thomas Publications, 1993.

Lemonick, Michael D. "It Takes More Than Food to Cure Starvation." *Time*, December 21, 1992.

Long, Roger. "The Truth About Andersonville Prison." *Blue and Gray*, Volume 3, Issue 3. Special Andersonville Edition. Columbus, Ohio: Blue and Gray Enterprises, 1985.

McElroy, John, Private, Company L., 16th Illinois Cavalry. *This Was Andersonville*. Edited by Roy Meredith. New York, N.Y.: The Fairfax Press. First published by the author in 1879. Revised by the editor in 1957. Republished in 1979.

McPherson, James M. *Battle Cry of Freedom, the Civil War Era*. Oxford University Press, 1988.

Mahood, Wayne. *The Plymouth Pilgrims*. Highstown, N.J.: Longstreet House, 1991.

Maile, John L. *Prison Life in Andersonville*. Los Angles, Ca.: Press of the West Coast Magazine, 1912.

Mallinson, David L. "The Andersonville Raiders." *Andersonville*. Eastern Acorn Press, 1983. First published in *Civil War Times Illustrated*, 1971.

Mann, Dr. T. H. "Plan of the Stockade and Surroundings at Andersonville." *Century Magazine*, July–August 1890.

Marvel, William. *Andersonville, The Last Depot*. Chapel Hill and London: University of North Carolina Press, 1994.

Massey, Mary Elizabeth. *Ersatz in the Confederacy, Shortages and Substitutes on the Southern Home Front*. Columbia, S.C.: University of South Carolina Press, 1952, 1993.

Meredith, Roy. *This Was Andersonville*. New York, N.Y.: McDowell Obolensky Inc. 1957.

Moran, Frank E. "Escape from Libby Prison." *American History Illustrated*, November 7, 1985.

Morsberger, Katherine and Robert. "The Judgment and Execution of Henry Wirz." *Andersonville*. Eastern Acorn Press, 1983. First published in *Civil War Times Illustrated*, 1976.

Murphy, Richard W. *The Nation Reunited, War's Aftermath*. Alexandria, Va.: Time Life Books, 1987.

National Archives, Record Group 92, *Quartermaster Consolidated File*. Referred to as NA, RG.

Page, James Madison. *The True Story of Andersonville Prison, a Defense of Henry Wirz*. New York and Washington: The Neale Publishing Company, 1908.

Parker, Elizabeth Leonard. *The Civil War Career of Henry Wirz and its Aftermath*. Master of Arts Thesis. Athens, Ga.: University of Georgia, 1948.

Poppenheim, Mary B., et al. *The History of the United Daughters of the Confederacy*. Under authority granted in convention assembled at Hot Springs, Arkansas, 1925.

Procedure for Executions, Department of the Army, Army Regulations, Section II, 633-15, Commercial Reprint, 1959.

Ransom, John. *Andersonville Diary, and List of the Dead*. Published by the author, Auburn, New York, 1881. Reprinted with a foreword by Bruce Catton, Berkeley Books, New York, 1986.

Reagan, Charles Wilson. *Baptized in Blood, the Religion of the Lost Cause*. Athens, Ga.: University of Georgia Press, 1980.

"*Report of the Joint Committee on the Erection of a Monument at Andersonville Georgia*." Senate: E. L. Freeman; House of Representatives: Walter H. Durfee, John T. Xenyon, L. F. C. Garvin. E. L. Freeman and Sons State Printers, 1903.

Robertson, James I. *Soldiers Blue and Gray*. New York, N.Y.: Warner Books, 1988.

Robertson, James I. *Tenting Tonight, the Soldiers Life*. Alexandria, Va.: Time Life Books, 1984.

Roth, David E. and Robin, editors-publishers. "The Human Interest Side of Andersonville." *Blue and Gray Magazine*, Volume 3, Issue 3.

Sheppard, Peggy. *Andersonville Georgia U.S.A.* Andersonville, Ga.: Sheppard Publications, 1973.

Stearns, Amos E. Edited by Leon Basile. *The Civil War Diary of Amos E. Stearns, A Prisoner at Andersonville.* Madison, Teaneck, Fairleigh, Dickinson University Press, London and Toronto, 1981.

Stevenson, Robert Louis. *The Ebb Tide, A Trio and Quartet.* New York, N.Y.: Charles Scribners Sons, 1905.

Stevenson, Randolph R., M.D. *The Southern Side of Andersonville.* Turnbull Brothers, 1876.

Stibbs, John, Brigadier General, 12th Ohio Volunteers. *Andersonville and the Trial of Henry Wirz.* Iowa Journal of History and Politics, January 1911.

Thompson, James West. "Andersonville Truth versus Falsehood." *Blue and Gray*, Volume 3, Issue 3. Special Andersonville Edition. Columbus, Ohio: Blue and Gray Enterprises, 1985.

Thomas, Benjamin P., and Harold M. Hyman. *Stanton, the Life and Times of Lincoln's Secretary of War.* New York, N.Y.: Alfred A. Knopf, 1962.

Trial of Henry Wirz, 40th Congress, 2nd Session, House Document 23, Washington D.C., 1868.

The United States War Department, *The War of the Rebellion: A Compilation of the Official Records of the Union and Confederate Armies*, 127 Volumes, Washington, D.C., 1880–1901.

Ward, Gregory C. with Rick Burns and Ken Burns. *The Civil War, An Illustrated History.* New York, N.Y.: Alfred A. Knopf, 1990.

Wheeler, Richard. *Sherman's March.* New York, N.Y.: Harper Perennial, 1978.

Unknown author. "Major Henry Wirz." *William and Mary College, Quarterly Historical Magazine*, January 1919.

Special Thanks To:

Guy Chastain

Steve Rowe

Bill and Barbara Roberts

Dennis Roberts

Bob and Joanne Steele

Jim Craeven

Gloria Emerson

William H. Warrick, M.D. and Family

Earl Pickins, M.D.

Maudie Valenti

Sally Theobold

INDEX